DISCARDED

COGNITIVE ANALYSIS OF SOCIAL BEHAVIOR

NATO ADVANCED STUDY INSTITUTES SERIES

Proceedings of the Advanced Study Institute Programme, which aims at the dissemination of advanced knowledge and the formation of contacts among scientists from different countries.

The series is published by an international board of publishers in conjunction with NATO Scientific Affairs Division

A	Life Sciences	Plenum Publishing Corporation
B	Physics	London and New York
C	Mathematical and Physical Sciences	D. Reidel Publishing Company Dordrecht and Boston
D	Behavioural and Social Sciences	Martinus Nijhoff Publishers The Hague, Boston and London
E	Applied Sciences	

Series D: Behavioural and Social Sciences – No. 13

COGNITIVE ANALYSIS OF SOCIAL BEHAVIOR

Proceedings of the NATO Advanced Study Institute on "The Cognitive Analysis of Socio-Psychological Processes", Aix-en-Provence, France, July 12-31, 1981

edited by

Jean-Paul Codol, Ph.D.
Université de Provence
Laboratoire de Psychologie Sociale
Aix-en-Provence
France

and

Jacques-Philippe Leyens, Ph.D.
Université Catholique de Louvain
Faculté de Psychologie
Louvain-la-Neuve
Belgium

1982

Martinus Nijhoff Publishers
The Hague / Boston / London

Distributors:

for the United States and Canada
Kluwer Boston, Inc.
190 Old Derby Street
Hingham, MA 02043
USA

for all other countries
Kluwer Academic Publishers Group
Distribution Center
P.O.Box 322
3300 AH Dordrecht
The Netherlands

Library of Congress Cataloging in Publication Data
Main entry under title:

Cognitive analysis of social behavior.

(NATO advanced study institutes series. Series D, Behavioural and social sciences ; v. 13)
Fifth summer school organized by the European Association of Experimental Social Psychology.
Includes bibliographical references and index.
1. Social psychology--Congresses. I. Codol, Jean-Paul.
II. Leyens, Jacques Philippe. III. European Association of Experimental Social Psychology. IV. Series.
HM251.C643   1982   302   82-7903
ISBN 90-247-2701-4   AACR2

ISBN 90-247-2701-4 (this volume)
ISBN 90-247-2688-3 (series)

Copyright © 1982 by Martinus Nijhoff Publishers, The Hague.

All rights reserved. No part of this publication may be reproduced, stored in a retrieval system, or transmitted, in any form or by any means, mechanical, photocopying, recording, or otherwise, without the prior written permission of the publishers,
Martinus Nijhoff Publishers, P.O. Box 566, 2501 CN The Hague, The Netherlands.

Printed in The Netherlands.

ECC/USF Learning Resources
8099 College Parkway, S.W.
Fort Myers, Florida 33907-5164

PREFACE

The fifth Summer School organized by the European Association of Experimental Social Psychology was held in Aix-en-Provence (France, from July 12 to 31, 1981. Previous schools had taken place in The Hague (The Nederlands) in 1966, Leuven (Belgium) in 1967, Konstanz (Germany) in 1972 and in Oxford (Great-Britain) in 1976.

This is an important activity of the European Association and has always met with great success. This time, 130 applications were received while only 50 could be accepted, given the format adopted for the Summer School. They represented many different countries and institutions.

To fully understand the aims of such a Summer School, especially of the present one, it is probably best to consider first its organization.

Participants were graduates or young postdoctoral students in experimental social psychology. For three weeks they worked in five teams of ten participants each under the mentorship of a senior researcher. Each of five staff members had suggested a special topic of study in which they were interested, well before the start of the session. This enabled the teams to be determined early enough for the participants to be able to prepare for the sessions. In Aix, in the magnificent surroundings of an old convent, afternoons (and often evenings as well) were spent discussing theoretical issues arising from the suggested topics and in planning research to test specific hypotheses. Some groups ran pilot studies and analyzed them or worked on data already collected before the Summer School. The topics investigated covered different areas connected to cognitive approaches of social psychology :

- Application of reasearch in cognitive psychology to the study of attitudes and opinions (E. Burnstein)
- Perception des similitudes et différences entre individus (J.P. Codol)
- L'identité sociale (J.C. Deschamps)
- The attribution theory (J.M.F. Jaspars)
- Implicit personality theories : How they change (J.Ph. Leyens)

In previous Summer Schools, English had been the only working language. However, this time two groups were conducted in French (lead by Jean-Paul Codol and Jean-Claude Deschamps) and the other three groups in English. The organizers, however, had carefully constituted the groups so that no language discrimination between them would occur : for instance, French speaking natives participated in "English" teams and vice-versa.

In this organization, mornings were devoted to lectures delivered by the staff members or by well-known invited speakers. More will be said about these later since the lectures constitute the content of the present work.

One important word now about the financial aspect of the enterprise. Board and lodging are offered to all participants so that money does not constitute the ultimate criterion of selection (for participants and for their country of origin as well). This very basic goal was achieved thanks the support of NATO who contributed on behalf of those participants coming from NATO countries. For the other participants, funds were obtained from the Centre National de la Recherche Scientifique (France), the Université de Provence, and some European laboratories. Needless to say that we are most grateful to all these institutions for their help. Our debt to them will become even more apparent when we have specified our aims in conducting such Summer Schools.

Training in experimental social psychology exists in most countries but its quality can vary tremendously. This is due to differences in national financial constraints and, also, to differences in the rate of development of that science in various countries. Also, it seems that European social psychologists often have more contacts with colleagues of other continents than with their own continent. All of our Summer Schools have tried to compensate for this heterogeneity while maintaining cultural specificities and identities. With that in mind, Mediterranean countries were our special "targets" in this particular Summer School. As usual, we are confident that we succeeded in another aim : special intellectual liaisons were effected resulting in joint programs of research involving several countries which are now ongoing.

The title of the Aix-en-Provence Summer School was : "The cognitive analysis of socio-psychological processes". The present book tries to convey some bits of its extremely stimulating atmosphere.

The first two chapters of this volume argue that behavior, and especially social behavior, has been a neglected entity, at least at the theoretical level. Indeed, both Jaspars and Upmeyer assert that there has been an overemphasis on verbal responses as substitutes for behavior in situ; this state of affairs may explain why social psychology has always so badly needed a theory of correspondence between cognitions or attitudes and behavior. Jaspars, then, presents two versions of a dual representation model to show how representations and behavior can be related to each other in a multivariate model by a system of rules. Upmeyer, on the other hand, develops his model of attitude and illustrates how an internal representation should be approached across different modalities.

How is it that the impact of communication has so little to do with the recall of its content ? This question, which goes back to attitude polarization studies, is raised by Burnstein and Schul in the following chapter. They show, empirically, how the persuasiveness of implicit information can be analysed at different stages of a processing model. These stages are respectively : initial encoding, elaborative encoding, integration and decision. This approach undoubtedly gives a new flavor to the field of social influence and has implications as well for other areas such as artificial intelligence, for instance.

"At the beginning are the social representations"; so, at least, pleads Moscovici in chapter 4. According to this author, the history of (cognitive) social psychology can be divided into three phases, each of them characterized by a well-known concept: social attitudes, social cognitions and finally social representations. Moscovici does not like Agatha Christie's hero, Hercule Poirot, and is unhappy with the present research on social cognitions. To him, this research is old concepts in new wrappings. Before speaking of biases and errors, one should consider the relevant social representations.

This latter idea is pursued empirically by Flament. This specialist of graph theory analyses the (cognitive) schemata which underly the equilibrium bias discovered by Heider. His results lead him to conclude that this bias can only be fully understood given the social representation of an egalitarian and undifferentiated group.

In chapter 6, and within the general framework of implicit personality theories, Leyens asks three questions. Are psychologists more prone than others to <u>favor</u> dispositional explanations ? Is it an error ? Does it <u>have</u> detrimental consequences ? All the answers are : yes. Some general suggestions are offered concerning the causes of this state of affairs and its remedies.

Palmonari is also interested in the work of psychologists and tells us how Italian psychologists perceive psychology and their work or practice. Four different representations emerge and they have strong implications for the Italian psychologists' training, profession and identity. One of the aims of this research was to find ways to build a new curriculum for Italian psychologists; the social representations of their discipline is, however, so heterogeneous and dogmatic that the author concludes that they cannot serve the aim he had envisaged.

In chapter 8, Tajfel opens what could be considered as the last section of this volume. He selectively reviews in it some of the experimental studies he and his team have recently conducted on intergroup behavior. He does so by linking the experiments around a few central processes and concepts : social categorization, social comparison and social identity.

Some of these ideas are developped by Deschamps in the following chapter. In four experiments, this author shows that there is a covariation between inter-group and inter-individual categorizations (or differentiations) : one leads to the other and vice versa.

Finally, in the last chapter of this volume, it is the concept of identity which is reviewed. Codol attempts to define what should be understood by "personal" and "social" identities. Within this framework, he discusses investigations about the search for similarities and differences with other people. In his opinion, the search for differences is most important.

Let us hope this volume will also offer a flavor of "differences" to his readers.

Claude Flament was the director of the Summer School. Jean-Claude Alric prepared it. Marie-France Pichevin was successful in overcoming all the practical problems. When typing the manuscripts, Roseline Van Dyck attempted to master the idiosynchrasies of each of them. Elisabeth Sousa and José Marques helped in the preparation of the indices. To all of them we owe a great debt.

Jean-Paul Codol,
Jacques-Philippe Leyens.

CONTENTS

Preface.. V
Contents... XI

J.M.F. JASPARS
Social Judgement and social behaviour : A dual representation model.. 1
    The social legacy of gestaltpsychology............ 1
    Pseudo-cognitions and substitute behaviour........ 7
    Attribution, integration, representation and evaluation.. 9
    Cognitive representation, social judgments and social behaviour................................... 20
    The dual representation of social reality......... 23
        A path analytical model....................... 23
        A multivariate model.......................... 32
    References.. 44

A. UPMEYER
Attitudes and social behaviour........................... 51
    Introduction..................................... 51
    Historical background............................ 53
        The measurement approach...................... 53
        Cognitive consistency......................... 54
        The prediction model.......................... 55
    Unsolved problems................................ 57
        The origins of attitudes...................... 57
        Selection of beliefs.......................... 58
        Selection of attitude objects................. 58
        Object evaluation and object choice........... 59
        Causal links.................................. 59
        Defining behaviour............................ 62
    Goal directed attitudes and behaviour............ 63
        Goal-attitude................................. 64
        Instrumental attitude......................... 65
    Judgements, announcements and behaviour.......... 66
        Cross-modality matching....................... 66
        Biases in two-alternative responses........... 68
        Biases in magnitude responses................. 70
        Stimulation for related literature............ 71

Schemata, scripts, and behaviour	74
Conceptual work	75
Research lines	77
Artificial intelligence research	78
Memory research	79
Illness schemata	80
Concluding comments	81
References	82

E. BURNSTEIN and Y. SCHUL

The cognitive analysis of a persuasive argument	87
Study 1. A correlational analysis of the persuasiveness and informativeness	89
Study 2. Basic operations in opinion formation	91
Method	95
Physical matching or Semantic matching	95
Impression formation	95
Results	97
Study 3. Time required to form an opinion with informative and uninformative arguments	98
Method	99
Results	99
Study 4. The representation of informative and uninformative arguments	102
Method	105
Results and discussion	106
General discussion	107
References	110

S. MOSCOVICI

The coming era of representations	115
Rediscovering the social mind	115
Cognitive social psychology. Reform or revolution.	117
The art of asking why : From lore to science	120
From social cognitions to social representations	128
Who is the real naive psychologist ?	136
Waiting for Godot	141
References	147

C. FLAMENT
Du biais d'équilibre structural à la représentation
  du groupe.. 151
    Introduction.. 151
    Biais, schèmes et représentation.................... 152
    Décomposition du schème d'équilibre................. 154
    Axiome de parcimonie et situation de stress......... 156
    Axiome de groupage et schème d'équivalence.......... 158
    Amitié et hiérarchie................................ 160
    Le groupe égalitaire................................ 162
    Image du groupe et différenciation.................. 164
    Conclusion.. 167
    Bibliographie....................................... 168

J.Ph. LEYENS
Implications des théories implicites de personnalité
  pour le diagnostic psychologique......................... 171
    Les théories implicites de personnalité............. 172
    L'erreur fondamentale............................... 176
    Pourquoi les psychologues sont davantage sensibles
      à la personnalité ?.............................. 178
      Différence entre acteur et observateur........... 178
      Les conceptions théoriques du psychologue........ 179
      Accessibilité et fonction des traits de
        personnalité................................. 181
      Le cadre de travail du psychologue............... 183
    S'agit-il d'une erreur chez les psychologues ?...... 184
    Les conséquences de l'erreur fondamentale chez
      les psychologues................................. 191
    Quels remèdes envisager............................. 194
      Le problème de la formation théorique............ 197
      Le problème des ressources thérapeutiques........ 197
      Le problème de l'empathie........................ 198
      Le problème des taxonomies....................... 200
      Le problème des diagnostics nuancés.............. 201
    Bibliographie....................................... 202

A. PALMONARI
On becoming a psychologist : A field-study in Italy..... 207
    Method.. 210
      Intuitive individuation of social represen-
        tations...................................... 210
      Building a grid for the content analysis......... 210
      Classification of the interviews'contents
        according to the grid........................ 211
      Verification of the internal consistency of
        the protocols................................ 211

The scientific status of psychology	214
Working activity = goals and intervention strategy	216
Psychologist's professional identity	220
The psychologist's professional training	221
Discussion	222
References	226

H. TAJFEL

Experimental studies of intergroup behaviour	227
Experimental social psychology and the realities of social conflicts	227
The interchangeable individuals	232
Social categorization and social competition.	233
Social comparison and awareness of group membership	239
Conclusion	242
References	243

J.C. DESCHAMPS

Différenciations entre soi et autrui et entre groupes. Recherches sur la "covariation" entre les différenciations inter-individuelles et inter-groupes	247
Recherches sur les différenciations inter-individuelles et inter-groupes	253
Expérience 1. Effet de la catégorisation inter-groupes sur les différenciations inter-individuelles	253
Expérience 2. Effet de la solidarité-compétition	259
Expérience 3. Différenciations entre groupes et entre individus identifiés par leur appartenance catégorielle	261
Expérience 4. Effet de la fusion-individualisation	263
Bibliographie	264

J.P. CODOL

Differentiating and non-differentiating behavior. A cognitive approach to the sense of identity	267
The sense of identity	268
Cognitive apprehension : a few general points	268
Cognitive apprehension of the self : Dimensions of the sense of identity	273
Constructing the sense of identity	273

In search of a social recognition of
   identity.. 283
      Self-image and social images of the self..... 283
      The desire for social recognition of the
         self : limits and conflicts................ 288
References.. 291

SOCIAL JUDGEMENT AND SOCIAL BEHAVIOUR

A dual representation model

> J. M.F. Jaspars
> University of Oxford

The social legacy of Gestaltpsychology

It is not uncommon in the history of science that different investigators arrive almost simultaneously, but independently of each other, at similar ideas for the explanation of certain phenomena. New insights reflect very often just as much the Zeitgeist as the originality of individual researchers. Merton (1961) and Boring (1957) have shown that the occurence of multiple discoveries is not limited to the natural sciences, but is also a regular feature in the development of the social and behavioural sciences.

One of the recent instances of such a development in social psychology is the remarkable coincidence of a number of influential publications around 1957, by such authors as Asch (1956), Festinger (1957), Heider (1958), G.A. Kelly (1955) and Osgood et al. (1957), all emphasizing the importance of an ordered and interdependent cognitive representation of reality for understanding social behaviour. The explanation for this sudden burst of interest in cognitive aspects of social behaviour is probably fairly complex and presumably of more interest to a historian of science than to a social psychologist. However, in order to evaluate certain recent developments in social psychology i.e. ethogenics (Harré, 1977), social skills theory (Argyle and Kendon, 1967) and in order to present my own point of view in a proper perspective, I would like to make a few remarks about the development of social psychology during the last 20 years.

Although social psychology has been severely criticized for its a-social, a-historical, mechanistic and deterministic model of man (Holzkamp, 1977-1978; Harré and Secord, 1972; Plon, 1974; Gergen, 1978) it is also true and almost trite to state that many social psychologists have always assumed "the physical and objective properties of social stimulation and incentives... to be less significant for the analysis of social behaviour than their subjective counterparts" (Zajonc, 1969). The lack of systematic dependence of social behaviour on objective, physical properties of stimuli has prompted social psychologists to focus on cognitive representations of social stimuli, rather than on their physical properties. Moreover it appears that "no social psychologist today seems to question the general assumption that, cognitions, whatever else they may be, are organized wholes of interdependent parts" (Zajonc, 1969).

These formulations immediately suggest that contemporary cognitive research in social psychology is strongly influenced by Gestalt psychological ideas. I do think that this is indeed the case, even to a much larger extent than is often realized. First of all there is a very direct link between the Gestalt tradition and the work of Asch (1946, 1956) and Heider (1958). The influence of the impression formation and conformity studies by Asch on research in information integration (Anderson, 1974, Wyer, 1974, Slovic and Lichtenstein, 1971) and conformity, obedience and influence of minorities (Allen, 1966, Milgram, 1974, Moscovici and Faucheux, 1973) is well known. Less welldocumented is the fact that these highly influential publications of Asch can be traced back to two earlier articles of Asch on the principles of social judgment and attitudes. (Asch et al. 1938, 1940). In the first of these two articles Asch states explicitly that the aim of these studies is to investigate to what extent principles of perception, which have been formulated by Gestalt-psychology, also apply to processes of social judgment. It is interesting to note that the two principles formulated by Asch foreshadow quite clearly his two later publications and the two research traditions referred to above. The first principle states that the judgments of a single situation are related to each other by a person in accordance with an underlying attitude of acceptance or rejection. The second principle states that a standard having an authoritative source tends to alter an individual judgment in its direction. The experiments performed by Asch on which these two principles are based appear to be exceedingly simple and do not fully support his conclusions. However, the experiments do show that social judgments are influenced by the nature and source of new information. In the first four experiments Asch studies the correlation between rankings of intelligence and honesty for ten photographs of adolescents and shows that the original "spontaneous" correlation of r = .75, is practically unaltered by information about the "true" ranking of intelligence if the latter confirms the initial impression of the Ss. (r = .80). However, if the "true" ranking for intelligence correlates only r = .12 or r = -.50 with the initial impression of intelligence, the correlation between rankings of intelligence and honesty drops to r= .63 and r= .30 respectively. Thus, Asch argues in this paper and in several more recent studies, that new information does not only change the final impression of e.g. honesty, but also the relation between the various elements constituting that impression. This can be shown even more clearly by regarding the judgment of honesty in these experiments as the outcome of a simple additive process of information integration in which the subject combines in a linear fashion his own initial impressions of intelligence and honesty with the information provided by the experimenter about the true nature of the differences in intelligence of the stimulus person.

As can be seen in Table I it is quite easy to predict the final judgment of honesty with a linear regression model, when new information confirms the already formed impression or when new information is uncorrelated with the initial judgment. In the latter case the initial impression has a negative effect and the new information is accepted instead, whereas in the first case the initial impression receives the highest weight in the formation of a final judgment . The results of experiment four are, however, much more interesting because they show that <u>an additive information integration</u> model does less well when contradictory information is provided. This is of course precisely the point which is taken up much later by various cognitive consistency theories (Festinger, 1957, Heider, 1950, Osgood, et al. 1957). But Asch already showed the effect of cognitive consistency in these first experiments, inspired by perceptual research of Gestalt psychologists.

The same direct relation between the Gestalt tradition and a cognitive approach in social psychology can be shown to exist in Heider's work. Most recent studies on cognitive consistency and attribution refer usually to Heider's psychology of interpersonal relations (Heider, 1958), but the two fundamental principles of balance and unit-formation were already formulated in several earlier publications (Heider, 1944, Heider and Simmel, 1944). Heider has recently denied that these principles were directly influenced by Wertheimer's formulation of the similar Gestalt principles (Ickes and Harvey, 1978) of unit-formation and pragnanz, but it is hard to believe that Heider was only influenced

TABLE I

Linear Regression Equations for Honesty
Judgments in Experiments 2,3,4
of Asch et al. (1938)

	$r_{IQ_i - IQ_t}$		R
Exp 2	1.00	$H_f = 0.76\ H_i + 0.12\ IQ_i + 0.12\ IQ_t$	.94
Exp 3	0.12	$H_f = 1.08\ H_i - 0.55\ IQ_i + 0.35\ IQ_t$	.95
Exp 4	-0.50	$H_f = 0.29\ H_i + 0.31\ IQ_i + 0.15\ IQ_t$	.54

where

$r_{IQ_i - IQ_t}$ = correlation between initial ranking of intelligence and true ranking provided by psychologist

H_f Final ranking of honesty

IQ_i Initial ranking for intelligence

IQ_t true ranking for intelligence provided by experimenter in his thinking by his informal observation of daily life and the reading of Spinoza's ethics, when he spend the early part of his academic career in the company of Meinon, Köhler, Wertheimer, Lewin and Koffka.

Of course the Gestalt-like structural principles of Heider's cognitive theory of interpersonal relations have been recognized as such by various social psychologists (Zajonc, 1969) but it is remarkable that the research which followed appeared to overlook some of the essential features of Heider's theory and therefore developed research strategies which seem to have led into blind alleys. Perhaps, the best known examples of such research are the numerous studies which have been devoted to the testing of Heider's balance theory. The principle of balance derives from Heider's earlier work on the perception of causality and unit-formation, and is basically a hypothesis about the dynamic state of cognitive units which tend towards steady states. Much research, however, has been devoted to the particular "generalization that states of balance tend to be preferred over disharmony". (Heider, 1958,204). Crockett (1977) who has recently reviewed the evidence in great detail finds that the balance principle is not strongly confirmed in pleasantness studies, whereas inference, prediction, learning and recall experiments present very strong evidence in favor of the operation of Heider's balance theory. This should not come as a surprise, given the fact that the primary derivation of Heider's theory is that imbalanced states are characterized by stress which produces changes in the cognitive organization. Whether such cognitive stress is experienced as unpleasant is another matter. Because balanced and unbalanced cognitive structures also reflect to some extent more or less rewarding actual social situations (Newcomb, 1953), pleasantness ratings are typically also affected by the attitude towards the other person and the agreement the subject has with the other person. This could have been seen already in the results of the very first experiment conducted by Jordan to test balance theory in this particular way. However, instead of simply comparing the pleasantness ratings of the 4 balanced and the 4 unbalanced triadic situations, a more refined analysis can be achieved by treating the perceived relations as predictor variables in a polynomial regression. Since the difference between the 8 possible triadic situations can be rewritten in terms of 7 uncorrelated variables (Wyer, 1974) including main effects of the perceived relations and their first and second order interactions, it is relatively easy to calculate the multiple regression equation for pleasantness. For the averaged data provided by Jordan the equation is :

$$p = .55S + .08V + .26O + .18SV + .05SO + \underline{.57VO} + \underline{.50SVO}$$

where S, V and O are defined as :

S = relation of p and o
V = relation of o and x
O = relation of p and x

The results of this analysis quite clearly show that there are three variables of about equal importance in predicting the degree of perceived pleasantness in these situations : the liking of P for O, the agreement of P and O and the balanced or unbalanced nature of the three perceived relations. Overall the prediction is perfect (R = 1.00), which is of course to be expected with 7 parameters and 8 values to be predicted, but the 3 most important variables of which the balance parameter is one, do explain 89 % of the variance which is less trivial. The essential feature of balance theory in such situations is, however, that it predicts the nature and strength of the third cognitive relation on the basis of the basis of the two other elementary relations. If interpreted in this way, the principle of cognitive balance can easily be quantified either in a vector model or a distance model and generalized to more complex cognitive structures. I have shown elsewhere (Jaspars, 1966, 1967, 1968, 1969, 1972, 1974, van de Geer et al., 1965) that the effect of the principle is strongest when the cognitive representation on which the judgments are based is less complex and the perceived sentiment relations imply unilaterality (Coombs, 1964) and decentration (Piaget, 1932). Moreover it was shown that anticipation of interaction transforms the balance effect into a positivity effect (Jaspars et al., 1974).

It is the latter finding which is of special interest because it reveals perhaps why the originally perceptual nature of Heider's theory has prevented the further development of the theory so as to include implications for social behaviour. To my knowledge almost no studies have been devoted to the effect of cognitive balance on social behaviour, although such an effect can be shown to exist over and above a positivity effect, at least in non-verbal communication (Jaspars, 1973, Jaspars et al., 1974). As Zajonc (1969) has pointed out, the Gestalt approach tends in fact to ignore the consequences of behaviour. It does not consider the possibility that the individual may interact with the perceived stimulus or that he may change or affect it. Application of the Gestalt approach to social psychology, however, necessarily implies an extension beyond the scope of experience and takes into account the fact that cognitive relations may exist "because of an (approximately) corresponding social reality." Newcomb's theory of interpersonal relations (1953) and research by Flament and his associates (Flament, 1979) are explicitly based on this assumption. The interesting point of Newcomb's work is, however, that it shows only that agreement and balance effects are indistinguishable if a positive relationship between persons is maintained in actual interaction. The studies by Flament and his colleagues (Flament, 1979) are more important in this respect, because they show an actual reversal of the positivity and generalization effect (Crockett, 1977), when the typical cognitive balance experiment is carried out in a realistic social situation. In their experiments workers appear to prefer negatively balanced relations with management over positively balanced relationships.

All this illustrates the point I am trying to make in this introduction. The Gestalt origin of cognitive research in social psychology has led to a neglect of one of the basic aims of such research which is to explain social behaviour by taking into account the subjective or internal representation of the social (stimulus) situation which gives rise to this behaviour. One wonders to what extent the unmistakable phenomenological overtones of cognitive research in social psychology (van de Geer and Jaspars, 1966) has produced the emphasis on cognitive coherence. As Asch has pointed out there are large areas to which such research has not noticeably contributed. Among these where the study of language-behaviour and social action in relation to social cognition (Asch, 1969). The challenge for and appeal of a cognitive approach of social psychology was primarily, as Shaw and Costanzo have pointed out (1970) "to seek a theoretical framework which is methodologically sound but which gives cognizance to the richness and complexity of the phenomenal world of the individual. The emphasis is "upon humanistic and phenomenological concepts without at the same time sacrificing rigor".

Pseudo-cognitions and substitute behaviour

I am about to reverse the conclusion I have just reached because, on closer inspection, a curious paradox manifests itself in research on social cognitive processes. The three or four main areas of research which developed in the wake of the original work by Asch and Heider are concerned with impression-formation, or information integration, attribution theory and implicit representations of personality traits, emotions, social relations, and, quite recently, with social situations. The common denominator in all these studies is, at least in theory, a concern with the mental processes which give rise to internal representations of the social environment. Since it is impossible to have direct access to such processes or representations, research in social cognition is always indirect and relies upon inferences made from overt responses. The unfortunate consequence of this dilemma is that in most research overt responses, usually in the form of verbal reports, have simply been treated as pseudo cognitions or as a substitute for other behaviour. The effect of these research strategies is, of course, that one does not deal, in fact, with cognitive representations at all, but with direct S-R connections of a different kind. Although this is true for any study of human information processing it is very important to realize that the simple substitution of an overt response for an internal stimulus makes more sense in certain cases than in others. When we are studying responses which intuitively can be interpreted as subjective counterparts of the stimuli it seems reasonable to view such responses as more or less veridical reports of experienced sensations. Research in psychophysics and many experiments on memory and attention are of this kind (Norman, 1976). However, when the response is not a reported sensation but a <u>reaction</u> of a <u>different</u> kind, more complex models will probably be needed to describe the S-R connection. The complexity of internal processes will presumably increase even more when we are interested in reactions to <u>stimuli</u> which are quite <u>different</u> from the stimuli eliciting the reported sensations. The recent work in language processing by Schank and Abelson (1977) and Anderson (1976) should convince any social psychologist that the task of explaining social behaviour by referring to social cognitive processes must be much more complicated than we have realized until now, because we are dealing very often with the problem of predicting complex or global behavioral reactions to stimuli on the basis of verbal responses to symbolic and generalized representations of these stimuli. In other words it makes quite a difference whether one tries to relate physical features of facial expressions to verbal classifications of emotions (Fryda, 1969; Ekman, 1975) or to predict how a particular Chinese couple will be treated in a restaurant on the basis of a verbal promise that Chinese people in general are welcome (La Pierre, 1934).

Most research in social cognition has not attempted to develop a differentiated description of the cognitive processes involved in social judgment and social behaviour. Only very limited models are available at the moment, most of them dealing with the relations between social judgments and verbal stimuli (Anderson, 1974; Rosenberg, 1969). The results of these studies are, however, of some importance for the development of a more complex cognitive model of social behaviour and social interaction, because they allow us to simplify certain aspects of such a more complex model.

Attribution, integration, representation and evaluation.

Contemporary research in social cognition can be divided into three or four areas which appear to correspond to different phases in the social judgment process. In order to form a judgment about another person or a social issue the observer, it is assumed, must first attribute the observable cues or stimuli to the cause of the observed phenomenon. A major distinction in recent attribution studies has been, of course, the attribution of another person's behaviour to either some latent, more or less invariant, disposition of the person or to some environmental cause. Once the attribution has been made, the observer faces the task of integrating the inferences made on the basis of his observations with already available information or, to put it in another way, to arrive at an overall cognition based on at least two separate items of information. Attention has been paid especially to situations in which there are apparent contradictions between cognitions resulting from different sets of information. Finally the subject is thought to arrange all the available information in a cognitive system which has been described as a cognitive structure (Lewin, 1948), a personal construct system (G.A. Kelly, 1957), a conceptual system (Hagendoorn, 1976), or cognitive schemata (Bartlett, 1932).

Whether these different processes can indeed be interpreted as sequential parts of an overall cognitive process, is perhaps less important at the moment than the realization that there are certain formal similarities between the three processes. Whether we are dealing with the attribution of causality in perceived behaviour, or with the integration of various items of information or even with the construction of an implicit cognitive system, the basic problem is to find the rules used by the observer to combine information into some final overall judgment.

As Slovic and Lichtenstein (1971) have pointed out, much of the recent work in social information processing has been accomplished in two basic schools of research : the regression and the Bayesian approaches. The former research tradition is exemplified by the correlational paradigm (Sarbin and Bailey, 1966), Brunswick lens model (Dudycha and Nayen, 1966), the ANOVA paradigm (Hoffman, 1968), functional measurement (N. Anderson, 1974) and conjoint measurement (Luce and Tukey, 1964). Two remarks should be made about these models. In the first place these models are an attempt to mimick or reconstruct the social judgment process as an additive form of information integration, but there are important differences between the various models which tend to be overlooked in most discussions.

Linear regression models of information processing do in fact form distinct groups of models. The <u>correlational paradigm</u> and Brunswick's lens model are simple S-R models which require the observer to make quantitative evaluations of a number of stimuli, each of which is defined by one or more quantified characteristics. The correlational analysis consists of calculating the linear multiple regression equation or the linear discriminant function to determine how each of the quantified characteristics is weighed by the observer in order to arrive at the final evaluations. Brunswick's lens model only adds to this analysis the comparison of the judge with the true state of affairs i.e. the multiple regression equation for the actual criterion value i.s.o. the judge's prediction. Introspection and Gestalt psychology suggest that cues are often used in a non linear and configurational manner. In fact a good deal of research on impression formation since Asch's first study in 1946 has been devoted to the question of configurational information processing. In theory a linear regression model can take such interaction effects into account by incorporating crossproduct terms in the equation, but because a reliable estimation of weighing coefficients requires large numbers of cases, various researchers prefer the use of analysis of variance to describe complex judgmental processes (Slovic and Lichtenstein, 1971).

Essentially different from the application of the correlation paradigm are studies which use subjective quantifications of stimuli in order to predict the final complex judgment. In this case we no longer have an S-R, but an R-R model, because we are relating responses made in isolation, to a response made to stimuli presented in combination. It should be realized that the responses to the stimuli in isolation can still be of two different kinds. These responses can either be interpreted as subjectively experienced sensations which are thought of as the cognitive counterparts of the stimuli or they may be considered final (evaluative) responses based on each of the stimuli in isolation. The difference between two types of responses can perhaps be clarified by a simple example.

In most diagnostic work one can make a prediction on the basis of objective cues. However, such cues can be perceived, interpreted, coded or diagnosed differently and they may have a certain predictive utility in isolation and/or in combination.

Usually the perceived cue is granted the status of an implicit, intervening variable although it is in fact an overt response. However in a theoretical model we treat it as a pseudo-cognition, which is not the case for the predictive response based on cues in isolation. The hypothesised causal relations in this case can be represented as in the following diagram:

FIGURE I

Path Diagram for Cognitive Integration Processes

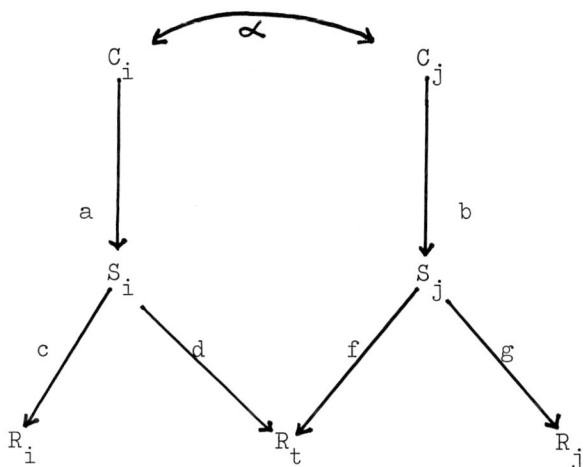

Error components are not labelled

where C_i and C_j are the objective cues or stimuli

S_i and S_j the subjective representations or perceptual responses

R_i, R_j, R_t are the responses based on the cues in isolation or combination

α = the correlation between cues

It should be realized that the diagram presented in FIGURE I is only one of a number of theoretically possible models. The purpose of this example is only to point out that, irrespective of the nature of the particular model we use, the relationship of the final overall judgment to cues, perceptual responses and separate predictive responses are quite different. If one considers e.g. the correlations which can be expected on the basis of this model between the separate cues, internal representations or predictive responses and the overall response, we find that

$$r_{Rt.Ci} = ad + \alpha\, bf$$

$$r_{Rt.Si} = \alpha + a\, bf$$

$$r_{Rt.Ri} = cd + ca\alpha\, bf$$

Comparison of those three correlation coefficients shows immediately that the correlation between the overall response and separate predictive responses must be lower than the correlation between the overall response and the internal representation. We also see that, depending on the correlation between cues (α), the veridicality of the internal representation (a) and the "response strength" (c) , the values of the correlations may vary with respect to each other. If e.g. the representation is veridical (a=1) $r_{Rt\ Ci}$ and $r_{Rt\ Si}$ are equal and there is no need to introduce a subjective counterpart of the objective cue. But the reverse is not true, because these correlations can be similar for any value of $\underline{a}$, as long as the strength of $\underline{d}$ is equal to the value of α bf.

The distinctions made here also have important implications for the perennial debate about averaging vs summating models of information integration. It can be shown (Jaspars, 1976) that a linear regression model encompasses both an averaging and an additive model, because the specific form of integration depends on the correlation between cues or internal representations. If the correlation approaches 1 the linear regression model becomes an averaging model, if the correlation approaches 0 a summative model results.

The S-R and R-R regression models of information integration should be clearly distinguished from the functional measurement models developed by N.Anderson (1970, 1974) and the conjoint measurement model of Luce and Tukey (1964). Both models are in a true sense models which relate internal representations to the overall response under the assumption of additivity. The main difference between the two approaches is that conjoint measurement uses only ordinal properties to obtain subjective scale values of stimuli, whereas functional measurement treats judgment at the interval scale level. This difference has recently become less important since even nominal judgments can be used to obtain estimates of subjective values at the interval level by alternating least squares procedures (de Leeuw et al. 1976, Young et al. 1976). The unique feature of both models and the recent developments in additivity analysis is that subjective scale values are inferred from the final responses to compound stimuli. In terms of the path-diagram presented in FIGURE I we obtain a direct estimate of the values for S_i and S_j weighed by the path coefficients. When all measures are expressed in standard scores one can directly obtain the weights for the internal representations and thus the correlation between R and O_i, without actually having to use a measure of S_i by e.g. a verbal report of the S. This approach allows us then to test whether such verbal responses can indeed be considered as substitutes for subjectively represented stimuli.

It should be pointed out that functional measurement is by no means restricted to simple additive information processing but it is surprising to see how often a linear regression model produces fairly accurate predictions whether it relies on objective or on subjective stimulus values or even on response values in isolation (Anderson, 1974). Slovic and Lichtenstein (1971) who have reviewed the literature of the S-R models, report for artificial tasks correlations between .80 and .90 and for complex tasks correlations between .70 and .80. This does not mean that Gestalt configurational or interaction effects do not occur in complex social judgments. Such effects have been reported in many studies (Jaspars, 1966, Slovic and Lichtenstein, 1971). In subsequent experiments others showed that simple additive models produce a systematic bias by under - or overestimating extreme values. Verhoeven (1970), Warr (1971), Israël (1973) and Schümer (1973) showed moreover that interaction effects are more likely to occur when part of the information presented is ambiguous and Van der Kloot (1975) found that when Ss were asked to make multiple judgments based on compound stimuli, a degeneration of the information processing seemed to take place to such an extent that only the most relevant information for a particular judgment was taken into account.

The conflict between a Gestalt model and additive models of information integration was to some extent resolved at a fairly early date because Yntema and Torgerson (1961) showed that whenever prediction variables are monotonically related to a criterion variable, a simple linear regression model can be very accurate even if interaction effects are known to exist. Even in the extreme case where all effect is due to interaction, an additive model will achieve quite accurate predictions simply because a weighed score on the independent variables will correlate very highly with the sum of these variables.

What has been said about linear regression models of information processing is to a large extent also true for probabilistic models in general and in particular for Bayesian models (Slovic and Lichtenstein, 1971; Warr, 1970; Jaspars, 1976).

Anderson (1974) is very critical of a Bayesian approach and simply states that there is no doubt that it is wrong. Also the results of the extensive work by Wyer (1974) is considered by Anderson as disappointing. There are, however, two important differences between the linear regression models and probabilistic models. First of all probabilistic models are always R-R models. This is e.g. immediately evident in the case of the Bayesian model, where one is primarily interested in the revision of judgments due to the impact of new data. It is often not realized or at least not mentioned explicitly in most studies that the standard application of Bayes' theorem ($\Omega_1 = LR \, \Omega_0$) presupposes that the data are conditionally independent, which amounts to saying that Bayes theorem does not take interaction effects into account and is essentially a summative model when a logaritmic transformation is used. The similarity of Bayes theorem to R-R linear regression models becomes even more clear if one rewrites it, so that the final judgment can be related directly to judgments based on each datum separately. In ratio form we get :

$$\frac{P(A/B \cap C)}{P(\bar{A}/B \cap C)} = \frac{P(A/C)}{P(\bar{A}/C)} \cdot \frac{P(A/B)}{P(\bar{A}/B)} \cdot \frac{P(\bar{A})}{P(A)} \quad \text{(Jaspars, 1976)}$$

This is in fact Wyer's concept identification model in ratio-form for which it is not necessary to assume that B and C are independent. If this is not the case Wyer's model becomes :

$$P(A/B \cap C) = \frac{P(A/B) \cdot P(A/C)}{P(A)} \cdot \frac{P(B) \cdot P(C)}{P(B C)}$$

This model is directly comparable to a linear regression model which takes into account the intercorrelations between the predictor variables. This comparison brings out another extremely important difference between functional and conjoint measurement on the one hand and all other models on the other hand. In probabilistic and linear regression models the weighing of the information which enters into the overall judgment is determined _a priori_ on the basis of intercorrelations between the predictors and the correlations of the predictors with the criterion : in functional and conjoint measurement the subjectively weighed scale values are obtained _a posteriori_ . Although this has the great advantage that one does not need pseudo cognitions or substitute responses, the distinct drawback is that both approaches do not constitute theoretical models in a substantive sense. One may be able to show e.g. that integration theory can be applied to attribution processes, but that does not mean that one can determine under which conditions e.g. responsibility will be attributed more to the person or to the situation. Research in social judgment could benefit, however, greatly from a combination of both approaches, as I will argue in the last part of this chapter (see also Fincham and Jaspars, 1979).

The difference between a priori models based on substantive theory and a posteriori descriptions, is also discussed by Warr (1970), who argued, moreover, quite rightly that one should study a priori models comparatively. In his own studies Warr shows that virtually all models produced very high correlations with the final judgments and only very slight deviations were found in all cases. However, in only one case did he find an acceptable regression gradient. This appears to be a sophisticated union set model, which is basically an additive model taking into account the perceived interrelationships of the information in set theoretical terms. Verhoeven and Jaspars (Verhoeven, 1972) showed that for the same data equally good predictions could be obtained with a complete Bayesian model which takes into account conditional dependency.

Although the debate about the exact nature of the integration of social information is by no means finished, it seems clear that one can safely conclude that additive information integration models can predict judgments of complex social stimuli very well. Although there are indications that the process of information integration is more complex and may require a model which takes into account configurational effects, such effects do not appear to occur very often and are usually fairly weak compared to the main effect of the information presented.

This means that complex internal representations of interrelated social judgments can be constructed with, by now widely available, procedures for multivariate analysis, multi-dimensional scaling and hierarchical cluster analysis.

These methods have been extensively used to study the representation of trait inferences, semantic differentiation, personal constructs, conceptual systems (Hagendoorn, 1976) and social situations. These studies are noticeably different from research on the representation of knowledge in long term memory and language processing. I believe that the study of social judgment processes and especially studies dealing with representational aspects would benefit greatly from the latter approaches developed in cognitive psychology, because so often social jugdments are based upon information presented in linguistic form. We have concerned ourselves mainly with formal characteristics of cognitive representations such as consistency, complexity, differentiation, etc, and we disregarded almost entirely the nature of the cognitive elements which are the constituents of such cognitive representations. Consistency e.g. was seen as a very general principle operating irrespective of the specific relations involved. The same is true for such characteristics as concreteness and cognitive complexity which are probably much more domain specific than has hitherto been realized (Hagendoorn, 1976). The point is not that we do not have some idea of how to classify personality traits, emotional states, social behaviour and social relations and even social situations, but it is highly unlikely that we would be able to predict, on the basis of cognitive representations, in these terms, how people would answer questions about social situations or what kind of alternative interpretations (paraphrases) they could give (Schank and Abelson, 1976), let alone that we would be able to predict how they would actually behave in the situation. No attempt has been made until recently, to relate cognitive representations to social behaviour. We have satisfied ourselves with the study of the formation of cognitive representations through processes of attribution and information integration but refrained from developing a theory about the production of social behaviour based upon such representations. To the extent that we have studied the relationships between social behaviour and subjective representations we have merely used verbal judgments as pseudo cognitions or as substitutes for overt action. No wonder that we have been puzzled by the fact that in many cases judgments do not seem to be related to behaviour. In the cognitive tradition of social psychology this problem has clearly been neglected. It is interesting to note therefore that some recent development in social psychology have been concerned much more with the genesis of action with social skills and social performance and the rule governed nature of social behaviour (Argyle, 1969, 1978; Argyle and Kendon, 1967; Collett, 1977; Harré, 1977; Clarke, 1975). Both Argyle's social skill model and Harré's ethogenics pay a good deal of attention to the perceptual aspects and subjective meaning of the social situation, but they do so in a way that is essentially different from the traditional cognitive approach in social psychology. In Argyle's original social skill model social behaviour is interpreted as an organized, coordinated activity in relation to a situation which controls the activity, in the sense that the outcome of actions are continuously matched against some criterium of achievement or approach to a goal, according to which the action is corrected (Argyle and Kendon, 1967). Social action is seen as being under direct control of the sensory output and is thus affected by cognitive processes. On the other hand selectivity of perception appears to be determined by the aim of the actor. There thus appears to be an intimate relation between social behaviour, the way in which the actor perceives the situation and the reactions of the other person. There is, however, very little direct evidence about perceptual and translation processes in actual social interaction. In 1967 Argyle and Kendon concluded that there was room for much more work especially on the information selected and made use of within the ongoing activity of social interaction. Quite recently Argyle reemphasized the importance of the perception of the other's reaction as part of skilled social performance, but the evidence referred to is mainly concerned with the judgment of emotions, interpersonal behaviour and personality characteristics in general, not with the relation between the perception of the other person and social behaviour in the situation itself. To be sure there is a great deal of evidence on _where_ and _when_ people look during social interaction (Argyle and Cook, 1976) but to what extent do these studies tell us something about _what_ people perceive, _what_ sense they make of what is going on and how they will behave (Argyle, 1978). Although gaze was selected for study by Argyle and his students because the social skill model suggested the importance of visual feed-back, it appears that gaze - which is both a behavioural signal and an information channel - has been studied much more often as the dependent variable in communication situations than as the independent or intervening variable influencing behaviour. Perhaps the only experiments which are relevant in this research are the studies in which vision is interfered with in various ways (Argyle, Lalljee and Cook, 1968; Jaspars, 1973; Jaspars et al., 1973 a,b,; Jaspars et al., 1974) although the evidence here is largely in the form of verbal accounts after the interaction situation.

Nevertheless the social skill model makes one point very clear. In order for the actor to match the outcome of his actions against some criterion and correct his own behaviour accordingly, some form of representation is assumed which is directly related to the action in the situation. It is on the basis of corrective action that we make inferences about the internal representations of the actor. Or to put it in another way, by following the behaviour of the actor and changes in the situation over time, we can estimate the parameters of the representation which is implied by the covariation of responses of the actor and changes in the environment. In this sense the original social skill model is directly comparable to an S-R correlational approach. In later developments of the social skill model Argyle has also included the direct influence of previous responses of the actor on his current behaviour, thereby introducing an R-R component in the model. In both versions of the social skill model it seems reasonable to assume the mental representation of the social situation, which is implicit in the corrective behaviour of the actor, is quite different from the representation which can be inferred from a person's general classification of social situations.

In Harré's ethogenics a similar notion can be found. In explaining intelligibility and warrantability of actions Harré argues that social psychologists may propose hypotheses as to the cognitive resources of people on the basis of the structure of the action sequence observed. However, Harré also states that "the ethogenic method is based upon the assumption that the very same cognitive resources can be employed in another task, the explication and justification of the manifested patterns of action in speech" (Harré, 1977, 285) . Harré claims, moreover, that account analysis yields much the same sort of hypotheses about a person's cognitive content and organisation as does the analysis of action sequences in microsociology. In addition Harré takes great pains to point out that accounts which precede, accompany and follow actions in the form of statements of rules, implicit or explicit exposition of meanings and stories and anecdotes should not be interpreted as introspective causal explanations, although some accounts may have that character. Still, accounts reveal the cognitive groundings of the individual's social competence from which an ideal competence of the milieu (local ethography) can be abstracted. Accounts also reveal the social semantic system of the individual, i.e. his social knowledge of situations and the proper action sequences. Account analysis, moreover, reveals TOTE hierarchies of social life and knowledge of "the rules" which apply in particular situations. In addition the fine structure of accounts can be investigated by studying the interrelations of distinct concepts which occur in accounts by Kelly's REP techniques. Whatever it is that accounts and account analysis reveal, it is obvious that accounts are closely related to particular actions in specific situations. In fact accounts are part of the action in the situation. In earlier studies of verbal social interaction or communication, accounts

were probably treated as specific forms of social behaviour
(say category 5 and 6 in a Bales observation scheme, Bales, 1950)
In a sense then we are back at our R-R models of social behaviour,
except that we are talking now about quite different responses.
In orthodox social judgment studies most researchers are concerned with verbal reactions to generalized and symbolically represented social stimuli; in ethogenics we are concerned with
speech, preceding, accompanying and following the very actions
we try to explain or understand. Again we must ask how the internal representation, which according to Harré is implicit in
both accounts and action, is related to representations which
are not directly related to action in a particular situation.

The most interesting aspect of the development, exemplified
by the social skill model and by ethogenic theory, from my point
of view, is that both approaches have tried to resolve the
perennial and neglected problem of relating social cognition to
social behaviour, by replacing the notion of a <u>general</u> cognitive
representation (cognitive structure, personal construct system,
conceptual system, attitude) with <u>situation specific</u> representetions directly related to the behaviour. One might argue that
this theoretical manoeuvre does not solve anything at all but
merely substitutes the problem of relating cognition to action
with the new problem of relating general cognitions to specific
ones. In a way this is true. But there is another side to the
issues raised by the "new look" social skills model and the
"new paradigm" approach of ethogenics. By emphasizing that action-immanent representations are possibly different from general
representations, both approaches force us to look in a quite different way at the problem of the relation between social judgments
and social behaviour. Because the question is not whether social
judgment and social behaviour are correlated, but whether social
judgments and social behaviour can be interpreted as manifestations
of the same underlying cognitive representations. People may not
always do what they say, but that does not mean that what they
say in one situation and what they do in another is not influenced
by the same thoughts or ideas. It would make sense therefore to
study the relationship between social judgment and social behaviour
as an indirect relationship brought about by a common cognitive
representation.

Cognitive representation, social judgments and social behaviour

There are two areas of social psychological research where the discrepancy between the expressed thought and action has baffled many researchers and produced considerable despair among social scientists. Both areas of research have to do with evaluative social judgments. The first one deals with the problem of the relationship between <u>moral reasoning</u> and <u>moral conduct</u> and the related area of cognition and action under conditions of <u>forced compliance</u>. The second area of research has to do with the relationship between <u>attitudes and behaviour</u>. In both fields of study a remarkable lack of correspondance between judgment and behaviour has been reported. Brown (Brown and Herrnstein, 1975) has recently called the discrepancy between moral thought and action a paradox. The paradox lies in the fact that most people or at least most American college students appear to attain a conventional "law and order" morality in making judgments about Kohlberg's moral dilemma's but subjects coming from the same population appear to be capable of deceitful conformity (Asch, 1956), willing to endanger another's life (Milgram, 1974) and destroy property (Zimbardo, 1969) and are indifferent to life and death problems of strangers (Latané and Darley, 1970). One can of course argue that the Ss in Kohlberg's studies were making judgments about other people in imaginary situations, whereas the subjects in the other experiments were personally faced with a moral dilemma in an actual situation. However this argument is not very convincing when one takes into account that observers grossly underestimate the extent of immoral behaviour of others and themselves. In forced compliance situations Nuttin (1974) found discrepancies of more than 90 % in the cases of counter-attitudinal advocacy and corruption between judgment and behaviour. In attitude research the famous study of La Pierre (1934) showed a similar discrepancy between actual behaviour and verbal promises.

How are we to account for these discrepancies and what is the significance of these discrepancies for the problem of the relation between action and cognition ? In the case of moral conduct Brown points out that the stage of moral development is in fact irrelevant for moral conduct. One can be moral or immoral for 6 different sets of reasons in Kohlberg's conception of morality. Brown argues that persons first of all have to consider a situation in moral terms, but if they do have identical moral conceptions they may choose different actions because they have no high degree of moral concern or feel little personal responsibility. In addition to all this, the situation may introduce factors not prefigured in verbal descriptions of the Kohlberg type.

The important point of Brown's preliminary model of moral reasoning and moral conduct is that he does not deny that Kohlberg's very general theory of moral reasoning does not play a role at all in moral conduct, but that the moral conception of the situation is not determined only by the stage of the individual's moral reasoning. His moral choice depends in addition upon other psychological factors, whereas moral action does depend on this choice and situational factors. Subjects in Kohlberg's experiments reflect apparently in an unperturbed fashion their way of moral reasoning in abstracto, whereas their moral conduct in the experiments discussed, reflects in addition the moral conception of the situation, other psychological factors and situational constraints.

Similar explanations have been offered in reviews of attitude-behaviour research (Wicker, 1969; Schumann and Johnson, 1976; Fishbein and Ajzen, 1977). Wicker (1969) simply reviewed the literature at the time, arrived at a rather pessimistic conclusion about the attitude-behaviour relationship, but did not go beyond a simple enumeration of the factors which might have disturbed the relationship. In their recent quite extensive review of attitude-behaviour studies, Fishbein and Ajzen (1977) made two quite obvious points. The correlation between evaluative judgments and actual behaviour increases when the attitude object is more specific and the congruence between the object of action and judgment is higher. Fishbein and Ajzen do not offer a theoretical model which encompasses these two factors and goes beyond the already formulated attitude theory. (Fishbein and Ajzen, 1974, 1975). Schuman and Johnson (1976) and Alwin (1973) are actually the first authors who try to construct a theoretical model which takes other factors into account in a systematic and interrelated fashion. First of all they make a number of highly relevant distinctions which seem to have escaped the attention of previous researchers, and which coincide with some of the points which I have tried to make before (Jaspars, 1975, 1978, 1979). They distinguish between elicited verbal attitudes and spontaneous verbal attitudes, between manifest expressions of attitudes and latent or true attitudes, between broad and narrow conceptions of attitudes. With respect to the attitude-behaviour relationship they make the same point Fishbein and Ajzen make about conceptual congruence, but more important is that they emphasize also the distinction between what I have called <u>discrepancy</u> of judgment and behaviour and (un) <u>relatedness</u>. The A-B discrepancy and A-B relationship are quite different and essentially unrelated phenomena.

Because they have not been clearly distinguished a great deal of confusion has arisen in the literature. Lack of correlation or the presence of discrepancies between what people say and what they do does not mean that their behaviour is not related to what they say. Even if large discrepancies exist one may still predict reliably behaviour from attitudes or vice-versa.

Any theory attempting to relate social judgments to social behaviour should therefore take into account at least the following points :

1. Both verbally or otherwise expressed judgments about social stimuli and overt behavioural responses in a particular situation should be seen as expressions or manifestations of latent, underlying dispositions which include an internal, cognitive representation of the social stimulus situation.
2. The internal representations implied by judgments and behaviour in the situation are not necessarily the same, at least a dual representation is therefore necessary. There may be first of all a lack of conceptual congruence in the sense that the behaviour is a response to a different stimulus situation compared with the judgment. Conceptual congruence is affected by differences in _time_, _generality_ and the _symbolic_ or _actual_ nature of the stimulus presentation. Action is usually observed with respect to actual and specific stimuli whereas judgments are very often observed with respect to generalized symbolic representations of the stimulus. Differences in time of measurement should take account of the fact that social judgments obtained before or after the action have a different theoretical status.
3. Other factors which may influence social judgments and social behaviour may or may not be similar. To the extent that they are they will influence the consistency and/or relationship of social judgments and social behaviour. The most common condition is the situation where social factors act as constraints against the expression of the latent representations in behaviour, but not in social judgment.

These points will be taken into account in two versions of a dual representation model I will present in the last paragraph, together with empirical evidence for the model. Before presenting the model I would like to point out that it should be considered as a sort of "minimax" model in the sense that I want to consider the minimum number of factors necessary to explain a maximum number of results of empirical studies. The first version of the model is expressed in the form of a causal network which allows path-analysis of the relations between the variables involved. It is therefore a model which considers variations in unidimensional responses and representations. This version of the model shows some similarity to the model proposed by Alvin (1973) and Schumann and Johnson (1976 and 1980) but it is more complex in that it does not treat "other" factors as uncorrelated error variances. In doing so it can explain more of the empirical results we are interested in, although it is harder to test, because of a greater number of relations that have to be inferred. The second model is multidimensional and regards social behaviour in a particular situation as an interrelated set of reactions to a complex stimulus situation, which can be conceived of as the result of a latent representational structure and a system of transformational rules. To apply the latter notion such structures are treated as matrices which can be analysed by various multivariate techniques which are akin to the functional measurement and conjoint measurement approaches. One interpretation of this approach which has certain attractive features is to consider social behaviour as a reflection of the structure which the individual creates in the environment by behaving in a particular way, and it is this action-immanent structure of the situation which can be recovered by unfolding the hierarchical or sequential order which can be observed in the behaviour.

The dual representation of social reality

a. A path analytical model

The path analytical model presented in FIGURE II makes certain assumptions which may not be immediately evident from inspection of the diagram and which therefore should be spelled out explicitly.

First of all the path diagram does not make an explicit distinction between behaviour and behavioral intentions in order not to introduce unnecessary complications. There is some empirical justification for this decision (Fishbein and Ajzen, 1974) but more important is the theoretical consideration that any discrepancy which may arise between intentions (whatever they may be) and action is in most cases the result of accidental social interference which is not foreseeable. To the extent that such factors are foreseeable it is assumed that they are already included in the intentions. I have in mind here factors like the abilities or the skills which allow the individual to carry out the action, or the environmental difficulties which may prevent him to accomplish e.g. a certain task. Unforeseeable factors, like sudden unexpected events which change the course of action are treated in the model as random influences.

Secondly although the model implicitly includes a time parameter in relating the general representation to a specific representation and to behaviour, it is in a more general sense not a dynamic model which goes through various states and allows for feedback of changes in the environment on the specific representation nor does it have reciprocal influences which would allow for a change of the general representation under the influence of changes in the specific representation. Such elements can however be build into the model, but so far this has not been done.

In the third place various factors which are introduced should in fact be considered as linear combinations of a number of other quite separate and more fundamental or primitive influences which if introduced individually into the model might show that certain path coefficients will take on completely different values. One factor which is extremely important in this respect is the factor which I have summarized under the label of social and psychological constraints. The term constraints is in itself somewhat misleading because one can easily conceive of personal and environmental factors which enhance behaviour. However, in most empirical research dealing with the problem of the relation between social judgment and social behaviour these factors very often take on the nature of factors which limit the response alternatives of the individual. The constraints which may have an influence on social behaviour are generally of 5 different kinds. First of all there may be personal constraints in the form of the ability, skills, relevant personality characteristics or temporary states of the individual. In short everything Heider (1958) includes under the factor "power", when he discusses effective personal forces. These are the personal forces which together with certain environmental difficulties determine what a person can do in a situation. The second group of factors can presumably best be described as material constraints. This is not to say that we are dealing here only with the non-social environment, because in many cases such constraints will be manmade and part of the social structure or material culture in which the individual lives. Available resources, financial or otherwise, which are relevant for carrying out a certain task are probably the most relevant and most general case of such constraints. The three other groups of factors I am referring to are more clearly social, but it is important to allow at least for a distinction between interpersonal constraints, structural constraints and cultural constraints. The interpersonal constraints correspond to such well known factors as requests and commands, which are based upon symmetrical sentiments and asymmetrical power relationships between persons. Structural constraints refer to social influences related to the <u>positions, roles and functions</u> of the individuals in the social structure or more specifically in various social institutions such as the family, the educational, the economic, the political and the cultural institutions which constitute the social structure. And finally the immaterial cultural constraints which take on the form of <u>social norms</u> or <u>social values</u> which again may be institutionalized in various ways. If there is to be any practical value in the model I present here it will probably be necessary to specify exactly which constraints operate in particular circumstances before any generalizations can be made.

These remarks apply in the similar sense to the other ultimate factors of the path diagram. The psychological factors which are not part of the social and psychological constraints I have just mentioned, are also multivariate. The most obvious factors here are various personality dimensions which are related to certain formal characteristics of general representations such as concreteness and abstractness, cognitive differentiation, complexity and consistency.

The general representations themselves are probably also domain specific. In fact we have developed in social psychology only an implicit psychology which deals with the representation of human relations, personality, emotions, social behaviour and social situations, but the scope of the world of mental representations is almost without limit. Recent French research on social representations has emphasized the social origin and the collective nature of such representations in addition.

Finally, the factor describing the social stimulus situation is itself a complex set of stimulus and situational context variations. However, as we have seen in the discussion about information integration, it appears that these factors in their effect on social judgments combine to a large extent in a linear fashion and can thus be conceived as a compound single stimulus or situation factor.

After these introductory remarks we are ready to look at the implications of the model itself.

FIGURE II

Path Analytical Model for the Relationship between Social Judgments and Social Behaviour

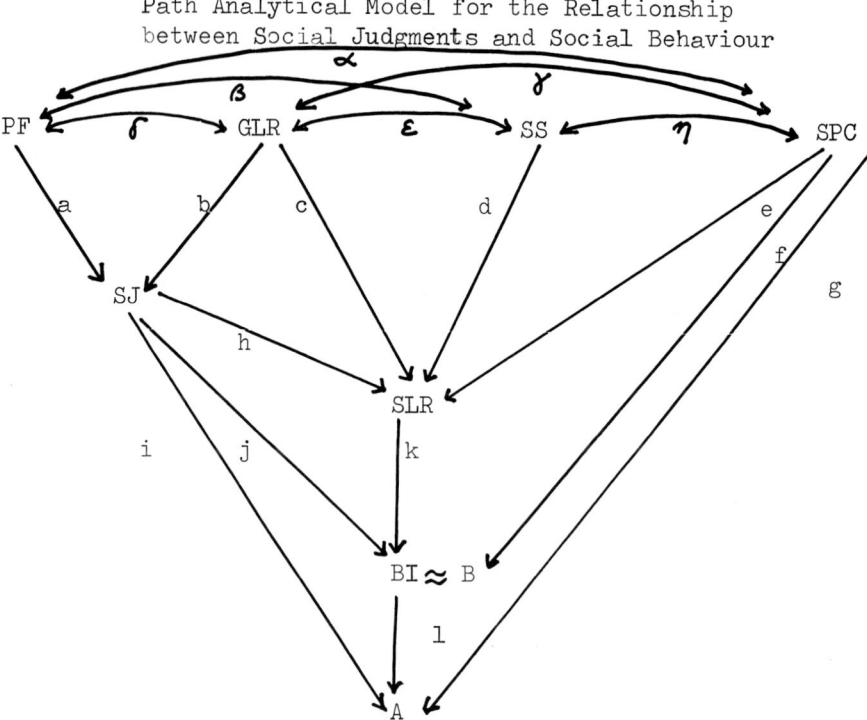

where PF = other psychological factors influencing social judgments
GLR general latent representation
SS stimulus situation
SPC social and psychological constraints
SLR specific latent representation
BI≈B behavioral intention and behaviour
SJ social judgment
A account given afterwards
a-h path coefficients
  correlations between ultimate variables

As can be seen in FIGURE II the path diagram contains 2 latent variables (GLR and SLR) and 6 variables which are, at least in principle, accessible to measurement. This means that we can in fact solve the equations for all parameters because 15 equations are given by the correlations between the 6 variables, whereas 4 more equations can be obtained from the restriction that the squared coefficients of paths ending in the same variables must add

up to one, if all variables are expressed in standard scores.
If we include the error factors for the variables SJ, SLR, B and
A there are in fact exactly the same number of equations as coefficients which have to be determined. This would however be quite
an undertaking for the complete model, but it is very likely
that in many specific situations certain relations can safely be
neglected. In many cases we can probably neglect the direct influence of the social judgment on the specific representation (reactivity) and behaviour (effort to be consistent) if social judgments are obtained under conditions of anonymity. Furthermore it
is not clear whether we would have to assume that social constraints have a direct influence on specific representations, behaviour and accounting or whether such influences manifest themselves through correlations with other ultimate variables.

For the theoretical analysis of the relationship and consistency of social judgments and social behaviour such uncertainties
are of less importance, because the conclusions which can be
drawn from a comparison of various equations and coefficients
which can be derived from the model, will not be affected by
these differences.

The correlations and consistencies which are of interest
are the relationships between the behaviour in the situation,
the apriori social judgments and the posterior accounts. Theoretically we are mainly interested in the relationship between
the general and the specific representations and the relationship
of the specific representation to behaviour. For the complete
model the following equations are obtained if we leave out all
error components

$SJ = aPF + b\ GLR$
$SLR = hSJ + cGLR + dSS + eSPC$
$B = jSJ + k\ SLR + f\ SPC$
$A = iSJ + lB + gSPC$

In terms of ultimate variables we get :

$SJ = a\ PF + bGLR$
$SLR = ahPF + (bh+c)\ GLR + dSS + eSPC$
$B = a(j+kh)PF + (bj+kbh+kc)GLR + dkSJ + ekSPC$
$A = a[i+l(j+kh)]\ PF + [ib+l(bj+kbh+hc)]\ GLR + ldkSS + (elk+g)SPC$

In order to avoid unnecessary cumbersome equations and comparisons I will consider in most cases only situations where we can
assume that the correlations between the ultimate variables are
negligible. This means e.g. that the correlation between social

judgments and social behaviour which for the complete model would be :

$$r_{SJ.B} = j + hk + bck + a\delta ck + a\beta\alpha k + a\alpha ek + a\alpha f + b\epsilon dk$$

reduce to

$$r_{SJ.B} = j + hk + bck$$

The correlations between social judgment and social behaviour could thus be decomposed in

j' a direct influence of the judgment on the behaviour in an effort to be consistent (consistency effect)

hk an indirect effect due to reactivity (h)

bck the joint effect of the general representation on social judgment and specific representations

aδck an indirect effect through the correlation of personal factors and the general representation, e.g. personality differences in cognitive differentiation, abstractness, etc.

a$\beta\alpha$k
b$\epsilon\alpha$k — indirect effects through the correlation of individual differences and variations in the stimulus situation which may be present especially in field studies, where selection may occur or in studies where the stimulus can be defined by the person.

aαek
aαf — indirect effect through the correlation of social constraints and individual differences e.g. through the effect of structural and cultural factors on personality or the incorporation of norms and values in a person's general representation.

The decomposition of the correlation coefficient of social judgment and behaviour shows immediately why there may not be a positive correlation between judgment and behaviour in many cases. Even if the effects of the judgment itself and the effect of the general representation are positive these effects may easily be offset by all the indirect effects which come about through the correlation of personal factors with situational influences, which have opposite effects on behaviour. The decomposition of the correlation coefficient makes also clear why differences between field studies and experiments may occur, because with random assignments of Ss to stimulus situations some indirect effects on the correlation will disappear which may lead to an increase or decrease of the correlation depending upon the nature of the effect of the situation.

In general one would expect that the correlation between judgment and behaviour will increase when similar or positively correlated additional factors determine both judgment and behaviour. Marais (1975) studied this effect in a series of experiments. In a first study he showed that a behavioral measure and a verbal measure of attitudes towards black South-Africans among Afrikaans speaking South-Africans correlated significantly ($r = .26$), whereas both measures did no show a relationship with a disguised perceptual measure of the same ethnic attitude. Although it is not possible to rule out other explanations, this result can be predicted on the basis of the path diagram, if one assumes that disguised measures are in general not influenced by social constraints whereas both verbal and behavioural measures may be. So we see that in this particular case a relationship between a verbal social judgment and social behaviour is found, but presumably because both are affected by the same social factors.

In a more extensive experiment disguised (pupillary responses, eye movements, sorting task) and undisguised (semantic differential, attitude scale) measures were used to study attitudes towards authority among Dutch students. It was found that undisguised verbal measures showed positive intercorrelations, whereas disguised measures correlated negatively with the verbal indices. This result is easy to understand if we assume that there was a negative correlation between the attitude towards authority and the norms influencing the expression of these attitudes.

In a third study Marais showed that reported Church attendance among English speaking South-Africans could be predicted better from verbal measures of the attitude towards the church ($r = .48$) than from disguised measures ($r = .28$). An interesting point was that selfreported church attendance correlated significantly with scores on a social authority scale ($r = .37$) among English speaking South-Africans, but not among Afrikaanders, which may be the reason why in the latter group verbal and disguised measures did not show any difference.

In a final study Marais manipulated social constraints but did not succeed in producing any change in behaviour or evaluative judgments, although the correlation between evaluative judgment and behaviour decreased somewhat ($r = .38$ vs $r = .28$) compared to a control condition. This difference was not apparent when the γ coefficient was used ($\gamma = .39$).

The use of a γ coefficient in studies of this kind is based upon Campbell's differential threshold notion (Campbell, 1963) The idea of a differential threshold follows directly from a simplified path model where social constraints do influence behaviour in the situation, but not social judgments.

If the ultimate variables are uncorrelated the correlation $r_{SJ.B}$ = j + hk + bck will not be affected by a change in social constraints, but the expression of the latent representation in behaviour becomes less likely than its expression in a verbal judgment, because the latter is not influenced by variation in social constraints. There is, however, an interesting complication. Since the behaviour and the judgment very often take the form of an act or decision which only allows for dichotomous classification, we may expect that an asymmetrical relationship will develop. The interesting point is that under such conditions there is in fact a complete association between judgment and behaviour, but not an absolute association (Kendall and Stuart, 1961,2,540). A measure of complete association (such as γ), which takes this asymmetry into account should therefore indicate a stronger association than a symmetrical measure (φ) of complete association. When $\gamma > \varphi$ we may assume that the relationship between judgment and behaviour is asymmetrical and different thresholds affect judgment and behaviour.

When studies on the relationship between evaluative judgments and behaviour are reanalysed and cast into a dichotomous scheme such asymmetries occur often. A very good example is a study by Cowdry, Kenniston, and Sabin (1970) on the attitude of American students against the war in Vietnam and the signing of a petition against the war. All students who signed the petition appear to have negative attitudes towards the war and all students who had pro-war attitudes did not sign the petition, thus producing a complete association between verbal judgments and social action.

It is important to realize that there are important differences between evaluative statements made before an act is performed and accounts given afterwards, as can be inferred from the path diagram. In general one will expect that the correlation between behavioural variables and account variables is higher than between behaviour and social judgment, because the same social constraints which have a direct influence on behaviour can also influence the account. It is also likely that the behaviour itself influences the account. The same asymmetry should however occur when accounts are obtained afterwards. A study by Bellin and

Kriesberg (1969) illustrates this point very nicely. In this
study potential applicants for public housing were asked to indicate their interest in public housing. Overall the results
show the typical asymmetry in the sense that people who had already applied for public housing all said that they were also interested in public housing. Among the people who had not applied,
a lack of interest indicated that people were not likely to
apply in the future. The difference between the two conditions
can furthermore be illustrated by including in the prediction of
behaviour in the Bellin and Kriesberg study, the material and social constraints. Since the account after the act includes the
same constraints as the act, the prediction (or rather postdiction)
does not require the inclusion of these constraints, whereas this
is not the case when one has to predict behaviour on the basis of
interests expressed beforehand. It turns out that this is indeed
the case in the Bellin and Kriesberg study. To predict behaviour
from social judgment one has to add the interaction between interests and normative constraints, but to predict behaviour from
a-posteriori accounts only requires knowledge of interests.

Although it is quite important from a practical point of view
to be able to predict behaviour in a specific situation on the
basis of expressed social judgment and perceived social constraints
it is of more interest theoretically to show that behaviour is
related to the latent representation which is postulated in the model. Assuming no reactivity, no direct effect of judgment on behaviour and uncorrelated ultimate variables, we can easily see that the
correlation between the latent representation and behaviour must
always be higher than between the social judgment and behaviour
since under these conditions,

$$r_{SJ.B} = bck$$

the influence of the specific latent representation on behaviour
(k) will increase with an increase in $r_{SJ.B}$, a decrease in the
reliability of the social judgment and a decrease in the strength
of the relationship between the general and the specific latent
representation. This might be due to lack of conceptual congruence, the time which elapses between the measurement of the social
judgment and the social behaviour or the degree of specificity
of the specific latent representation. It seems reasonable to
assume therefore that under most circumstances, with intermediate
degrees of reliability, congruence and specificity, the correlation between the specific latent representation and the behaviour
in the situation will be higher than the correlation between the
social judgment and the social behaviour in question. Obviously

more predictions can be derived from the path model presented here, but a more important consideration is to realize that so far we have been dealing only with single representational, judgmental and behavioural **variables**. The notion of a representation intuitively implies multidimensionality and it is for this reason that we will have to consider a more complex model of the relationship between social judgment and social behaviour.

A Multivariate model

The weakness of the path analytical model presented in the preceding section is that it is impractical to include more than two types of responses and even more difficult to consider reactions to more than one stimulus. A multivariate model attempts to overcome this problem by interpreting individual social behaviour in a particular situation as the complete set of S-R relations. The set of S-R relations can be interpreted as an off-diagonal sub-matrix of an intact matrix of <u>all</u> relations between stimuli and responses. The S-R matrix thus implies a matrix of R-R relations (a response matrix) and a matrix of S-S relations (a stimulus matrix) as can be seen in FIGURE III.

FIGURE III

The S-R matrix as an off diagonal sub-matrix
of the intact S-S, R-R, S-R matrix

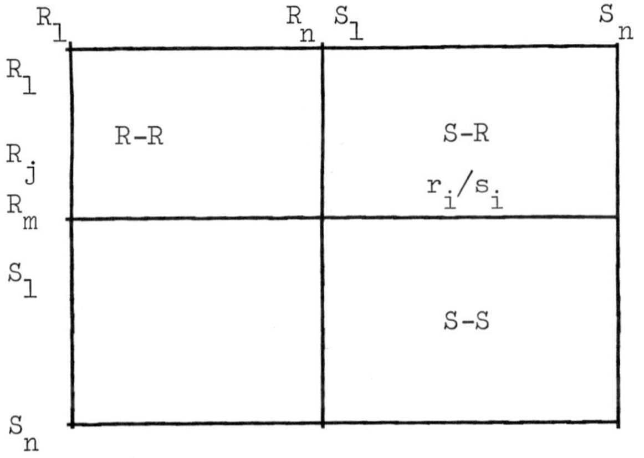

	$R_1 \ldots R_n$	$S_1 \ldots S_n$
R_1 R_j R_m	R-R	S-R r_i/s_i
S_1 S_n		S-S

$S_1 \ldots \ldots S_n$ are stimuli

$R_1 \ldots \ldots R_n$ are responses

$p(r_j/s_i)$ conditional probability of response j given stimulus i

It is important to realize, however, that different S-R matrices may imply the same or different S-S matrices. It is this fact which provides us with the possibility to relate social judgment and social behaviour to each other, because social judgment can simply be regarded as another set of responses which is related to the same set of stimuli and also implies a particular stimulus structure. Given the two stimulus structures, the one implied by the actual behaviour in the situation and the other implied by the social judgments made about the stimuli, we can now directly investigate the relationship between the two structures. There are various ways in which relationship can be expressed. We can simply correlate the two sets of S-S relationships or we can analyze first both stimulus matrices and determine subsequently a transformation matrix relating one stimulus structure to the other. I have discussed elsewhere several examples of the relationship between cognitive structures based on the analysis of similarity judgments and comparable structures based on preferential choice behaviour (Jaspars, 1966). In one experiment 6 male students in psychology at the University of Leiden were asked to volunteer as "social stimuli" for other students of their class (N = 31). The experiment was carried out at the end of the first year. We may assume therefore that the students knew each other fairly well. In one part of the experiment the 31 students who served as judges were asked to judge the psychological similarity between the 6 stimulus students, by the method of multi-dimensional rank-orders (Torgeson, 1958;262). In another part of the experiment the judges used the method of paired comparisons to indicate their liking for each of the 6 students. A Thurstone scale was constructed on the basis of the preferential choices and a multi-dimensional scaling analysis was performed for the similarity judgments. A multiple correlation of $r=.98$ between the preference scale and a weighed combination of the first two dimensions of the cognitive structure was found, thus indicating that the preferential choices of the judges could be derived very well from the cognitive structure which was obtained independently.

FIGURE IV

Similarity Structure Generated by
Six Stimulus Persons

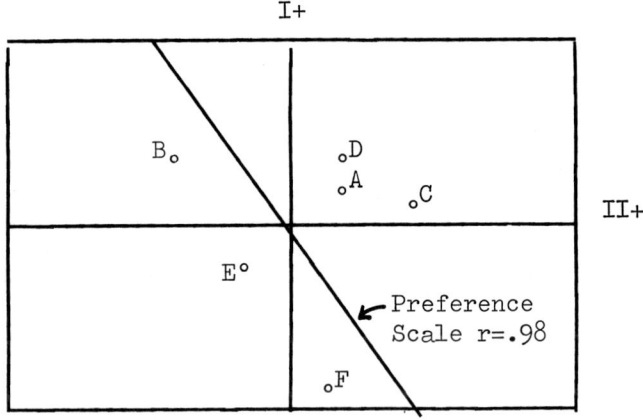

Essentially the same results were found for a set of quite different stimuli. In another experiment (Jaspars et al. 1965, 1972) 120 Dutch children were asked to judge the degree of similarity for 15 pairs of countries and to indicate their preference for each of the six countries constituting the fifteen pairs. The experimental methods used in this experiment were the same as in the previous study. For the older children in this study again a very high multiple correlation was found between the cognitive representation of the six countries based on the similarity judgments and the Thurstone scale based on their preferential choices (r=.97). (See Figure V)

FIGURE V

Similarity Structure for Six Countries
(Sixth Grade; N=24)

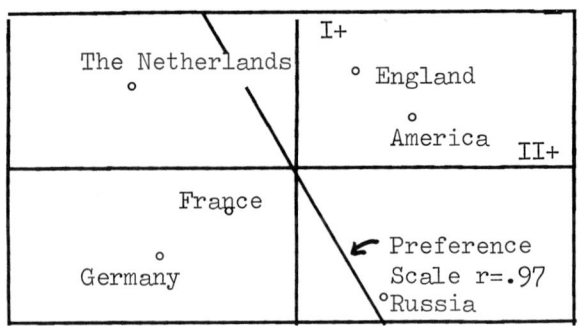

Because agreement between Ss is very high it also follows that individual preferential rankorders can be related in a similar way to the joint cognitive representation (Jaspars, 1979). In other cases such a simple relation between preferential choice and cognitive representation does not exist. A clear but relatively simple example is the relationship between the preference for particular family compositions and the perception of these configurations (Goldberg and Coombs, 1962; Delbeke, 1965; Coombs, Dawes and Tversky, 1970). There is considerable variation between individuals in the type of family they prefer. If we consider only the number of children and disregard sex differences for the moment, we see that e.g. in Delbeke's study (Delbeke, 1965; Jaspars, 1966) a clear bimodal distribution of preferences exists which indicates that approximately 25 % of the Ss prefer a family with two children whereas 40 % of the Ss prefer a family with 5 children. For the Ss who prefer small families (2 or 3 children) there is not a very high linear relationship between cognitive structure and individual preferential ranking, but such preferential orders can be derived by unfolding (Coombs, 1964; Coombs, Dawes and Tversky) from the joint cognitive structure in this particular case. Another, and perhaps more interesting, way to look at this problem is to reverse the question and instead of asking whether individual preferential choice behaviour can be predicted on the basis of the joint cognitive structure of the Ss, we can ask whether the cognitive structure implied by the set of preferential choices is the same as the cognitive structure obtained by direct similarity judgments or some other type of social judgment. In the study of the family preferences this is quite clearly the case, at least qualitatively. In the case of the judgments of the 6 stimulus persons we find that there is not enough variation in the preferential behaviour to reconstruct the cognitive structure underlying the individual preferential rankorders by unfolding analysis, but an approximation of this method of analysis shows that there is indeed a high degree of correspondence between the cognitive structure obtained on the basis of similarity judgments and the cognitive structure obtained by unfolding the individual preferential rankorders (Jaspars, 1966). In the case of the preferences for different countries there was again so much agreement among the Ss that an unfolding analysis was impossible.

In these examples we have concerned ourselves not with the relationship between cognition and "actual" behaviour, but with the relationship between cognitive representations based on similarity judgments and preferential, or comparative evaluative judgments. The point of these examples is, however, to argue that

FIGURE VI

The Relation between Rules, Cognitive
Representation (Map) and Behaviour
Multivariate Model

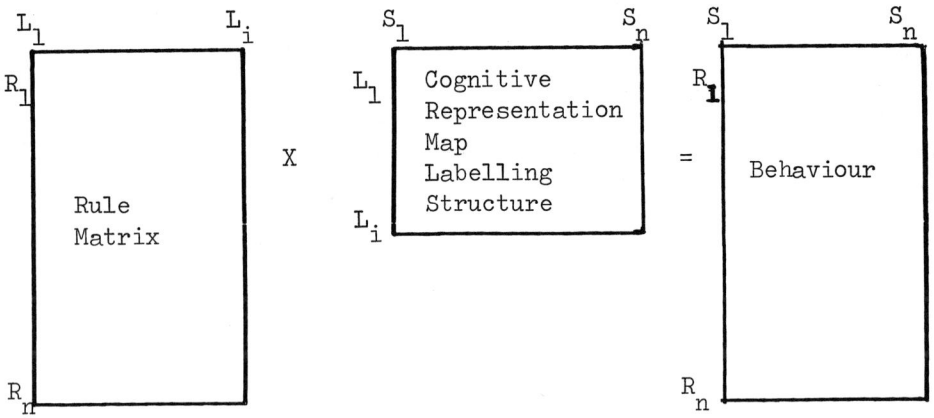

where S = stimulus
       R = overt response
       L = verbal response or label

<u>all behaviour</u> can be interpreted an a similar way i.e. an individual's reaction to a set of stimuli creates an order among the stimuli by virtue of the fact that particular S-R relationships are stronger than others.

Another way of relating behaviour to cognition is therefore suggested by the fact that both social judgments and overt behavioural responses can be interpreted as two off-diagonal matrices. To relate these two matrices to each other we have to find a transformation matrix which postmultiplied by the social judgment matrix will give the best approximation to the stimulus-response matrix. Thus

$$B = R.M$$

where B is the matrix of stimulus-overt response connections
M is the matrix of social judgments of the stimuli
R is the transformation matrix

If B and M are given we can find R by solving the matrix equation.

$$R = BM'(MM')^{-1}$$

I would like to argue that one can interpret the transformation matrix which I have introduced here as a rule system which allows us to relate the cognitive representation of the stimulus situation to the response system which we can observe. Or to put it in a slightly different way, the social judgments of the stimuli are considered as a mapping of the stimuli, into a labelling structure, to which also the overt responses are related by a system of rules. FIGURE VI illustrates the above matrix equation in more detail.

A direct application of this approach can be found in an experiment conducted by van der Kloot (1975). In this experiment 37 first year psychology students of the University of Leiden were asked first of all to rate the probability that someone who possesses one particular trait also possesses another one out of a set of 8 traits. These traits were selected because they had the highest loadings on the first two dimensions obtained in another study (van der Kloot, 1975). The traits are : aggressive, unsociable, cooperative, dominant, submissive, passive, pessimistic and rational. All 56 ordered pairs were rated on an 11 point scale ranging from 0 to 100 percent.

In the second part of the experiment which took place two weeks later, Ss were placed in front of a video-monitor. The Ss were informed that they were about to see a group discussion

TABLE IIa

Loadings of Verbal Reaction Categories
on Two Discriminant Dimensions

Categories	Unrotated		Rotated	
	I	II	I	II
social-emotional positive	.624	.760	-.024	.938
social-emotional negative	-.883	.436	-.953	-.247
task-oriented positive	-.440	.443	-.623	.048
task-oriented negative	-.238	-.026	-.164	-.175

TABLE IIb

Projections of Stimulus Persons
on Two Rotated Discriminant Dimensions of Task Two

Stimulus Person	Dimension	
	I	II
1	-.172	-.762
2	-1.548	-.737
3	.876	.075
4	.844	1.423

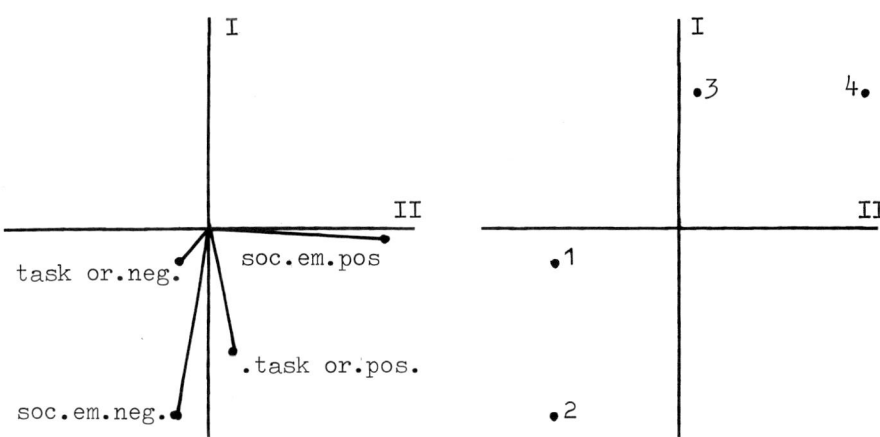

FIGURE VII. Plot of the loadings of the verbal reaction categories (left figure) and of the projections of the stimulus persons on two rotated discriminant dimensions.

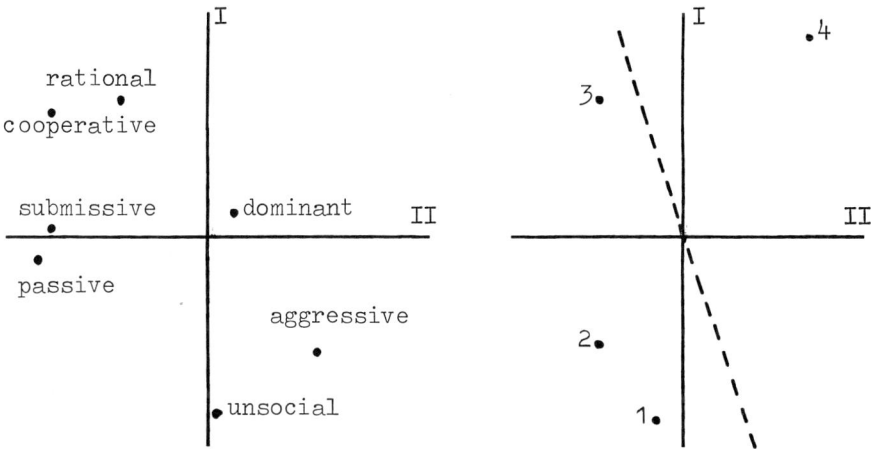

FIGURE VIII. Plot of the loadings of eight personality traits (left figure) and of the projections of the stimulus persons (right figure) on two rotated discriminant dimensions of task five.

in which four persons discussed the problem of a 13 year old delinquent boy. A short biography of the boy was read to the S and he was asked to "participate" in the group discussion by reacting to statements and opinions of the discussants. The S was told to join in the discussion as if he were an actual member of the group. The S was asked to speak into a microphone placed in front of him and he was given a set of earphones to hear the sound track of the videorecording.

The reactions of the S were recorded on one track of a stereo taperecorder. The group discussion was recorded simultaneously on the other track. The videorecording consisted of a 20 minute discussion of the well-known Johnny Rocco case by four graduate students in social psychology of the Department of Psychology of Leiden University . In the discussion the four discussants held different views about the treatment of the boy varying from advocating leniency to proposing very hard treatment. After the discussion the S was given the same 56 ordered pairs of adjectives and asked to rate the conditional probabilities again but now for the specific situation of the members of the group. The Ss were also asked to rate the four participants on a 7 point scale composed of the 8 personality traits already mentioned. In the first place a semi-metric multidimensional scaling analysis was performed on the two sets of subjective conditional probability matrices. Two highly similar two-dimensional structures were found indicating that by and large the general labeling structure did not change when applied to the particular situation. Only one slight change was observed. The trait "pessimistic" is more strongly associated with aggression and dominance, which makes sense because the participant who was most pessimistic about the future of Johnny Rocco dominated the discussion in an aggressive way. In the second part of the analysis the verbal reactions of the Ss to the 4 participants in the group discussion were transcribed from the tape, together with the group discussion and were scored according to the four major categories of Bales observation scheme (Socio-emotional negative, socio-emotional positive, task oriented active, task oriented passive). The direction of each act was scored by assigning it to one of six categories, where category one to four stood for the four members of the discussion group, category 5 represents the group as a whole and category 6 is the experimenter. The scoring was performed by 7 judges. The coefficient of generalizability which was calculated for the 7 judges was $p = .997$ which indicates that the scores could very well be generalized over judges. In order to analyze the Ss' verbal reactions towards the group discussants an S-R matrix (stimulus persons-response categories) was calculated for each S. These data were then used as input for a canonical discriminant analysis on the four stimuli so as to achieve maximum discrimination between the four stimulus persons with the aid of the differential behavioral reactions of the Ss. It was found that the four stimulus persons had two significant difference dimensions (cumulative $\chi_2 = 158.41$; df = 12 $p < .001$) of which the first could be interpreted, after varimax rotation, as active task behaviour with negative socio-emotional behaviour related to it. Very often behaviour of this kind appeared to consist of remarks like : "I don't agree with you; I think..." The second rotated dimension appeared to consist almost exclusively of positive socio-emotional behaviour. The complete double structure of stimulus persons and response categories is given in TABLE II and FIGURE VII.

As can be seen in TABLE II and FIGURE VII the Ss reacted in general fairly positively to stimulus person 4 and 3, but rather negatively to persons 1 and 2. Since stimulus person 4 tended to a rather lenient position and stimulus person 1 advocated the harshest treatment it is not difficult to guess what position most Ss favored.

This is confirmed by the canonical discriminant analysis of the ratings of the 4 stimulus persons on the eight personality traits. Again two significant dimensions were found ($\chi_1 = 96.17$ $\chi_2 = 16.10$ with 10 and 8 df) which could be interpreted in the same way as before; the first dimension describing distinction between cooperative and unsocial behaviour, the second dimension emphasizing the opposition of dominant and submissive behaviour. The results together with the positions of the stimulus persons on the first two dimensions are presented in TABLE III and FIGURE VIII.

As can be seen in FIGURE VIII the structure of the stimulus persons which is obtained on the basis of the social judgmental accounts after the interaction, is fairly similar to the structure which is implied by the actual interaction with the stimulus persons. Only the positions of stimulus person 1 and 2 are apparently reversed. This reversal is nevertheless very important because it reveals precisely the point I want to make which is that the cognitive representation underlying the verbal interaction with the stimulus persons is not necessarily the same as the one obtained from social judgments. If we want to relate these two structures to each other in this particular study we see that it is mainly the first social judgment dimension which contributes

TABLE III

Loadings of Eight Personality Traits
on Two Discriminant Dimensions of Task Five

Traits	Dimensions			
	Unrotated		Rotated	
	I	II	I	II
aggressive	-.243	.657	-.410	.568
unsocial	-.567	.172	-.593	.013
cooperative	.144	-.523	.279	-.465
dominant	.116	.265	.041	.286
submissive	-.145	-.458	-.017	-.480
passive	-.193	-.559	-.036	-.591
pessimistic	-.981	-.014	-.942	-.277
rational	.261	-.318	.337	-.237

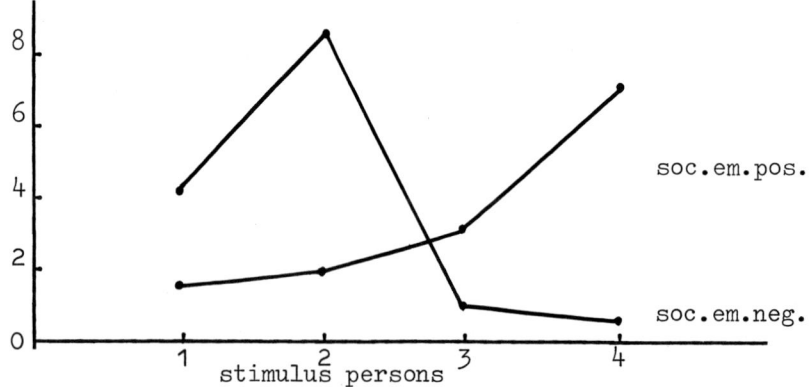

FIGURE IX. Mean number of social emotional negative and positive acts for the four stimulus persons.

to the canonical correlation with the interaction dimensions. Since the first social judgment dimensions correlates highly with the sociometric choices made by the Ss in the same experiment, it is clear that the first dimension is mainly evaluative in nature. Both interaction dimensions are related to this evaluative judgment dimension but in different ways. The easiest way to represent this relationship is to look simply at the frequency of positive and negative interactions with the 4 stimulus persons. FIGURE IX represents these relationships.

As can be seen in FIGURE IX positive and negative interactions are related in different ways to the evaluation of the stimulus persons. The higher the evaluation of a stimulus person is the more positive a S will interact with him. The opposite, however, is not true for negative socioemotional behaviour. There appears to be a monotonic relationship up to a certain point between evaluation and negative social interaction. Beyond this point the relationship is reversed. This finding is similar to the results obtained by Schachter (1951) with respect to the reaction to deviants in small groups. Members who hold deviant opinions in a small group attract a good deal of interaction up to a certain point. If deviants do not change their opinion in the direction of the majority opinion of the group, the group loses interest in them and ignores the deviants. This is what seems to happen in the van der Kloot experiment. The person who holds the harshest opinion (n°1) is evaluated negatively and is largely ignored. Because van der Kloot expressed both the social judgment data and the social interactions in a canonical form it is easy to see how social judgment and social behaviour can be related to each other.

First of all we have seen that the 8 traits which are used to describe people in general do form the same two dimensional implicit personality theory when applied to the 4 stimulus persons. When these 4 persons are subsequently rated on these traits it appears that they are mostly differentiated along an evaluative dimension. The reactions of the Ss to the stimulus persons do require, however, a two dimensional representation. To relate the action structure to the social judgment structure a system of two transformation rules is required. The first rule implies that positive socio-emotional behaviour should increase with an increase in positive evaluation. The second rule implies an increase of negative socio-emotional and active task behaviour with a decrease in positive evaluation. Of course these two rules could have been formulated also in a direct relationship with the labelling structure, but since the first dimension of this structure is evaluative in nature we would have obtained practically the same results.

REFERENCES

Allen, V.L. Situational factors in conformity. In L. Berkowitz (Ed.), <u>Advances in experimental social psychology</u>. Vol.2. New York : Academic Press, 1966.

Alwin, D.F. Making inferences from attitude-behaviour correlations. <u>Sociometry</u>, 1973, <u>36</u>, 253-278.

Anderson, N.H. Functional measurement and psychophysical judgment <u>Psychological Review</u>, 1970, <u>77</u>, 153-170.

Anderson, N.H. Cognitive algebra : Integration theory applied to social attribution. In L. Berkowitz (Ed.), <u>Advances in experimental social psychology</u>. Vol.7. New York : Academic Press, 1974.

Anderson, J.R. <u>Language, memory and thought</u>. New York : Wiley, 1976.

Argyle, M. <u>Social interaction</u>. London : Methuen, 1969.

Argyle, M. <u>Social interaction</u>. London : Penguin, 1978.

Argyle, M. and Kendon, A. The experimental analysis of social performance. In L. Berkowitz (Ed.), <u>Advances in experimental social psychology</u>. Vol.3. New York : Academic Press, 1967.

Argyle, M., Lalljee, M. and Cook, M. The effects of visibility on interaction in a dyad. <u>Human relations</u>, 1968, <u>21</u>, 3-17.

Asch, S.E. Studies on the principles of judgments and attitudes II. Determination of judgments by group and by ego standards. <u>Journal of Social Psychology</u>. 1940, <u>12</u>, 433-465.

Asch, S.E. Forming impressions of personality. <u>Journal of Abnormal and Social Psychology</u>, 1946, <u>41</u>, 258-290.

Asch, S.E. Studies of independence and conformity. IA. Minority of one against a unanimous majority. <u>Psychological Monographs, General and Applied</u>, 1956, Whole no. 416.

Asch, S.E. Gestalt theory. In D.L. Sills (Ed.), <u>International Encyclopedia of the Social Sciences</u>. Vol.6. London : Mc Millan, 1968.

Asch, S.E., Block, H. and Hertzman, M. Studies in the principles of judgments and attitudes I. Two basic principles of judgment. <u>Journal of Psychology</u>, 1938, <u>5</u>, 219-251.

Bales, R.F. <u>Interaction process analysis</u>. Cambridge, Mass. : Addison-Wesley, 1950.

Bartlett, F.C. <u>Remembering</u>. C.U.P. : Cambridge, 1932.

Bellin, S.J. and Kriesberg, L. Relationship among attitudes, circumstances and behaviour : the case of applying for public housing. <u>Sociology and Social Research</u>, 1967, <u>51</u>, 453-469.

Boring, E.G. <u>A history of experimental psychology</u>. New York : Appleton, Century-Crofts, 1957.

Brown, R. and Herrnstein, R.J. <u>Psychology</u>. London : Methuen, 1975.

Clarke, D.D. The use and recognition of sequential structure in dialogue. <u>British Journal of Social and Clinical Psychology</u>, 1975, <u>14</u>, 333-339.

Collett, P. (Ed.), <u>Social rules and social Behaviour</u>. Oxford : Blackwell, 1976.

Coombs, C.H. <u>A theory of data</u>. New York, Wiley, 1964.

Coombs, C.H., Dawes, R.M. and Tversky, A. <u>Mathematical psychology</u>. Englewood Cliffs : Prentice Hall, 1970.

Cowdry, R.W., Kenniston, K. and Sabin, S. The war and military obligation : private attitudes and public actions. <u>Journal of Personality</u>, 1970, <u>28</u>, 525-549.

Crockett, W.B. Conceptual rules and the understanding of social relations. Un published manuscript, University of Kansas, 1977.

Delbeke, L. <u>Konstruktie van een voorkeursruimte met behulp van multidimensionale schaal-methoden</u>. Academisch Proefschrift: Leuven, 1965.

Dudycha, A.L. and Nayen, J.C. Characteristics of the human inference process in complex choice behavior situations. <u>Organizational Behaviour and Human Performance</u>, 1966, <u>1</u>, 110-128.

Ekman, P. and Friesen, W.V. <u>Unmasking the face</u>. Englewood-Cliffs: Prentice Hall, 1975.

Festinger, L. <u>A theory of cognitive dissonance</u>. Evanston, Illinois: Row Peterson, 1957.

Fincham, F. and Jaspars, J. Attitudes of responsibility to the self and others in children and adults. <u>Journal of Personality and Social Psychology</u>, 1979, <u>37</u>, 1589-1602.

Fishbein, M. and Ajzen, I. <u>Belief, attitude, intention and behaviour : An introduction to theory and research</u>. Reading, Mass. : Addison-Wesley, 1975.

Fishbein, M. and Ajzen, I. Attitude-Behaviour relations : A theoretical analysis and review of empirical research. <u>Psychological Bulletin</u>, 1977, <u>84</u>, 888-918.

Flament, C. Schèmes d'équilibre et représentations sociales. Paper presented at the Colloquium on Social Representations. Paris, 1979.

Frijda, N.H. Recognition of emotion. In L. Berkowitz (Ed.), <u>Advances in experimental social psychology</u>, Vol. 4, New York: Academic Press, 1969.

Geer, J.v.d., Jaspars, J., Tajfel, H. and Johnson, H. On the development of international attitudes. Rapport HSP 001-65. Psych. Inst. University of Leyden, 1965.

Geer, J.v.d. and Jaspars, J. Cognitive functions. *Annual review of Psychology*, 1966, 17, 145-176.

Gergen, K.J. Experimentation in social psychology. A reappraisal. *European Journal of Social Psychology*, 1978, 8, 507-529.

Goldberg, D. and Coombs, C.H. Some application of unfolding theory to fertility analysis. In *Emerging Techniques in Population Research.* Proceedings of the 1962 Annual Conference of the Milbank Memorial Fund. N.Y. Milbank Memorial Fund, 1962.

Harré, R. The ethogenic approach : Theory and practice. In L. Berkowitz (Ed.), *Advances in experimental Social Psychology*, Vol.10. New York : Academic Press, 1977.

Hagendoorn, A. *Conceptuele systemen.* Proefschrift Katholieke Universiteit Nijmegen, 1976.

Heider, F. Social perception and phenomenal causality. *Psychological Review*, 1944, 51, 358-374.

Heider, F. The psychology of interpersonal relations. New York: Wiley, 1958.

Heider, F. and Simmel, M. An experimental study of apparent behavior. *American Journal of Psychology*, 1944, 57, 243-259.

Hoffmann, P.J. Cue consistency and cofigurality in human judgment. In B. Klimmentz (Ed.), *Formal representation of human judgment.* New York : Wiley, 1968.

Holzkamp, K. Die Ueberwindung der wissenschaftlichen Beübigkeit psychologischen Theorien durch die kritische Psychologie. *Zeitschrift fur Sozialpsychologie*, 1977, 8, 1 Teil, 1-22, 2 Teil, 78-97.

Holzkamp, K. Empirische Forschung in der Psychologie als historische Rekonstruktion und experimentelle Reduktion. *Zeitschrift fur Sozialpsychologie*, 1978, 9, 78-83.

Ickes, W. and Harvey, J.H. Fritz Heider : A biographical sketch. *Journal of Psychology*, 1978, 98, 159-170.

Israel, J. and Tajfel, H. (Eds.), *The context of social psychology. A critical assessment.* London : Academic Press, 1972.

Jaspars, J.M.F. *On social perception.* Proefschrift Leiden University, 1966.

Jaspars, J.M.F. *De vrienden van mijn vrienden.* Openbare les. Univ. Pers. : Leiden, 1967.

Jaspars, J.M.F. A structural approach to social perception. Invited paper presented at the annual conference of the social psychological section of the British Psychological Society, 1968.

Jaspars, J.M.F. A modification of Heider's balance theory. Paper presented at the Conference on Mathematical models in social psychology, Aussois, France, 1969.

Jaspars, J.M.F. Synthese van cognitieve conflicten. In J. Loenen and K. Gevers (Eds.), <u>Syntese als aktiemodel</u>, Assen : van Gorkum, 1972.

Jaspars, J.M.F. Cognitieve evenwicht en ogencontact. <u>Nederlandse Tijdschrift voor Psychologie</u>,1973,<u>28</u>,51-65.

Jaspars, J.M.F. Person perception and social cognition. A discussion of major problems. In K.W. Tilley (Ed.), <u>Leadership and management appraisal</u>. London; The English U.P 1974.

Jaspars, J.M.F. The future of social psychology. Paper presented at the general conference of the European Association for Social Psychology, Bielefeld, 1975.

Jaspars, J.M.F. The study of cognitive processes in social psychology. Paper presented at the International Congress of Scientific Psychology, Paris, France, 1976.

Jaspars, J.M.F. The coming of age of European social psychology. Presidential adress. General meeting of the European Association of Experimental Social Psychology. Weimar, 1978.

Jaspars, J.M.F. Attitudes and social representations. Paper presented at the Colloquium in social representations. Paris, France, 1979.

Jaspars, J.M.F., Geer, J.P.v.d., Tajfel, H. and Johnson, N. The development of nationalism in children. <u>European Journal of Social Psychology</u>, 1972, <u>2</u>, 347-369.

Jaspars, J.M.F., van Kreveld, et al. : Cognitive balance, selfinvolvement and anticipation of interaction. <u>Nederlandse Tijdschrift voor Psychologie</u>, 1974, <u>29</u>, 535-551.

Jaspars, J.M.F.,v.d. Oever, T. and v.Gils, A. Cognitive balance and visual interaction. <u>Nederlandse tijdschrift voor Psychologie</u>, 1974, <u>29</u>, 557-568.

Kelly, G.A. <u>The psychology of personal constructe</u>. New York: Norton, 1955.

Kendall, M.G. and Stuart, A. <u>The advanced theory of statistics</u>. New York : Hafner, 1961.

Kloot, W.A.v.d. A cognitive structure approach to person perception. Doctoral Dissertation, Rijks Universiteit Leiden, 1975

Kohlberg, L. Stage and sequence. The cognitive developmental approach to socialisation. In D. Goslin (Ed.), <u>Handbook of socialisation, Theory and Research</u>. Chicago : Rand Mc Nally, 1969.

La Pierre, R.T. Attitudes versus actions. <u>Social Forum</u>, 1934, <u>13</u>, 230-237.

Latané, B. and Darley, J.M. The unresponsive bystander : Why doesn't he help ? New York : Appleton-Century-Crofts, 1970.

Leeuw, J.de, Young, F.W. and Takane, Y. Additive structure in qualitative data. An alternating least-squares method with optimal scaling features. Psychometrica, 1976, 41, 471-503.

Lewin, K. Resolving social conflicts. New York : Harper, 1948.

Luce, R.D. and Tukey, J.W. Simultaneous conjoint measurement : a new type of fundamental measurement. Journal of Mathematical Psychology, 1964, 1, 1-27.

Marais, H.C. Multiple indications of attitudes. Ph.D. Thesis, University of Port Elisabeth, 1975.

Merton, R.K. Singletons and multiples in scientific discovery. A chapter in the sociology of science. Proceedings of the American Philosophical Society, 1961, 105, 470-486.

Milgram, S. Obedience to authority. New York : Harper and Row, 1974.

Moscovici, S. and Faucheux, C. 1973. Social influence, conformity bias and the study of active minorities. In L. Berkowitz (Ed.), Advances in experimental social psychology. Vol.6, New York : Academic Press, 1973.

Newcomb, T.N. An approach to the study of communicative acts. Psychological Review, 1953, 10, 393-404.

Norman, D.A. Memory and attention. New Yrok : Wiley, 1976.

Nuttin, J.M. The illusion of attitude change. London : Academic Press, 1975.

Osgood, C.E., Suci, G.J. and Tannenbaum, P.H. The measurement of meaning. Urbana : University of Illinois Press, 1957.

Piaget, J. Le jugement moral chez l'enfant. P.U.F.: Paris, 1932.

Plon, M. On the meaning of the notion of conflict and its study in social psychology. European Journal of social psychology, 1974, 4, 389-436.

Sarbin, T.R. and Bailey, D.E. The immediacy postulate in the light of modern cognitive psychology. In K.R. Hammond (Ed.), The psychology of Egon Brunswik. New York: Holt, Rinehart, Winston, 1966.

Schachter, S. Deviation, rejection and communication. Journal of Abnormal and Social psychology, 1951, 46, 190-207.

Schank, R.C. and Abelson, R.P. Scripts, plans, goals and understanding : An inquiry into human knowledge structure. Hillsdale, N.J.: Erlbaum, 1977.

Schümer, R. Context effects in impression formation as a function of the ambiguity of test traits. European Journal of Social Psychology, 1973, 3, 333-338.

Schumann, H. and Johnson, M.P. Attitudes and behavior. Annual Review of Sociology, 1976, 2, 161-207.

Shaw, M.F. and Constanzo, P.R. Theories of social psychology. New York : McGraw Hill, 1970.

Slovic, P. and Lichtenstein, S. Comparison of Baysian and regression approaches to the study of information processing in judgment. Organizational Behavior and Human Performance, 1971, 6, 649-744.

Torgerson, W.S. Theory and methods of scaling. New York : Wiley, 1958.

Verhoeven, T. Over impression formation. Doctoraal scriptie. Katholieke Universiteit, Nijmegen, 1972.

Warr, P.B. and Smith, J.S. Combining information about people; Comparisons between six models. Journal of Personality and Social Psychology, 1970, 16, 55-56.

Wicker, A.W. Attitudes vs actions : the relationship of verbal and overt behavioral responses to attitude objects. Journal of Social Issues, 1969, 25, 41-78.

Wyer, R.S. Cognitive organization and change : an information processing approach. New York: Wiley, 1974.

Young, F.W., Leeuw, J. de and Takana, Y. Regression with qualitative and quantitative variables : an alternating least squares method with optimal scaling features. Psychometrika, 1976, 41, 505-529.

Zajonc, R. Cognitive theories in social psychology. In G. Lindzey and E. Aronson (Eds.), Handbook of social psychology. Reading, Mass.: Addison-Wesley, 1969.

Zimbardo, P.G. The human choice : individuation, reason and order versus deindividuation, impulse and chaos. In W.J. Arnold and D. Levine (Eds.), Nebraska Symposium on motivation. Vol. 17, Lincoln, Nebraska : Univ. of Nebraska Press, 1969.

ATTITUDES AND SOCIAL BEHAVIOUR 1)

A. Upmeyer 2)

Technische Universität Berlin

INTRODUCTION

The purpose of this chapter is to present a theoretical framework which relates attitudes to social behaviour. Once the framework has been developed we are able to derive testable hypotheses for new empirical work.

The need for more theory has been claimed by Fishbein & Ajzen (1975) in the most comprehensive and thorough publication on the state of the field in the seventies. The claim is derived from their critique of the so-called other variable approach, saying that a lack in consistency between attitude and behaviour may be due to the operation of other variables that influence behaviour. As a consequence we have to detect those other variables in continuous empirical research; the domains suggested as a source to find these variables are often labelled as "personality" and as "situation".

---

1) This chapter was also supported by a research grant entitled "Mapping attitudes into verbal and behavioural response modalities" from the Deutsche Forschungsgemeinschaft to the author. The grant is part of a frame of projects (Schwerpunktprogramm "Attitudes and Behaviour")coordinated by the author.

2) The author has been deeply influenced by discussions and a seminar with Dr.Harry S. Upshaw who spent an academic year as a Fulbright visiting professor at the Institut für Psychologie, Technische Universität Berlin.

Although the idea that other variables operate if unpredicted results occur is always true it does not provide us with a strategy of detection. Also consider the extreme of a random selection of a variety of other variables. It will always provide us with a limited number of variables predicting a part of the variance of behaviour. However, for our systematic understanding of the underlying processes such a procedure confounds more than it solves. Finally, since the domains of personality and situational variables are exhausting the universe of relevant variables in this field, nothing is gained by dropping these names.

A second justification to develop more theory springs from the fact that our ability to predict social behaviour from attitudes is still rather limited (Wicker, 1969) although some progress has been made in the seventies (Ajzen & Fishbein, 1980). Our general deficiency contrasts sharply with the enormous amount of money spent by government agencies and private institutions in the industrialized countries to measure and monitor the attitudes and values of people. The representative assessment of what Turner & Krauss (1978) called the subjective state of nations is increasingly used by western policy-makers because traditional expert judgements turned out to be even more fallible than the results from the social sciences.

In some areas of inquiry, e.g. voting behaviour, the prediction of actual voting from voting intentions was surprisingly accurate in some elections. However, on other occasions, i.e. when a landslide change occured, voting has been much less precisely predicted. The election of President Reagan is a most recent example of such a failure. This and other instances of poor results suggest that our analytical tools are good if the predicted event is a continuation of a stable trend and if the measurement of behavioural intentions is contingent to the actual behaviour. Long-term predictions seem to require more than a simple question on what a person is going to do. This is particularly true in other areas of application, e.g. health prevention or energy saving - where the psychological homogeneity of the introspectively gained predictors and the actual behaviour is rather low.

In order to be able to make long-term predictions we have to start a conceptual discussion first. For example, is it valid to equate a behavioural intention to vote for a party with the attitude towards the party ? Fishbein & Ajzen (1975) clearly separated these two concepts, but they restricted the measurement of intentions to verbal reports on what a person is going to do in the near future. They did not analyse the process of intention formation and we do not learn from them how people build action plans.

How can we conceive social behaviour ? In voting behaviour, the analysis of the motor performance to put a cross on a ballot sheet does not tell us anything on the meaning of voting. Why is this behaviour, then in contrast to verbal behaviour ?

I believe that a brief examination of the history of attitude research in social psychology will yield some valuable information to answer these and other questions.

HISTORICAL BACKGROUND

In sketching the history of the attitude and behaviour issue, I will not present the details of numerous conceptual contributions which have been identified in the literature (e.g. by Ostrom,1968). Rather I will confine myself to those ideas implicitly contained in the majority of publications in a certain period.

1. The measurement approach

Empirical research in the attitude area boomed in the thirties after Thurstone (1928, 1931) proposed that "attitudes can be measured". Thurstone (1946) defined "attitudes as the intensity of positive and negative affect for or against a psychological object". (p. 39). The theory behind this definition states that persons share beliefs, i.e. knowledge statements concerning an object. Since beliefs usually load on a variety of specific dimensions it was reasonable to select one important common dimension, i.e. the evaluation of beliefs. Evaluations can be conceptualized as quantitative values on a scale ranging from an extreme negative pole through neutrality to an extreme positive pole. Thurstone's theory implies that all the evaluations of beliefs towards an object coming into mind when an object is presented, are averaged and the average is defined as an attitude. In other words an attitude is a compound of a number of evaluations or affects. On the operational level, the Thurstone scale, evaluations of beliefs were averaged over persons.

Thurstone's approach had some important consequences for the development of the field. It led to an explosion of empirical as well as laboratory research. It stimulated other attempts to construct attitude scales (Likert , 1932;Guttman, 1944; Osgood, Suci & Tannenbaum, 1957; Edwards, 1957), using the evaluation dimension. Although a diverse conceptual discussion continued to flourish in the forties and fifties, theorists and applied researchers seemed to agree, at least tacitly, with Thurstone's basic notion.

2. Cognitive consistency

In the period between 1950 and 1970 the top issue and most of the research was devoted to <u>cognitive consistency</u> principles (Heider, 1958; Abelson & Rosenberg, 1958; Abelson, Aronson, McGuire, Newcomb, Rosenberg & Tannenbaum, 1968). Applied to the intrapersonal cognitive structure, cognitive consistency suggests that a person has a desire to balance his/her cognitions. For example, if my attitude is positive towards a certain politician I perceive my friend's attitude towards the same man also as positive. However, if such a perception appears to be subjectively invalid, a tension emerges to restore the imbalance. In this example, balance can be achieved by starting to dislike one's friend.

Consistency theories are typically concerned with internal states which are assessed by verbal reports on introspection. In order to operationalize those reports researchers have used attitude scales and <u>ad hoc</u> rating scales thus drawing upon Thurstone's influence. Irrespective of how elaborate the dependent attitude variables were, the large majority of studies relied on evaluation as the underlying dimension.

One theory within the group of consistency theories is particularly interesting for the attitude and behaviour discussion. Dissonance theory (Festinger, 1957, 1964) states that a change in the internal representation of an evaluation of a belief will occur as a consequence of having elicited a specific behaviour. For example, if somebody engages voluntarily to tell another person that a boring task is exciting and if this claim cannot be justified by high payment he or she comes to like the task more than before (Festinger & Carlsmith, 1959). Here a behaviour seems to have a causal effect on the attitude as a dependent variable.

For our discussion below it should be noted, however, that it is not the compliance behaviour, but the amount of payment forming the independent variable in this famous experiment. Also behaviour is theoretically treated as a cognitive element thus having the same conceptual status as non-behavioural elements, like attitudes. Although a behavioural element may be usually more resistant to change as compared to other "soft" elements, dissonance theory allows for cases where values are stronger than internal representations of behaviour (Festinger, 1964). Thus, dissonance theory basically treats attitude-behaviour consistency in the same way as other consistency theories do, i.e. as an interplay of latent variables. This I believe is the reason why we find an abundant usage of verbalized reports and scales, but very rarely choice behaviour as the dependent variable in dissonance research.

3. The prediction model

In the recent decade with the rediscovery of field experimentation, social behaviour has been increasingly scrutinized. Wicker (1969) in his influential review of the literature documented how rarely behaviour was subjected to empirical analysis as compared to verbal reports or scaling. He also tabulated the amounts of covariance between attitude and behaviour and concluded that, on the average, the relationship between the two variables is discouragingly weak. Although the strength of covariation varied across studies and averaging them is not a sophisticated idea, the overall picture led to a loss of confidence in the attitude concept itself (e.g. Abelson, 1972). Wicker's review was in line with a general trend of distrust in dispositional variables (e.g. Mischel, 1968). However, he did not provide a theoretical explanation why the state of the research is so desolate. Rather, he shares the view of other researchers who tried to progress in the field by using prediction models. I feel that the research activities in the seventies are predominantly concerned with prediction.

This trend started when researchers like Fishbein (1963) and N.H. Anderson (1971) applied models of impression formation of attitudes. Their basic theory did not go beyond Thurstone's approach, i.e. to evaluate beliefs and form a compound of these evaluations to define attitudes. However, the composition rule of the compound was intensively discussed and subjected to many empirical tests. The results were that the prediction of attitude from beliefs improves if one substitutes Thurstone's simple average idea by some sort of weighted averaging. Despite empirical evidence that doubts the universality of a single model (Schümer & Cohen, 1968) and some critique of the functional measurement approach (Krantz & Tversky, 1971) the predictability from more sophisticated models certainly improved. Since the present contribution is supposed to be predominantly theoretical, I will not go into further details. However, for the understanding of Fishbein & Ajzen's as well as Bentler's recent research on the prediction of behaviour it is of benefit to trace it back to former solutions (Bentler & Speckart, 1979, 1981).

A substantial refinement of those former predictions has been introduced in the seventies as the concept of behavioural intention by Ajzen & Fishbein (1973, 1977) and Fishbein & Ajzen (1975). This can be interpreted as an attempt to summarize a host of so-called "other variables" mediating attitudes and behaviour. Indeed, the introduction of intention did improve the prediction of behaviour (Ajzen & Fishbein, 1977).

The most recent version of the intention concept has been incorporated into a "theory of reasoned action" (Ajzen & Fishbein, 1980). According to the theory, the immediate antecedent of a person's behaviour B is his/her intention I to perform the behaviour B. Equation [1] depicts that intention itself is a function of two other additive factors : the person's attitude towards the behaviour A_B and perceived social pressure or subjective norm SN.

$$B \sim I = W_1 A_B + W_2 SN \quad [1]$$

The relative importance of A_B and SN to predict I depends on weights W_1 and W_2 which vary across behaviours and across individuals. Intention will predict behaviour B only if intention has not changed before B is performed. To be able to obtain a reasonably good prediction it is also required that intention and behaviour are related to the same target, action, context and time elements.

Ajzen and Fishbein's concept of intention can be seen as an effort to specify more precisely the action or conative component of attitudes. They are making a difference between the general attitude towards an object and the specific attitude towards a behaviour addressed to the object in question. For example, in the famous early study by LaPierre (1934) restaurant owners were asked "Will you accept members of the Chinese race as guests in your establishment ?". According to the Ajzen and Fishbein analysis the question does not reflect the general attitude towards Chinese but the attitude towards a specific behaviour at the reception. It seems that the SN factor may moderate the answer to the intention question as well as to actual behaviour.

Fishbein and Ajzen obtained stronger effects of intentions to predict behaviour as compared to general attitudes by using multiple regression analysis. However, Bentler & Speckart (1979, 1981) found that the attitude effect and the intention effect on behaviour may vary considerably in size - depending on content area under investigation. They used path analytic models to differentiate between latent and observed variables and to test different theories of the relationship between attitudes and behaviour. Although we need more research to be confident on the stability of the models suggested in this type of analysis, causal modeling seems to be a superior methodological approach as compared to traditional regression analysis if latent variables are analyzed (see Bentler, 1980).

One drawback of the research in predicting behaviour is the fact that self-reported behaviour has much more often been used as the dependent variable than actual behaviour. Again LaPierre's findings are a dramatic demonstration that even reports on intentions and actual behaviour may fall apart.

UNSOLVED PROBLEMS

In this section I will evaluate critically the state of the field as depicted in the historical report.

1. The origin of attitudes

The apparent agreement on defining attitude as an evaluation of an object imposes a major problem if we ask where this evaluation is coming from. Thurstone, Anderson, Fishbein & Ajzen, and others derived the overall evaluation implied in an attitude from a finite set of evaluations of single beliefs. However, the progress achieved by this idea is rather limited, because a given belief already carries on an evaluation by itself. If we ask where the evaluation of a belief stems from it will probably be said that it relies on still other pieces of information with their own affect loadings. As a result, the definition gets lost in an infinite regression. Therefore, the progress of the information integration approach lies in the composition rules developed, but it does not define the origin of evaluations independently.

2. Selection of beliefs

When an applied researcher administers a Thurstone attitude scale, he/she provides a set of beliefs in terms of attitude statements which have to be checked for agreement or disagreement. By this kind of exposure the respondent may be induced by beliefs he did not know before. Since an attitude is defined as the average of evaluations of beliefs, the average can be affected by the new beliefs and result in an attitude change by definition. In fact, Thurstone conceptualized attitude change as due to new information off the centre of the distribution of old information.

By way of contrast, suppose we allow a person freely associate his/her beliefs about an object and in a second step we ask for evaluations of the generated beliefs. The attitude score resulting from this method may deviate from the Thurstone scale score considerably. If we speculate where the anticipated difference between the two alternative operationalisations is coming from, we have to recall where the Thurstone statements emerged from.

The designer of an attitude scale usually collects a large <u>variety</u> of attitude statements related to an object. I suspect the <u>range</u> of statements he/she prepares for the item analysis is larger than the individual ranges of beliefs known by the majority of respondents. Suppose, now, a respondent's range of acceptable beliefs is located on the negative side of the total attitude continuum and he/she is exposed to yet unknown belief statements on the positive side. It seems likely that a few of these new items are accepted by the respondent and will lead to an attitude change artifact if Thurstone's average model is correct. I am using the term "artifact" because the attitude shift is due to the measurement device, not to the former internal state of the respondent.

There is a second effect of selectivity of beliefs which might be relevant to behaviour. Apart from interview situations a person may carry out a certain behaviour related to his/her attitude. In this case, the beliefs are retrieved from long-term memory and their mean evaluation scores form the attitude towards the object related to the behaviour in question. Will the set of beliefs retrieved always exhaust the set of stored beliefs ? Or will it be representative at least ?

From all that we know about human memory, both answers are negative. The retrieval process in the situation where a behaviour is influenced by one's attitude is likely to be <u>cued recall</u>, i.e. the attitude object plus some other aspects of the behavioural situation are serving as cues and will yield non-representative subsets of beliefs. As a consequence of the impression formation models the resulting attitude will be situation-specific. If we want to explain or predict this process we need to have a theory on both the attitude object and the situation in which social behaviour occurs.

3. Selection of attitude objects

In an interview situation beliefs as well as attitude objects are presented by the interviewer. By comparison, a behavioural situation invokes objects (1) as potential means to do something or (2) as targets supposed to be affected by the behaviour. All the other objects in a behavioural situation are less salient and can be considered as background information or noise (3).

The attitude judgement given in an interview may heavily depend on the categories (1), (2) or (3). Background objects will likely result in unstable attitude responses. By contrast, a target object if addressed in the interview will be much more stable. Finally an object as a means will generate a variety of different attitude states depending on its function of target activity. For example, a party leader (as the attitude object) can be evaluated positively if the target activity is the career of a member of parliament. However, he appears to be negative in the context of deviant party line voting. Note in this example, that both the deviant policy and one's own career are positive targets. Thus for category (1) we expect stable attitudes of varying averages on the evaluation dimension.

4. Object evaluation and object choice

The concept of evaluation is an attribute or property attached to an object, person, group, event, or idea. It certainly adds to the structural knowledge in psychology if we know how an object is evaluated. However, if we want to analyse behaviour this knowledge is insufficient because an evaluation does not imply the dynamic sources for a particular behaviour. By analogy, our knowledge that a table is white does not provide us with information on why it breaks. The table may "behave" by breaking if the impact is a karate strike. For the analysis of both attitude and behaviour we have to incorporate a motivational source for the behaviour.

Daveney (1964) argued that we do not choose objects when we act. Rather we are choosing state of affairs featuring objects in order to perform a certain action. A theory of behaviour has to specify alternative choices. The choice of the best-fitting alternative will then point to the state of affairs which a person is motivated to attain. To be able to choose, a person must know these alternatives and believe that they are attainable. It seems to be difficult to analyse social behaviour without invoking an aim orientation.

5. Causal links

Most theorists and researchers assume that an attitude is an antecedent of a behavioural consequence. Indeed, the attitude concept has been originally invoked to explain social behaviour. This kind of causal assumption is underlying interview research, in that one wants to predict behaviour from verbalized attitudes.

There are at least three lines of research where attitude and behaviour are conceived as related in the reverse causal direction : Bem's (1972) work on self attribution, Festinger's (1957, 1964) dissonance theory, and research on critical life events (see Dohrenwend & Dohrenwend, 1974; Datan & Ginsberg, 1975).

Bem argues that behaviour originates in a Skinnerian learning process without attitudes mediating a stimulus-response connection. Thus, the knowledge of an attitude cannot help to predict behaviour. Although people are communicating their attitudes Bem views these communications as <u>ex post</u> descriptions of behaviour. In other words people infer attitudes from behaviour in terms of self-attributions.

The debate on Bem's work showed that his proposition is both hard to prove and to disprove. In everyday experience it is hard to explain with Bem's theory why prisoners engage in hunger strike knowing that they will probably die for their attitude. Although the hunger strike itself may polarize the striker's attitude, it seems unlikely that the prisoner inferred the polarity of an attitude from his her behaviour. In addition, it is difficult to explain the hunger strike without some attitudes, e.g. to attain the status of a political prisoner.

On the other hand, there are occasions in life where Bem's inference hypothesis may apply. If somebody engages in an unplanned activity without much thought and is later asked to <u>justify</u> that activity we might obtain a self-related attitude interpretation by that person. The likelihood of an attitude-response is even increased if a researcher asking for the reason of the behaviour offers an attitude rating scale to assess the reason. Here as in other cases an interview can provide the cue to give an attitude response, which would never have occurred in self-generated behaviour. To summarize, the fact that subjects are giving responses on request should not be taken as a guarantee that something like an attitude exists. Even if these elicited responses are reliable we cannot be sure about their validity because situational factors can be used by subjects to stabilize their responses. One of these factors may be behaviour.

Festinger (1964) in his theory of cognitive dissonance conceptualized an attitude change after the performance of an attitude-contradicting behaviour as the reduction of internal tension - called "dissonance". Alternatively, the observed attitude change can also be interpreted as an attempt to justify one's own behaviour to the social environment by adjusting the attitude <u>response</u>, leaving the "true" attitude unchanged. Unfortunately, we have no method available yet to separate a "true" attitude from an attitude response. M. Deutsch (1973) has pointed out that a gambler or a nation in war may justify erroneous behaviour by showing consistency, i.e. by producing further behaviour of same kind. Moscovici (1972) theorized that a consistent response style is a necessary condition to influence other people. Eventually, we have learned that insisting on what we do is a means to be taken serious by other people.

Research on critical life events (Dohrenwend & Dohrenwend, 1974; Datan & Ginsberg, 1975) suggests that persons exposed to traumatic experiences like the death of one's spouse, readjust to their environment. As a consequence, they undergo attitude changes. The causal direction from an event to such changes may simply reflect the fact that all attitudes are learned. A more detailed analysis is possible by constructing the following causal paths (arrows are indicating the causal direction):

(1) Event ⟶ Attitude ⟶ Behaviour
(2) Event ⇌ Attitude
    ↘ Behaviour
(3) Event ⟶ Behaviour ⟶ Attitude

The analysis of the three paths relies on the assumption that the event did not occur as a result of one's own responsible behaviour. (If the assumption is wrong, dissonance theory is a more suitable approach). On a theoretical level, we have to ask which one of the three paths is most likely. I suggest that path (1) is the best candidate because readjusting to a new situation in one's life needs considerable planning. New plans will first affect latent variables, i.e. also attitudes before they are executed in terms of behavioural acts. In addition, it is plausible that a person receives feedback from his/her behaviour leading to a modification of his/her latent structure. Over time this process can be conceived as a series of cycles - an idea proposed by Miller, Galanter, & Pribram (1960). The process suggests that attitude and behaviour develop in parallel lines like path (2), although each cycle implies path (1).

Finally, path (3) can be exemplified by an empirical finding provided by Bentler & Speckart (1981). In one of their three content areas, namely in studying, they found that the studying behaviour had a "causal" effect on the subsequently measured attitude. That is, students may study because of an external influence, e.g. a social norm, and once the behaviour has occurred it tends to create positive attitudes. Alternatively, the result could be interpredted as the pleasure of having attained a studying goal;

this alternative is "external" to the causal model used by
Bentler and Speckart but their methodology could be fruitfully
applied if the external variable would be included in a modified
model. In sum, the results of Bentler & Speckart (1979, 1981)
and of Kahle & Berman (1979) suggest that the causal direction
of attitudes and behaviour is rarely reversed.

To summarize this section, I do not believe that Bem's and
Festinger's notions of attitudes are promising to explain behaviour.
I would like to treat them as special judgement phenomena to be
studied in their own right. The critical life event research does
not necessarily suggest a reversal in the causal chain of attitude and behaviour.

6. Defining behaviour

It has already become apparent that social psychologists
are preoccupied with the analysis of latent variables and care
much less about social behaviour. Elaborate theoretical propositions are concerned with attitudes, whereas behaviour has been
predominantly considered as some natural consequence. Given this
state of the field, it seems worthwhile to go backwards i.e. to
start to conceptualize behaviour and then to see what kind of latent variables may be limited to it.

Since any latent variable, like an attitude, relies on a
more complicated scientific inference process as compared to
observed overt behaviour, some researchers argued that behaviour
is the ultimate evidence of validity (Deutscher, 1969). I do not
fully agree with this, because observed behaviour may also lead
to complicated inferences when its meaning has to be interpreted.
For example, what does it mean when voters place a cross on a
ballot sheet ? If we don't consider the consequences a voter
expects from his behaviour, the observation of the act alone does
not make sense.

Fishbein (1973) provided a taxonomy of behavioural criteria
directed to measurement problems. He distinguished single-act
versus multiple-act and single observation versus repeated observation criteria. A single act is a two-alternative choice
between showing or not showing a single behaviour, whereas multiple
act comprises a variety of shown acts with respect to a given
target in a given situation. Repeated observation means that
the same behaviour is directed at different targets, in different
situations or at different times. In addition to these distinctions behaviour may be dichotomous (e.g. to breast feed or not)
or continuous (e.g. the time of breast feeding).

Fishbein's taxonomy enables a researcher to construct different behavioural indices which have different meanings. For example, a multiple-act criterion is a behavioural analogy to a collection of belief statements from an attitude scale. However, the similarities are limited, because self-generated behaviour does not reveal those acts which a person did not show overtly. Thus, it is difficult to construct scale values analogies for the observed acts.

Although Fishbein's system is useful to measure behaviour, it does not convey any explanatory meaning. When a scientific observer is facing a complex flow of behaviour, Fishbein does not provide him or her with a rationale of what kind of acts should be selectively analysed for a given purpose. We have to consider a behavioural theory to enable us to perform the required analysis.

GOAL DIRECTED ATTITUDES AND BEHAVIOUR

The theory presented here will draw upon the work by Lewin (1938) and McClelland, Atkinson, Clark & Lowell (1953) on motivation and goal-directed activity. It is assumed that behaviour leading to goal attainment will require more cognitive control and planning as compared to other kinds of behaviour, e.g. conditioned reflexes or highly automatized motor behaviour. In restricting the domain of behaviour, it is assumed that attitudes will play a more prominent role if actions are analysed and predicted.

According to McClelland et al. goal-directed activity starts with a need to reach a goal and is terminated when the goal is consumed. After consumption the same goal may or may not be set up again and a similar activity may occur. The need to attain a goal emerges and accompanies the behaviour when a person anticipates the state of goal consumption. The behaviour is instrumental for reaching the goal, i.e. persons will use means and try to remove obstacles. They are also appreciative of any help from other persons.

Goals can be distinguished by a variety of attributes :
(1) some goals require a short-term activity, e.g. picking a restaurant to get food. Other goals need more time, e.g. getting married or receiving a Ph. D. degree. (2) Two or more goals can be compatible or incompatible. For example, if I want to enjoy myself on Lanzerote I am not able to play games on my computer. (3) If a goal implies a positive target, e.g. a friend, he will probably be approached. By contrast, a biting dog will be avoided or sprayed with a can. (4) A single sequence of behaviour may

subsume several goals. For example, if the final exam of a student is graded an A, she will catch the attention of her professor, get more dates, and receive a more generous payment check from her father. (5) For some goals, there may exist a strategy to guarantee consumption **permanently**. If I feel a strong need for swimming, I can concentrate my scattered activities like going to lakes, indoor pools, long distant beaches etc., if I build my own swimming pool. (6) Finally, goals may be ranked according to their importance for an individual or group.

The concept of goal-directed action simultaneously offers some solutions to the problems posed above. If a researcher knows the goal of a subject, the selection of the object of inquiry is much less arbitrary. The attitude towards the object can be defined by its facilitating or obstructive function towards the selected goal. Part of the instability of object evaluations can be eliminated if the function of the object does not vary over several different goals. A person supposed to report on his or her attitude towards an object will normally select implicitly a goal-frame unknown to an interviewer; if the goal is assessed or presented by the interviewer, some of the "error" variance can be partialled out or reduced by referring to a single goal only.

Furthermore, if we know the function of an object within a goal-attaining activity, it is easier to describe the subset of beliefs selected by the person holding the goal. For attitude scale construction the attitude statements may be selected less arbitrarily as traditionally if the framework of goals is priorly assessed. The single evaluations of beliefs will reflect their instrumental value so that the problem of an infinite regression is solved.

We can now go a step further and define attitudes more rigorously. So far, I used the terms objects, target, and goal loosely with respect to bipolar attributes, like approach/avoidance, instrumentality and positivity/negativity. Basically, I suggest there are two latent constructs implying a valence attribute : goal-attitude and instrumental attitude.

1. Goal-attitude

Goal-attitude is always positive and can vary in strength. A goal-attitude of zero strength indicates the non-existence of that goal. At a first glance it seems that this definition contradicts Lewin's approach and avoidance concept. For example, if pain avoidance is a goal, pain is of negative valence. However, the goal can be defined as the complement of pain avoidance, i.e.

comfort seeking; this state is conceptualized as always being positive. Pain, then, is a target implicit in the goal, whereas the goal is a positive state which can be consumed.

In the McClelland et al. (1953) system the concept of <u>need</u> is an equivalent to what I called goal-attitude. Other theorists have labelled it <u>value</u> (Rokeach, 1973); Rokeach's values are conceived as "basic" because they generalize over a variety of goals and thus, can be considered as ultimate goals. A major problem with very general goals is the difficulty in deriving specific action plans and behaviour from them.

Another term used as a substitute for value, need, or goal-attitutde is <u>preference</u> (see Fischhoff, Slovic & Lichtenstein, 1980). Applied to goals, it indicates that some are more important than others. However, as applied to action choices the term preference means that one alternative is better for goal-attainment than another. I would like to reserve this meaning for my second key term, i.e. instrumental attitude.

2. Instrumental attitude

Instrumental attitude refers to means and obstacles embedded in goal-directed behaviour that facilitate, handicap, or block that behaviour. The instrumental attitude can be expressed towards objects, persons, groups, institutions, ideas, events, or action units. More technically, an instrumental attitude is an internally represented quantity on a bipolar dimension with a positive and a negative end pole. In this respect, it is formally equivalent to Thurstone's, Anderson's and others' concepts of attitude. However, instrumental attitude $\underline{A_I}$ always refers to the evaluation of means $\underline{E_M}$ given a particular $\underline{GB_P}$ goal-directed behaviour plan $\underline{GB_P}$ or actual behaviour $\underline{GB}$:

$$A_I = f(E_M \mid GB_P \vee GB) \quad [2]$$

First, note that if the means expressed by $\underline{E_M}$ is an action unit, $\underline{E_M}$ is similarly defined as the attitude towards a behaviour $\underline{A_B}$ by Ajzen & Fishben (1980) except that $\underline{A_B}$ is not made conditional upon goal-directed behaviour $\underline{GB}$. Secondly, the instrumental attitude $\underline{A_I}$ towards the same means may vary depending on the time when the evaluation $\underline{E_M}$ is assessed. Prior to a goal-directed activity

E_M's instrumental attitude may be called "planned". After the activity E_M's instrumental attitude may have changed because the acting person received feedback. A difference between "planned" and "feedback" instrumental attitude may reflect the difficulties of an acting person to perform goal-directed behaviour.

JUDGEMENTS, ANNOUNCEMENTS AND BEHAVIOUR

Since instrumental attitudes have been defined as internal representations, we need to ask next how they are expressed externally in a (social) environment. Once we have developed such a response theory we will be able to measure internal representations.

The literature on attitude and behaviour has not expressed yet the need for such a theory. There seems to exist a tacit agreement that attitudes are measured by using standardized or non-standardized verbal reports, whereas behaviour is something different - "observable acts that are studied in their own right (Fishbein & Ajzen, 1975, p.335)". It should be acknowledged, though, that Fishbein & Ajzen (1975) suggested that "behavioural observations can be used to measure the person's attitude (p.357)". However, they discuss the issue within the tradition of Thurstone (1931), Doob (1947) and Campbell (1963) saying that a single attitude (e.g. liking a person) can generate a whole pattern of different behaviour. Also, Fishbein and Ajzen treated behaviour in a non- theoretical way, i.e. as an "indicator" of attitudes.

1. Cross-modality matching

In deviating from this tradition, I propose to transfer an idea, already developed in psychophysics, to the attitude and behaviour arena - the idea of cross-modality (Stevens, 1966; Stevens, Mack & Stevens, 1960). Basically, Stevens hypothesized that a given perceptual quantity can be expressed (matched) in any kind of response modality, e.g. by a number system like a scale, by drawing a line, by squeezing a hand dynamometer, etc. Upshaw (1969) let subjects express the strength of their moral beliefs into volumes of sand piled up on a table. Lodge, Cross, Tursky & Tanenhaus (1975) and Wegener (1978) demonstrated that attitudes can be expressed non-verbally and the results seem to have some advantages in test criteria as compared to category scales. Most of the research on cross-modality matching used ratio scales to let subjects match a quantity into motor behaviour.

How can this basic process be transferred to instrumental

attitude responses ? I will distinguish three types of processes.

(1) <u>Behaviour</u>. Since an evaluative dimension underlies our instrumental attitude concept we need to construct evaluative behaviour modalities into which the internal representation is to be expressed. If the attitude object is a person, this behaviour modality could be pro-<u>versus</u> anti-social behaviour, or in other words, helping <u>versus</u> aggression. Since helping and aggression can vary in strength, it must be possible to express an internally represented quantity into this response mode. The neutral point of the modality would be non-activity.

Note that the suggested mode is not restricted to motor behaviour like lifting a fallen person or hitting somebody on the head. It can be also a symbolic act having some definite consequences, e.g. spending more money on one's rent or filing a law suit against a landlord. If the attitude is expressed towards a material object the dimension could vary between maintenance and destruction.

(2) <u>Announcements</u>. As compared to behaviour an announcement is a claim to perform an act although that act will not necessarily be performed. Indicators are words like I will, I shall, I would like, etc. The evaluative content of an announcement will vary along the poles <u>assurance</u> and <u>threat</u>.

According to Ajzen & Fishbein (1980) this concept could have been labelled "intention" as well, but since intentions in their theory of reasoned action depend on attitudes towards a behaviour A_B and a subjective norm <u>SN</u> it would be confusing for readers to use the same term. Also in our model, subjective norm will have a slightly different function, as will be seen below.

(3) <u>Judgements</u>. This is the normal attitude response in field and laboratory research. A respondent will use evaluative language to express his internal state, e.g. in positive/negative numbers, in Osgood et al.'s (1955) semantic differential, or on a Likert scale. The reader will remember that I proposed a departure from the traditional methods, namely to expose an interviewee with belief statements to express his or her attitude. Rather, I suggested to omit beliefs and provide the goal context within which the attitude object occurs. It is clear that the attitude scale examples in this paragraph vary with respect to directness of measurement. Osgood's evaluation factor is certainly more context-free in terms of the content of beliefs than a Likert scale, and an <u>ad hoc</u> rating scale provides almost no content except the object.

Other things being equal, the spontaneous and the induced usage of the three types of modality is hypothesized to depend on the strength of the goal-attitude. More precisely, with increasing willingness to attain a goal a person is hypothesized to substitute judgements by announcements and announcements by behaviour. The association between the choice of the response modality and strength of goal attitude is higher if the responses are generated by the respondent instead of task-orientated responses in a measurement context.

My hypotheses on the matching or mapping process as well as the rank order of modalities only hold if a person is not skillful in performing either of the modalities. Among academics one is likely to expect that behaviour is the more difficult modality in which to perform, whereas among working class members verbal abilities may be less trained. I am not convinced that class differences make that strong a difference when persons are pursuing goals, but I wanted to emphasize that on the individual level my hypotheses may interfere with skills. This is mainly an empirical problem.

2. Biases in two-alternative responses

It is an advantage of the present conceptualisation that we can draw upon findings in judgement research to predict what will happen in behaviour if the modalities themselves do not make a substantial difference. Theories of judgement responses are by far better developed as compared to behavioural responses.

Upmeyer (1981) systematically summarized response-mapping effects for two-alternative choices and magnitude estimation. He used signal-detection methodology to analyse two-alternative response modes and separated response processes from sensitivity towards stimuli in various perceptual and memory experiments. Three factors appeared to be crucial for the understanding of biases in response processes : (1) perceived sanctions, (2) expectations, and (3) correspondences (value and descriptive correspondence).

Sanctions influence a response choice under external or internalized social pressure. Upmeyer (1971) demonstrated that subjects complying to the pressure exerted by the suggested response style of a group, independently increase their sensitivity towards the stimulus. As a theoretical derivative one can say that the response pattern distorts and masks the internal representation of stimuli.

Ajzen & Fishbein (1980) invoked a similar factor to predict their intention variable : social norms (see Formula [1] in this paper). This can be treated like internalized social pressure, although Ajzen & Fishbein also allow for external influences. The issue is not an easy one. Since I am concerned with the **expressiveness** of instrumental attitudes in this section I believe more strongly in the effect of external pressure in situ.
Our experimental experience taught us that social influences are particularly strong if they are exerted during the judgement task continuously over trials. Social influence is not as strong if it is conveyed before an ongoing task and not replicated during task trials.

On the other hand, being unable to justify a goal-attitude before oneself may lower the strength of goal attitude. For example, because of internalized social norms a person may not be able to justify having two lovers simultaneously. Given my distinction between goal attitude and instrumental attitude this person will not pursue vigorously the goal of getting a second lover, but he or she may express an instrumental attitude to the idea of a second lover favourably in a group of friends of the same sex. To summarize, I would like to reserve the term "internalized norms" for the motivational strength to reach a goal, and measure this influence by personal fantasy products.

Expectations were conceived by Upmeyer (1981) as a frequency distribution of stimuli. If a subject believes that stimulus A occurs more often than stimulus B - be it right or wrong - the response distribution will be affected in the same direction, i.e. the response identifying stimulus A will be given more often, and largely independently of a subject's error rate. This effect is well established in signal detection research (Swets, 1973).

As applied to behaviour the expectation principle means e.g. that a person prefers aggressive behaviour if, in a particular situation, aggressive stimuli are predominantly exhibited. No pressure may be involved here, although as a second factor pressure can augment or decrease aggression. The expectation principle simply means that in a behaviour choice situation, subjects take into account the stimulus distribution.

Correspondences are another factor which influence two-alternative response mapping (Upmeyer & Layer, 1974). A correspondence exists if the response mode variable happens to covary with a so-called third variable, i.e. a variable which is not the object of the present judgment task. If the response choice is uncertain and the status of the third variable is clear, <u>then</u> a subject will take the third variable as a guideline to determine his or her response. For example, a child playing the role of a devil will more likely insult than assure a co-actor for having done something because the devil's role is used as a guideline for eliciting responses. As compared to a situation without role playing the same behaviour of another person would not have been responded to by an insult.

Sanctions, expectations, and correspondence will operate more strongly if a person is insecure about his or her internal state. If a goal is important for a person and the means to attain the goal is obvious judgements, announcements, and behaviour are elicited more or less unbiasedly.

3. Biases in magnitude responses

If a subject wants or has to express an internally represented quantity or magnitude, the mapping process is more complicated than in a two-alternative choice situation. The most powerful judgement mechanism found here has been called the <u>range</u> or <u>perspective</u> principle (Upshaw, 1962; Parducci, 1965; Upshaw, 1969). According to this principle any subjective quantity is internally represented on a dimension with two finite end points, i.e. the perspective end anchors. If a quantitative response modality with finite poles is provided to the respondent, s/he will linearly transform the internal quantity to the response mode after the perspective end anchors and the scale poles are equated.

The internally represented end anchors thus serve as comparison standards. They may vary dramatically over situations. Suppose (1) the response mode is a bipolar rating scale with a fixed number of points and (2) an instrumental attitude has a fixed evaluative quantity over time. If one of the perspective end anchors remains constant and the other differs over situations, the same attitude will be expressed differently on the scale. This bias is well established in the social judgement literature and has been applied to attitudes (e.g. Ostrom & Upshaw, 1968). It has not yet been transferred to evaluative behaviour and announcements.

Upmeyer (1981) has argued that sanctions, expectations, and correspondences also apply to magnitude estimation. I will not repeat the arguments here.

One open problem is the assumption that the transformation from internal quantities to response mode variables is linear. From the studies performed by Upshaw and ∂oworkers as well as Parducci this assumption seems to be viable. Stevens, Mack & Stevens (1960) obtained various exponents of power functions when different physical quantities were transformed to response scales. Moreover, Rule, Curtis & Markley, (1970) received different exponents for a power function, transforming a stimulus dimension to the dimension of internal representation (as measured by MDS) and a power function transforming the internal dimension to a response scale. From these results it seems difficult, on a theoretical level, to predict the type of function relating internal representations to behavioural response dimensions. In order to be able to make empirical progress it is also mandatory to develop a metric for behavioural acts.

4. Stimulation for related literature

Since I did not find a publication which explicitly studied the matching process of an attitude into verbal, intentional and behavioural response modalities, I can only provide related experimental designs to stimulate more rigorous tests of our central hypotheses. The designs may be converted to a paradigm for the investigation of the model proposed above.

Research on the judgement of humour may contribute to such a paradigm (Cupchik & Leventhal, 1974; Leventhal & Cupchik, 1976). Subjects had to read cartoons of good and bad quality while they were observed to determine how far they expressed mirth non-verbally. The dependent variable ranged from 1 to 4 (no response, slight smile, full smile, laugh). They were also asked to evaluate the cartoons on a 7-point ad hoc rating scale according to the following questions. (1) How funny was the cartoon ? (2) Did you like the cartoon ? (3) Was it a good cartoon ?

For our purpose the "magnitude" of observed mirth and the rating scale can be conceived as two modalities across which a subject matches his or her attitude towards the cartoons. In this case, the behaviour was self-generated whereas the scale was administered for measurement purposes. For a variation, it seems possible to tell subjects to voluntarily express their attitudes in degrees of mirth so that both modalities are used in a task-orientated setting. One of the results of the authors suggests that this variation could work. The instruction to the subject to observe his/her expressive behaviour during the experiment successfully extinguished the "automatic" mirth response.

Note that the Cupchik & Leventhal study was limited to the positive side of an evaluative dimension. Probably, one could also use negative picture stories and the non-verbal utterance of disgust.

Moreover our principles of correspondence and/or of sanctions seem to have had an effect on Cupchik & Leventhal's variables. In a variation, one group of subjects received an audience feedback of equal intensity (taped or "canned" laughter) when they read the cartoons. Males were significantly affected by this manipulation. Cupchik and Leventhal (1974) tentatively concluded that "males used the audience response as information about the cartoon quality (p.435)". According to the theory presented here it is alternatively possible that their subjects used canned laughter to determine (bias) their <u>responses</u>. It would be worthwhile to investigate this hypothesis after making two modalities more homogeneous; it is hypothesized that the effect of the audience would operate in both response modes, i.e. be invariant over modalities.

A second paradigm to investigate our theory could be based on the well-known social learning studies by Bandura and coworkers (e.g. Bandura, Ross & Ross, 1963; Bandura 1971). In a typical experiment a video-taped person (the model) performs unusual aggressive acts towards a doll. After having seen the video film children are confronted with the doll in the room where the film has been taken and they can play there freely. The imitation of aggressive acts was shown to depend on reinforcement i.e. either directed to the subjects or vicariously to the model. If negative reinforcement was given first, subjects rarely showed aggression, but they imitated the aggressive acts as accurately as another group, if they got positive reinforcement in a repeated measurement condition. In his social learning theory, Bandura concluded that the acquisition of behaviour is a psychologically independent process as compared to the performance (or overt expression) of behaviour.

Whereas acquisition is mediated by attention to and encoding of stimuli, the decision to perform or not to perform a behaviour is affected by reinforcement.

It is primarily the invariance of the accuracy of performed behaviour over different valences of reinforcement that led Bandura to postulate the two processes. Accuracy indicates how well a behavioural unit is learned, stored, and reproduced. If a behavioural act is accurately stored we can assume that it can be used overtly to express an internal state. Bandura's experiments indicate that the usage is biased by reinforcement (or sanctions as we have called it). By contrasting accuracy and performance, one can be more certain that performance is a response process which can be studied in its own right.

A closer inspection of Bandura's paradigm reveals three issues related to our own interests. First, like in the studies of humour reported above, the paradigm is concerned with one side of the evaluative dimension only, i.e. in this case the negative side (aggression). If we want to use this approach to let people express their attitudes, we need the positive side, too. As suggested earlier this could consist of pro-social behavioural acts.

Secondly, if we allow for the decision between pro- and anti-social performance we could assess accuracy in both performance categories. This provides us with the opportunity to test whether accuracy is independent of positive and negative valence. As the Bandura paradigm stands now, the category of non-performance cannot be analysed because nothing can be observed here.

Finally, although Bandura, Ross & Ross (1963) used words and behaviour, they assessed accuracy as a total of all responses. For our purpose, it would be advisable to separate the two modalities and show that the performance process is invariant over modalities.

To classify what we have gained by the suggested expansion, I would like to compare it with a two-alternative judgement model i.e. signal detection theory. In a signal detection analysis two sets of stimuli (S_1 and S_2) are presented in a random order of succession of their elements and on each trial the subject responds in a two-alternative verbal response modality A, where S_1 is identified by A_1 and S_2 by A_2. In each set of answers A_1 and A_2 a subject will be right and wrong. Suppose A_1 and A_2 are used equally often and the percentage of correct answers is 70 % in both A_1 and A_2. If the subject changes his preference and uses A_1 more frequently than A_2 (because of sanctions, expectations or correspondences) the number of correct choices could be increased in A_1 and decreased in A_2 so that the sum of correct answers in the two categories is still 70 %. Such a result would indicate that the accuracy in identifying the stimuli is not independent of the preference of the response category. In other words, the response process itself has some effect on the internal representation of stimuli. By contrast, assume that after changing the preference, the percentage correct is 70 % in both A_1 and A_2. In this case, the response does not seem to affect the internal representation. As a consequence, our analytical tools to verify the independence of acquisition and performance and to conceptualize performance as a response process are greatly improved if we are going to use two exclusive behaviour categories within which we can make observations to measure accuracy.

SCHEMATA, SCRIPTS AND BEHAVIOUR

Thus far, we were concerned with how instrumental attitudes can be expressed in different response modalities, one being behaviour. Persons will show this kind of behaviour either to fulfill a task, e.g. as a subject in a psychological study, or to express their instrumental attitudes spontaneously or deliberately when they pursue goals.

The other type of behaviour is the goal-directed activity itself. It consists of a number of action units implying the objects evaluated in terms of their instrumental purposes. Since equation [2] has made instrumental attitude conditional upon goal activity, the knowledge of the content of goal activity seems to be indispensable.

If we focus on the assessment of instrumental attitudes we may avoid a descriptive analysis of goal activities by making subjects think in the context of one of their goals before letting them evaluate an object. Thus Snyder & Swann (1976) found a correlation of .58 between attitude and subsequent behaviour if subjects were thinking about a general issue before expressing their attitude. The correlation was .07 if they did not have the opportunity to think. If thinking in a goal-context is used as an analytical tool to improve the measurement of attitudes it could still be beneficial to have the details of that context available.

If we focus on the goal-directed activity itself we will not be able to avoid some descriptive work before we can start predicting that kind of behaviour. More specifically, we need to answer the following questions. What is an action unit ? How are action units organized in long-term memory ? How are action plans retrieved from memory and applied in a situation ?

1. Conceptual work

To answer the first question I will use here a concept that has become again very popular in psychology over the last five years or so, i.e. the schema concept (Bartlett, 1932; Bobrow & Norman, 1975; Rumelhart & Ortony, 1976; Taylor & Crocker, 1980). A schema is a cognitive structure representing the knowledge of a defined stimulus domain.

Scripts are a special kind of schemata. They form a set of expectations about an event sequence which can be used to understand actions or to perform actions rapidly (Schank & Abelson, 1977). Recently, Abelson (Note 1) has convincingly argued that scripts can be used to explain the relationship between attitudes and behaviour.

To introduce the details, consider the following example. Suppose a sport diver is planning a trip to the Red Sea. His goal is to enjoy the nature in the Sinai desert and shooting pictures of tropical fishes. Since the goal attitude is strong (say, .9) he will exhibit all kinds of goal-directed activities.

First, he needs general travel information which may be readily obtained from diving magazines. The activity to scan magazines can be called a script because of its routine nature; it consists of the following steps : (1) going to the diving club library, (2) reading tables of content, (3) selecting articles on the Red Sea and Israel, (4) noting local addresses, (5) noting addresses of travel agents. There is no problem involved in planning this action unit. It can be called a unit because both the beginning and the end is clearly defined. This script has been elicited because the subgoal of getting information and the knowledge about diving magazines has been associated in memory.

Let us compare reading magazines with an alternative : asking a club member who has been there. This activity is somewhat more difficult to perform because our diver has to ask questions without having a well-structured idea about what is necessary to ask. On the other hand, this activity is less time-consuming than reading many articles.

After having gathered information it appears that it is necessary to bring an air compressor in one's luggage because the local air-stations in the Sinai are too far apart. Two problems are emerging now. First our diver has to learn to operate the compressor. There is no schema or script available to take this for granted. So he has to get trained, to carefully analyse the manuals, buy maintenance material, etc. After a long time this activity unit may be converted into a script.

However, secondly, the problems involved in the operation of the compressor may not be predictable at the onset of planning, so that the goal has to be cancelled, postponed, or substituted by another goal. For example, one could buy a trip package to a hotel with an air-station. Since the hotel is touristy, the diver will not enjoy the nature of the Sinai as much and his attitude toward the new goal is only .7.

We can learn several things from the example :

(1) If a person wants to attain a goal the total activity falls into several pieces, called action units.

(2) Action units are partly anticipated in terms of schemata or scripts. Given a certain activity, schemata are arranged in a serial order and thus, they are organized in memory similar to episodes. However, since alternative activities may lead to the same goal, the knowledge of the time order does not have as much influence on the planning process as it has when episodes have to be reconstructed.

(3) Some action units may be absolutely necessary for reaching a goal. If the schema associated with this action unit tells the person that the action unit cannot be successfully performed, a person will give up the goal as long as the circumstances do not change.

(4) Often we find alternative action units which will lead to the same goal. In this case a person will choose the one which is easier to perform in terms of resources, time, and "scriptness". By scriptness I mean the degree of skill (more precisely : ease) required to perform it. The same criteria apply to alternative action plans.

(5) The **structure of planned action units** are assumed to be "top-down", though not strictly hierarchical. By top-down, I mean that one can usually start on top with a variety of ongoing action units which will finally lead to the same goal (down). They constitute a network with knots, the knots being the action units. The same action unit can appear within several paths from the various top entries to the goal.

(6) During the period of planning a person usually invokes an incomplete plan, i.e. a plan that does not contain all the action units which will be used later to really attain the goal. The person will develop a confidence rating on how complete the plan looks like. This rating will affect the realisation of the plan.

(7) During planning, and in a situation, a schema or action is elicited by cognitive or situational cues. Abelson (Note 1) proposed that an "action rule" is used by a person to verify the appropriateness of a script. For example, if somebody asks me for a light, I will use the answers to the following questions as an action rule : (a) Do I have a light ? (b) Did he ask politely ? Abelson believes that action rules are not necessarily consciously articulated.

Although the schema concept is plausible when applied to an ex-post explanation of a course of activities it is often difficult to use for prediction. Really existing schemata are often ill-defined and cannot be generalized over situations. It is also not clear if a schema can be further partitioned into smaller units; like "vignettes" or "scenes" in a script (Schank & Abelson, 1977), although this may be solved empirically (Bower, Black & Turner, 1979).

By definition, a schema or script is a cluster of knowledge. It deserves its label only if one can show that the elements belonging to the schema show a higher degree of interrelatedness than elements not belonging to the schema. This analysis has to be done empirically for the area in question before one can start to use it. Since the schema concept is so general it is very unlikely that we will detect concrete schemata that generalize over many diverse situations.

2. Research lines

In their review on schema research Taylor & Crocker (1980) distinguished three classes of social schemata about (1) individual persons, (2) roles of persons, and (3) events. The latter is particularly interesting for attitude and behaviour. Unfortunately, an inspection of the literature yields that the research on schemata is predominantly concerned with perception, cognition, and judgement; very little has been related to social behaviour.

Without presenting too many details I selected three recent research areas which are closest to our present interests : research on artificial intelligence, memory and illness schemata.

2.1. Artificial Intelligence (AI) research

Schank and Abelson's work on script theory is a fine example of interdisciplinary work between computer science and psychology. The work at Yale University is primarily devoted to the aim to make a computer understand natural language. Although cognitive psychology made numerous contributions to their work it did not suffice to write a programme that understands stories. Ideas from linguistics and philosophy as well as many ad hoc assumptions have to be worked into the programmes. The "test" of the appropriateness of these ideas is made by the user of the programme, i.e. by his or her judgement that the computer gave an intelligible response. Although the productive power of some of the programmes is amazing it may not readily be transferred to real human cognition or behaviour. On the other hand, I am convinced that the analytical work to establish programmes will be a valuable feedback for theorezing in cognitive psychology. To be fair, I would like to add that much of the work on schemata in psychology is also purely analytical without being on the level of precision in AI research.

Among the numerous publications from the Yale group a dissertation by Wilensky (Note 5) on the understanding of goal-based stories is close to our theme. His programme PAM (Plan Applier Mechanism) uses knowledge about intentions to make inferences. It shows its understanding by answering questions about novel stories - answers which are generated by the programme itself.

In building his programme Wilensky found that different approaches have to be used when a computer is supposed to understand a goal-based as compared to solving problems, i.e. to simulate goal attainment (p.57-59). However, he successfully used a goal classification and set of primitive planning structures proposed by Schank & Abelson (1977), which could also be fruitful in the descriptive work I postulated.

According to Schank & Abelson goals are classified as follows : (1) Satisfaction goals occur from hunger, sex and sleep. (2) Enjoyment goals are pursued for leisure and can be simultaneously attained with satisfaction goals, e.g. eating in a three-star restaurant. (3) Achievement goals are established to achieve abilities, possessions, and social positions. (4) Preservation goals involve the maintenance of a desirable state, like one's own health. (5) Instrumental goals are subgoals pursued for the sake of a more general goal. (6) Delta goals are a special kind of instrumental goals that occur frequently and can be achieved in many ways, e.g. changing one's location, one's knowledge or one's control of an object; obtaining social permission and employing an agent on one's behalf.

The primitive planning structures proposed by Schank & Abelson are called plan boxes and can be used both for understanding a goal-based activity and for the planning of an activity itself. A planbox has preconditions and a content. As soon as the preconditions are met, the content of the planbox can be transformed into action without training. One of the planboxes is called ASK - expressing a request to someone. A precondition requires that the planner is able to communicate. To insure this he may have to achieve the Delta goal of changing his location. Thus, a plan can be constructed by chaining different Delta goals and planboxes together.

An additional number of useful descriptive terms can be found in Wilensky's (1978) dissertation.

2.2. Memory Research

Whereas artificial intelligence researchers are feeding a computer with scripted stories they would like the machine to understand, empirical researchers in the memory area let subjects write up scripts and use them later in experimental settings. In a carefully done study, Bower, Black & Turner (1979) asked subjects to write a list of actions describing what students do if they go, for example, to a lecture. They asked them to provide a beginning and end of the script, and to include 20 actions in the right order of occurrence. For the Lecture script, only 4 out of 704 actions were uniquely given by one person (N = 32). In addition, the frequency with which particular actions of a script appeared were surprisingly reliable (ranging between .80 and .88 over scripts). Subjects also agreed highly in segmenting a given script into single scenes.

Furthermore, Bower et al. tried to analyse the role of memory in script processing. If some script actions were actually presented to subjects in the wrong order they tended to be recalled in the order logically predescribed by the script. Finally, the authors found a von-Restorff effect for obstacles and distractions in scripts by using written recall protocol as the method of retrieval.

To summarize, this article contains a number of useful diagnostics by which we can classify scripts as highly expected courses of events. I do not see any major problems in applying these techniques to goal-related activities.

2.3. Illness schemata

Preventive medicine tries to assess the circumstances under which a patient complies to preventive services. One advantage in investigating the relation of attitudes and behaviour in this field is the personal scheme of this preservation goal. Another advantage is the possibility to assess real behaviour.

Outstanding work in this area has been done by H. Leventhal and his coworkers. The research originated in the well-known study of fear-arousal by Janis & Feshbach (1953). Leventhal (1970) summarized a great number of his own and other's studies as follows. A health threat is conceived as a necessary, but not sufficient condition to follow a long-term recommendation for health protection. The level of fear appeared to be of little consequence in the formation of an awareness of the threat. More important for forming an action plan was precise information about the recommended behaviour. If this information and a threat coincides then a person is more likely to follow preventive suggestions. This research supports our view that behaviour needs both a motivation to reach a goal and an action plan to be able to perform goal-directed activity.

Johnson & Leventhal (1974) studied patients undergoing an endoscopic examination and demonstrated an interaction between fear and danger control. They prepared patients by providing information about the sensory experiences of the test, resulting in a reduction of fear. During the examination the patients used the information to exert control over swallowing the fiber optic tube and they showed less heart acceleration.

The study is an example that concrete planning for a preservation goal leads to successful attainment.

In a summary of more recent research Leventhal, Meyer & Nerenz (Note 2) described three schemata of different representations of an illness. For example, hypertensive patients were asked how long they expected treatment to last and what the outcome will be. Group 1 (the "acute episode" schema) expected a short-term treatment followed by being cured. Most of these patients pointed to a recent symptom and a specific time and place for the onset of hypertension and they attributed it to specific home and job stress.

Group 2 (the "cyclic" schema) expected the symptoms to subside for a period of time and then reoccur. Most of them were likely to report a random or repetitive symptom pattern and attributed the onset of their hypertension to diet and drinking.

Group 3 (the "chronic" schema) thought they would need long term treatment because they were old or their problems were inherited. They attributed the disease to physical damages.

It is interesting for our purpose that these schemata correlated with announced coping behaviour, i.e. the concreteness of an illness representation seems to covary with the concreteness of coping strategies . Leventhal, Meyer & Nerenz (Note 2) provide further information on cancer schemata that are associated with still other kinds of coping behaviour. To summarize, although most of this research is correlational and relies partly on verbal reports, it indicated that stimuli (symptoms) are cues for schemata which trigger specific goal-directed behaviour.

CONCLUDING COMMENTS

Our theoretical analysis and interpretation of empirical findings should stimulate new research along the following lines.

(1) In order to be able to link attitudes and behaviour we need to select goal attitudes of a sufficient strength. Without a strong motivational basis I believe we cannot expect that people spend much energy to display persistent behaviour. As a result of this general view the range of application of attitudes will be much more narrow than in former research. I feel that we simply cannot expect that attitudes apply to any conceivable behaviour.

(2) If it is true that behaviour depends on prior action plans and schemata, the contents of these schemata are likely to vary widely over situations and goals. Under these circumstances it seems advisable to choose a typical action-relevant topic, e.g. seeking medical services, saving energy, participating in political action, and analyse back towards the underlying schemata and attitudes.

(3) Given a relevant topic we should first identify a goal or the goals. Then we can start to descriptively analyse the set of possible action plans including their schemata and scripts. Finally, we can observe and question people pursuing this goal, and incorporate or classify this data within the system elaborated upon before. The system would also be a welcome frame to determine the relative meaning of <u>self-generated</u> action alternatives and recall data.

(4) The relative ease to perform an action plan will depend on the number of action units which can be characterized as scripts, i.e. highly expected event units in the course of reaching a goal. If a behaviour is based on less automatic schemata then the accuracy of information and skill training conditions will be decisive to predict behaviour.

(5) Instrumental attitudes may point to important action units as well as to objects implied in those units. Within a course of action they can be expressed in terms of judgements, announcements, and behaviour. Instrumental attitudes can be used as diagnostics to assess means to be acquired and obstacles to be removed in a goal.

(6) In field research on social behaviour the content of attitude items should be derived from goals. During the interview, the goal-context should be provided for the respondent prior to assessing an attitude rating.

A general conclusion to be drawn from this chapter is that attitudes are only a part of the cognitive variables we need to explain and predict behaviour.

REFERENCE NOTES

1. Abelson, R.P. Three modes of attitude-behavior consistency. To appear in : M.P. Zanna, C.P. Herman & E.T. Higgins (Eds.), Variability and consistency in social behaviors : The Ontario Symposium. Vol. 2. Hillsdale, N.J.: Erlbaum, 1981.
2. Leventhal, H., Meyer, D. & Nerenz, D. The common sense representation of illness danger. To appear in S. Rachman, (Ed.), Medical Psychology. Vol. 2. Pergamon Press, 1980.
3. Taylor, S.E. & Crocker, J. Schematic bases of social information processing. To appear in E.T. Higgins, C.P. Herman & M.P. Zanna, (Eds.), Social cognition : The Ontario Symposium on personality and social psychology. Hillsdale, N.J. : Erlbaum.
4. Upmeyer, A. Perceptual and judgmental processes in social contexts. To appear in : L. Berkowitz (Ed.), Advances in Experimental Social Psychology. New York : Academic Press, 1981.
5. Wilensky, R. Understanding goal-based stories. Research Report No. 140. Yale University. Department of Computer Science, 1978.

REFERENCES

Abelson, R.P. Are attitudes necessary ? In B.T. King & E. McGinnies, (Eds.), Attitudes, conflict, and social change. New York : Academic Press, 1972.

Abelson, R.P., Aronson, E., McGuire, W.J. Newcomb, T.M., Rosenberg, M.J. & Tannenbaum, P.H. (Eds.), Theories of cognitive consistency : A sourcebook. Chicago : Rand McNally, 1968.

Anderson, N.H. Integration theory and attitude change. Psychological Review, 1971, 78, 171-206.

Ajzen, I. & Fishbein, M. Attitudinal and normative variables as predictors of specific behaviors. Journal of Personality and Social Psychology, 1973, 27, 41-57.

Ajzen, I. & Fishbein, M. Attitude-behavior relations : A theoretical analysis and review of empirical research. Psychological Bulletin, 1977, 84, 888-918.

Ajzen, I. & Fishbein, M. Understanding attitudes and predicting social behavior. Englewood-Cliffs, N.J. : Prentice-Hall, 1980.

Bandura, A. Social learning theory. New York : General Learning Press, 1971.

Bandura, A., Ross, D. & Ross, S.A. Vicarious reinforcement and imitative learning. Journal of Abnormal and Social Psychology, 1963, 67, 601-607.

Bartlett, F.C. Remembering. Cambridge : Cambridge University Press, 1932.

Bem, D.J. Self-perception theory. In L. Berkowitz, (Ed.), Advances in Experimental Social Psychology. Vol. 6. New York : Academic Press, 1972.

Bentler, P.M. Multivariate analysis with latent variables : Causal modeling. Annual Review of Psychology, 1980, 31, 419-456.

Bentler, P.M. & Speckart, G. Attitudes "cause" behaviors : A structural equation analysis. Journal of Personality and Social Psychology, 1981, 40, 226-238.

Bentler, P.M. & Speckart, G. Models of attitude-behavior relations. Psychological Review, 1979, 86, 452-464.

Bobrow, D.G. & Norman, D.A. Some principles of memory schemata. In D.G. Bobrow & A. Collins (Eds.), Representation and understanding. New York : Academic Press, 1975.

Bower, G., Black, J.B. & Turner, T.J. Scripts in memory for texts. Cognitive Psychology, 1979, 11, 177-220.

Campbell, D.T. Social attitudes and other acquired behavioral dispositions. In S. Koch (Ed.), Psychology : A study of science. Vol. 6. New York : McGraw-Hill, 1963.

Cupchik, G. & Leventhal, H. Consistency between expressive behavior and the evaluation of humorous stimuli : The role of sex and self observation. Journal of Personality and Social Psychology, 1974, 30, 429-442.

Datan, N. & Ginsberg, L.H. (Eds.), Life-span developmental psychology. New York : Academic Press, 1975.
Daveney, T.F. Choosing. Mind, 1964, 73, 513-526.
Deutsch, M. The resolution of conflict. New Haven, Connecticut : Yale University Press, 1973.
Deutscher, L. Looking backward : Case studies on the progress of methodology in sociological research. American Sociologist, 1969, 4, 35-41.
Doob, L. The behavior of attitudes. Psychological Review, 1974, 54, 135-156.
Dohrenwend, B.S. & Dohrenwend, B.P. (Eds.), Stressful live events. New York : Wiley, 1974.
Edwards, A.L. Techniques of attitude scale construction. New York : Appleton, 1975.
Festinger, L. & Carlsmith, J.M. Cognitive consequences of forced compliance. Journal of Abnormal and Social Psychology, 1959, 58, 203-210.
Festinger, L. (Ed.), Conflict, decision and dissonance. Stanford, Ca. : Stanford University Press, 1964.
Festinger, L. A theory of cognitive dissonance. Stanford, Ca. : Stanford University Press, 1957.
Fischhoff, B., Slovik, P. & Lichtenstein, S. Knowing what you want : Measuring labile values. In T.S. Wallsten (Ed.), Cognitive processes in choice and decision behavior. Hillsdale; Erlbaum, 1980.
Fishbein, M. The prediction of behavior from attitudinal variables. In C.D. Mortensen & K.K. Sereno (Eds.), Advances in Communication Research. New York : Harper & Row, 1973.
Fishbein, M. An investigation of the relationships between beliefs about an object and the attitude toward that object. Human Relations, 1963, 16, 233-240.
Fishbein, M. & Ajzen, I. Belief, attitude, intention and behavior. Reading, Mass.: Addison-Wesley, 1975.
Guttman, L. A basis for scaling qualitative data. American Sociological Review, 1944, 9, 139-150.
Heider, F. The psychology of interpersonal relations. New York : Wiley, 1958.
Janis, I.L. & Feshbach, S. Effects of fear-arousing communications. Journal of Abnormal and Social Psychology, 1953, 48, 79-92.
Johnson, J.E. & Leventhal, H. Effects of accurate expectations and behavioral instructions on reactions during a noxious medical examination. Journal of Personality and Social Psychology, 1974, 29, 710-718.
Kahle, L.R. & Berman, J.J. Attitudes cause behaviors : A crossed-lagged panel analysis. Journal of Personality and Social Psychology, 1979, 37, 315-321.

Krantz, D.H. & Tversky, A. Conjoint measurement analysis of composition rules in psychology. Psychological Review, 1971, 78, 151-169.

LaPiere, R.T. Attitudes vs. actions. Social Forces, 1934, 13, 230-237.

Leventhal, H. & Cupchik, G. A process model of humor judgement. Journal of Communication, 1976, 26, 190-204.

Lewin, K. The conceptual representation and the measurement of psychological forces. Durham, N.C.: Duke University Press, 1938.

Likert, R.A. A technique for the measurement of attitudes. Archives of Psychology, 1932, 22, No.140.

Lodge, M., Cross, D.V., Tursky, B. & Tanenhaus, J. The psychophysical scaling and validation of a political support scale. American Journal of Political Sciences, 1975, 19, 611-649.

McClelland, D.C., Atkinson, J.W., Clark, R.A. & Lowell, E.L. The achievement motive. New York : Appleton-Century Crofts, 1953.

Miller, G.A., Galanter, E. & Pribram, K.H. Plans and the structure of behavior. London : Holt, Rinehart & Winston, 1960.

Mischel, W. Personality and assessment. New York : Wiley, 1968.

Moscovici, S. & Faucheux, C. Social influence, conformity bias, and the style of active minorities. In L. Berkowitz (Ed.), Advances in Experimental Social Psychology. New York : Academic Press, 1972.

Newcomb, T.M. An approach to the study of communicating acts. Psychological Review, 1953, 60, 393-404.

Osgood, C.E., Suci, G. & Tannenbaum, P.H. The measurement of meaning. Urbana, Ill.: University of Illinois Press, 1957.

Osgood, G.E. & Tannenbaum, P.H. The principle of congruity in the prediction of attitude change. Psychological Review, 1955, 62, 42-55.

Ostrom, T.M. The emergence of the attitude theory : 1930-1950. In A.G. Greenwald, T.C. Brock & T.M. Ostrom (Eds.), Psychological foundations of attitudes. New York : Academic Press, 1968.

Ostrom, T.M. & Upshaw, H.S. Psychological perspective and attitude change. In A.G. Greenwald, T.C. Brock & T.M. Ostrom (Eds.), Psychological foundations of attitudes. New York : Academic Press, 1968.

Parducci, A. Category judgement : A range-frequency model. Psychological Review, 1965, 72, 407-418.

Rokeach, M. The nature of human values. New York : Free Press, 1973.

Rule, S.J., Curtis, D.W. & Markley, R.P. Input and output transformations from magnitude estimation. Journal of Experimental Psychology, 1970, 86, 343-349.

Rumelhart, D.E. & Ortony, A. The representation of knowledge in memory. In R.C. Anderson, R.J. Spiro & W.E. Montague (Eds.), Schooling and the acquisition of knowledge. Hillsdale, N.J.: Erlbaum, 1976.

Schank, R. & Abelson, R.P. Scripts, plans, goals and understanding. Hillsdale, N.J.: Erlbaum, 1977.

Schümer, R. & Cohen, R. Eine Untersuchung zur sozialen Urteilsbildung : II. Bemerkungen zu verschiedenen konkurrierenden Modellen der Urteilsbildung. Archiv für die Gesamte Psychologie, 1968, 120, 180-202.

Snyder, M. & Swann, W. When actions reflect attitudes : The politics of impression management. Journal of Personality and Social Psychology, 1976, 34, 1034-1042.

Stevens, J.C., Mack, J.D. & Stevens, S.S. Growth and sensation on seven continua as measured by force of handgrip. Journal of Experimental Psychology, 1960, 59, 60-67.

Stevens, S.S. Matching functions betwwen loudness and ten other continua. Perception & Psychophysics, 1966, 1, 5-8.

Swets, J.A. The relative operating characteristic in psychology, Science, 1973, 182, 990-1000.

Thurstone, L.L. Attitudes can be measured. American Journal of Sociology, 1928, 33, 529, 554.

Thurstone, L.L. The measurement of social attitudes. Journal of Abnormal and Social Psychology, 1931, 26, 249-269.

Turner, C.F. & Krauss, E. Fallible indicators of the subjective state of the nation. American Psychologist, 1978, 33, 456-470.

Upmeyer, A. Social influence on discrimination and usage of scale. Psychologische Forschung, 1971, 34, 285-294.

Upmeyer, A. & Layer, H. Accentuation in attitude in social judgement. European Journal of Social Psychology, 1974, 4, 469-488.

Upshaw, H.S. Stimulus range and judgemental unit. Journal of Experimental Social Psychology, 1969, 5, 1-11.

Upshaw, H.S. Own attitude as an anchor in equal appearing intervals. Journal of Abnormal and Social Psychology, 1962, 64, 85-96.

Wegener, B. Einstellungsmessung in Umfragen : Kategorische vs. Magnitude-Skalen. Zuma-Nachrichten, 1978, 3, 3-27.

Wicker, A.W. Attitudes vs. action : The relationship of verbal and overt behavioral responses to attitude objects. Journal of Social Issues, 1969, 25, 41-78.

THE COGNITIVE ANALYSIS OF A PERSUASIVE ARGUMENT (1)

E. Burnstein

University of Michigan

Y. Schul

Hebrew University of Jerusalem

One of the more interesting puzzles for a theory of social influence is why the impact of a communication has so little to do with the ability to recall its content. In two experiments, Greenwald (1968), for example, obtained average correlations of .06 and .03 between the accessibility of a persuasive argument and its influence on opinion (for comparable results see Insko, 1964; Miller & Campbell, 1959; Watts & McGuire, 1964).
Our own interest in this problem was stimulated by observing similar effects in studies of attitude polarization in groups. The standard polarization experiment presents the members of a group with conflicting pieces of information in the form of a "choice dilemma". The group has to discuss the matter and come to a decision. As an illustration, one dilemma asks the members to decide whether a person should attend University X or University Y, given that : (i) X is highly prestigeful, but (ii) quite rigorous so that a good number of those who are admitted never receive their degree, while (iii) Y, though not at all prestigeful, is adequate, and (iv) sufficiently undemanding that virtually everyone who is admitted receives his or her degree. When people list the arguments that come to mind while pondering their choice

---

1. The research reported in this chapter was supported by a grant from the National Science Foundation.

(Ebbesen & Bowers, 1974; Vinokur & Burnstein, 1974; Vinokur, Trope, & Burnstein, 1975) they restate more or less precisely all of the four given facts (above) or make small extrapolation that require no additional knowledge beyond these facts (e.g., "You'd learn more at X"). Nevertheless the paraphrases are perceived by judges as relatively unpersuasive and the extrapolations as only moderately persuasive (Vinokur & Burnstein, 1978). Indeed, when these two kinds of arguments are presented to an individual, they have little effect on his or her opinion. The most persuasive arguments that members listed were not actually given in the statement of the dilemma. We consider them <u>implications</u> inasmuch as they are arguments that are implicit in, but not always retrievable from, the explicit content of a communication.

Retrieving implicit information involves finding a <u>useful</u> encoding structure. To illustrate, consider again the problem of whether to attend University X or University Y. In discussions of this dilemma an extremely persuasive argument is "You can always transfer from a really good school to a mediocre one so you might as well go to X <u>regardless</u>". Note that the argument is neither contained in, nor does it directly follow from the statement of the dilemma. Though implicit, it would remain inaccessible were not the content of the dilemma linked to and interpreted within "the structural record of past learning, that is, knowledge of the world" (Craik & Tulving, 1975), here, knowledge of the transfer option in the American university system. Note also that this knowledge may not come to mind immediately but only after an extensive search. Such an encoding structure constitutes a <u>schema</u> (Bartlett, 1932; Rumelhart & Ortony, 1977).

This suggests the persuasiveness of an argument depends on its <u>informativeness</u>, that is, on (i) the amount of implicit information it contains, (ii) the availability of a schema for activating this information, and (iii) the usefulness of the information in deciding between alternative positions, beliefs, solutions, courses of actions, etc. Within the traditional communication and persuasion literature, the evidence for this point of view is limited but consistently positive. Both Cacioppo and Petty (1979) and Greenwald (1968) had individuals list the arguments that came to mind following a persuasive communication. Presumably these ideas were implicit in the system of arguments that made up the communication and were activated as the result of schematic elaboration. In any case, the resulting opinion was much more closely related to the arguments generated in response to the communication than to those actually given in the communication itself. In addition, there are results suggesting that when the appropriate schema is unavailable (Tesser, 1978) or pre-empted (Burnstein & Vinokur, 1975; Tesser, 1978; Watts & Holt, 1979), the implications of an argument will remain inaccessible and inconsequential. The four studies presented below continue this line of work by demonstrating how the cognitive system processes persuasive arguments differently from unpersuasive ones.

Even though the amount of implicit information a statement contains (say, in its typical context) could be specified ahead of time, there is a good chance that when such propositions are juxtaposed in a persuasive communication, other implications will come to mind. These semantic interactions, being inherent in natural language, are probably impossible to eliminate. Nevertheless, their systematic effects can be controlled. We chose to do this by using a large number of communications in which the arguments would be selected and ordered at random. Evaluative descriptions of the form "Igor was stupid and cruel" lend themselves to this kind of manipulation. Note that the potential impact of the description is given by the trait's scale value or "likability" score (Anderson, 1968). If we consider these descriptions "arguments" in respect to the impression, then it can be said that the scale value of a trait is simply a reflection of how much this argument will persuade one that the person described is likable.

Study 1

A Correlational Analysis of Persuasiveness and Informativeness

Our first study compares the persuasiveness of a trait description with its informativeness. Persuasiveness is assessed by taking the absolute difference between a trait's capacity to produce a favorable or unfavorable opinion - its scale value in Anderson (1968) - and the mean scale value of this list. Thus, if a trait has either a very positive or a very negative impact, it is seen as persuasive, whereas if it is neutral, it is considered unpersuasive. Informativeness is indicated by the amount of implicit information that is activated when the trait is encoded in its typical context. To explore whether persuasiveness depends not only on semantic but also on non-semantic implications (e.g., the visual imagery associated with a trait), four different measures of implicit information were employed. These measures are described more fully in the Handbook of Semantic Word Norms (Toglia & Battig, 1978). The two that focus on semantic features were : (i) Meaningfulness, that is, ratings of the ease

Table 1

Correlations between Persuasiveness
and Measures of Implicit Information

	Persuasiveness	Meaningfulness	Number of Attributes
Meaningfulness	$.30^a$		
Number of Attributes	$.33^b$	$.52^b$	
Concreteness	.00	-.01	-.04
Imagery	.05	$.44^b$	.24	.61 Concreteness

$^a p$ .05
$^b p$ .01

with which a trait is associated with other traits; and (ii) Number of Attributes, that is, ratings of how many different sub-traits or attributes each trait contains. The two that focus on non-semantic features were : (iii) Concreteness, that is, ratings of the concreteness (versus abstractness) of the trait in terms of sensory experience; and (iv) Imagery, that is, ratings of the ease with which the trait gives rise to visual imagery.

Table I displays the correlations between these five indices for the 62 traits that appeared both in Anderson (1968) and in Toglia and Battig (1978). It can be seen that the impact of a trait is a positive function of its implicit semantic information and is unrelated to its implicit visual information. In order to generalize from these findings, an attempt was made to replicate them with a larger number of traits. In so doing, we sampled 180 trait descriptions at random from Anderson (1968) and asked subjects to rate how many other traits each given trait suggested or brought to mind. The correlation between this index of informativeness and persuasiveness was quite reliable (r (1/8) = .44, p .01). Finally, in order to validate these ratings we examined more directly whether they indeed corresponded to the activation of implicit information. This was done by sampling at random 40 trait descriptions from the 180 above and asking another group of 16 subjects actually to list all the other traits suggested by each of the given traits. As expected, the correlation between the number of traits written down by the subjects and estimates (ratings) of their number provided by the earlier sample was highly reliable (r (38) = .64, p .01). It is clear, therefore, that the impact of a trait description increases with its informativeness. Our next study is concerned with the operations that underlies this relationship.

Study 2

Basic Operations in Opinion Formation

The mental operations involved in opinion formation are partitioned into four classes : initial encoding, elaborative encoding, integration, and decision. The purpose of the present study is to demonstrate whether these are functionally discrete operations. This is done by observing the extent to which they are differentially sensitive to changes in the quantity and the consistency of information.

During initial encoding an argument undergoes perceptual analysis and segmentation (Newtson, 1973; Ebbesen, 1980). As a result it is transformed into symbolic structures or memory codes (e.g.,Posner 1978) so that each piece of information in the argument is associated with a separate memory code. Here initial encoding is induced by an orienting task that involves <u>physical matching</u> (Posner & Keele, 1967). That is to say, a set of traits are shown on a video monitor and individuals indicate when they have finished reading them. Immediately following this, the traits are replaced by a probe (a single trait) and individuals note whether or not the probe appeared in the previous set. The time needed to read a set indicates the processing required to prepare the traits for physical matching. The operations involved are taken to correspond to those of initial encoding, that is, each argument is encoded separately with minimal semantic analysis, perhaps none beyond what is performed automatically whenever such codes are activated by semantic material (the Stroop effect (Dyer, 1973) is a prime example of such a phenomenon; also, cf., Posner, 1972 for detailed discussion of automatic activation of one type of code by another). This suggests that initial encoding ought to be most sensitive to features associated with the separate elements in the set (e.g., the number of traits), and least sensitive to relationships between these elements (e.g., their consistency).

Once information has made contact with memory, <u>elaborative encoding</u> may occur. This involves associating the explicit information in an argument with schematic knowledge. The schema is conceived as a set of propositions that describe either some prototypical series of events (i.e., a <u>script</u>, in Schank & Abelson, 1977) or objects (i.e., a <u>frame</u> in Minsky, 1975; Friedman, 1979). The knowledge it contains has two functions : First, it specifies which arguments can be matched to or instantiate the schema. Second, when instantiation occurs, information contained in the argument is supplemented by schematic knowledge. The latter process occurs by default, namely, it "fills in" those features that typically occur in such a context when they are not explicitly given in the argument (Rumelhart & Ortony, 1977). Therefore, under elaborative encoding, the pattern of information activated by a trait description will include no only the memory codes that correspond to the description itself, but also implicit information, namely, representations of the default knowledge contained in the encoding schema (Carlston, 1980). For example, to argue that Igor is the "Robin Hood of Washtenaw County" implies that "he steals from the rich and gives to the poor", that "he fights oppression", etc. Such elaborations follow from instantiation of the interpreting schema. In our example this means that stereotypic knowledge about "Robin Hood" is applied to Igor.

It should be noted that some integration may occur during elaborative encoding. Of course, in principle, each trait in a description can be encoded within different schemata. On many an occasion, however, two or more traits will be interpreted within a single schema. As a result, rather than being represented piecemeal, these traits are chunked together and encoded as an <u>unified structure</u>. We refer to this process as <u>automatic</u> so as to stress that integration occurs unintentionally, as a consequence of comprehension and without conscious effort on the part of the individual. Generally, automatic integration will happen when two or more propositions are thematically related and there is a schema activated during comprehension that encodes this relationship (e.g., Ostrom, Lingle, Pryor, & Geva, 1980; Smith, Adams, & Schorr, 1978). This is discussed in more detail below in Study 4.

To induce individuals to elaboratively encode each trait description, they performed an orienting task that involves <u>semantic matching</u>. As in physical matching, individuals indicate when they have completed reading the trait set. However, when the probe-trait is displayed, the individuals are to say whether or not it is <u>similar in meaning</u> (rather than identical) to one of the traits in the set. The time used to prepare for semantic matching was taken to reflect the operations required for elaborative encoding. As in initial encoding, this process should also be sensitive to the amount of information, that is, the number of traits in a set. Furthermore, recall that if traits are automatically integrated, they are encoded within the same schema; otherwise they are encoded separately. Thus, in automatic integration the encoding of one element facilitates (primes) the encoding of another element - the knowledge structure used to interpret the former is immediately available to interpret the latter. This implies that when traits are automatically integrated, they will be processed faster than when they are interpreted one at a time within separate schemata (see similar findings in lexical priming (Meyer & Schvaneveldt, 1971; Schvaneveldt & Meyer, 1973)). Automatic integration is more likely when the traits in the set are consistent than when they are inconsistent. Therefore, we expect that under elaborative encoding (unlike initial encoding) processing time will vary with consistency.

Although inconsistencies do not have to be reconciled under elaborative encoding, they <u>do</u> under integration. This implies, first, that differences between the time to process consistent and inconsistent trait information ought to be more pronounced in integration than in elaborative encoding (or initial encoding); second, that integration should become more time consuming as the number of the to-be-integrated trait descriptions increases; and third, that the effects of increasing the number of to-be-integrated descriptions on processing time should be aggravated when the traits are inconsistent. The latter interaction reflects a characteristic of information structures in general and semantic networks in particular, namely, that the difficulty in reconciling inconsistent information will increase exponentially with the number of elements in the network.

Inconsistent arguments are a problem in opinion formation because they have to be interpreted coherently and no such interpretation comes readily to mind. These arguments simply do not make sense together in their normal context. Nonetheless, individuals can go ahead and integrate the arguments by discounting some (Abelson, 1968). Or they can continue to search for an alternative schema, one that is atypical (i.e., rarely activated in the situation and, hence, relatively inaccessible) but that will nonetheless accommodate all the arguments in a consistent fashion. Our conjecture is that the likelihood of calling an atypical schema is higher than that of discounting. The knowledge we have of people in real life is so rich that we are almost always able to take traits that are inconsistent in their typical context and find another context in which they would be consistent (e.g., ordinarily it is difficult to conceive of someone being "a good person" and "a thief", until we happen to think of "Robin Hood"). Whatever strategy is chosen, integration involves the reconciliation of inconsistencies. Hence, trait information will be represented in a more consistent fashion after integration than it had been before (Wyer, 1974).

Integration prepares the information for a final operation, the _decision_. This process interprets the now-integrated information within the context of an evaluative schema and translates the evaluation into a response format, such as a ten-point scale, a scowl, or a smile (see Upshaw's (1969) attempt to specify a model for such operations; also Parducci, 1965). It is important to note that the decision occurs _following_ integration, that is, after inconsistencies in the description have been reconciled. The decision process, therefore, should be invariant with the _initial_ consistency of the trait description. At the same time, it should be sensitive to the amount of information contained in the (integrated) description. The latter effect, however, is likely to be opposite to that we expect to occur during initial and elaborative encoding, that is, the more knowledge people have about someone they are to judge, the easier and the more rapid their decision, _once this knowledge has been integrated_ (Posner & Snyder, 1975).

Method

Sets of traits were constructed from the Anderson (1968) list so as to vary in respect to size and consistency : a set contained either two traits (the small sets) or four traits (the large sets) which were either consistent (all positive or all negative) or inconsistent (half positive, half negative). Subjects were seated in individual booths, equipped with a CRT monitor, two movable buttons labeled "yes" and "no", and a six button response box (buttons labeled from "1" to "6"). Presentation of the stimuli was controlled by a PDP-11 computer system with responses and reaction times recorded under the program control.

After practice, each experimental session was divided into two parts in the following order :

1. Physical matching or Semantic matching

During this part subjects performed one of the first two orienting tasks. Under physical matching a set of traits was displayed on the CRT and subjects had to press the "yes" button as soon as they had read the entire set. The set was erased from the screen following the subject's response. Immediately afterward, a probe trait was displayed. Subjects then had to press the "yes" button if the probe had appeared in the prior set, and the "no" button otherwise. Under semantic matching the instructions were similar to those for the physical matching task except for the matching criterion, that is, subjects had to press the "yes" button if the probetrait was similar in meaning to one of the traits in the set, and "no" otherwise.

2. Impression Formation.

All subjects then performed the impression formation task. During each trial a message appeared on the screen saying, "Person X is characterized by the following set of traits. How FAVORABLE is your impression of this person ?". Shortly afterward the message was erased and subjects were presented with one of the experimental trait-sets. They responded by pressing the button that corresponded to their impression (1-very unfavorable,,, 6-very favorable).

Table 2

Mean Latency (in seconds) as a Function of Set-Size and
Consistency Under Different Operations in Opinion Formation
(error rate in parentheses)

Operation:	Initial Encoding		Elaborative Encoding		Impression	
Set Size:	Small	Large	Small	Large	Small	Large
Consistent Sets	64.0(.01)	161.6(.02)	106.4(.07)	263.7(.17)	206.5	300.4
Inconsistent Sets	64.5(.00)	170.5(.01)	109.3(.09)	300.2(.20)	235.2	361.2

Note : Latencies are from correct trials in initial and elaborative encoding, and from all trials in impression formation.

Results

Regardless of the operation subjects responded faster to small sets than to large sets, and faster to consistent sets than to inconsistent ones (see Table 2). Moreover, as hypothesized, during impression formation the differences between large and small sets were more pronounced when traits were inconsistent than when they were consistent.

Both set-size and consistency, thus, had reliable effects under the three orienting task. This, however, does not mean that these factors are <u>equally important</u> for performing each operation. Indeed, it is quite possible that set-size and consistency explain different amounts of the variance under different operations. To assess this possibility, we computed the proportion of variance accounted for (<u>eta square</u>, Hays, 1963; Dwyer, 1974) by set-size and consistency in each of the three tasks. Table 3 presents these proportions. It is quite clear that in respect to explaining the total variance, the contribution of set-size <u>decreases</u>, and that of consistency <u>increases</u> as we move from initial encoding, through elaborative encoding, to impression formation.

Table 3

Proportion of Variance Explained by Set-Size and Consistency Under Different Operations in Opinion Formations

Operation	Set-Size	Consistency
Initial Encoding	.91	.001
Elaborative Encoding	.73	.008
Impression Formation	.31	.052

One assumption has been made about the temporal order of the four processes in impression formation, namely, the decision takes place after the information has been integrated. The remaining operations, however, may occur in cascade (McClelland, 1979) so that one begins before the other is completed (see Posner (1978) for the temporal order of activation of semantic and physical codes). It is reasonable and useful to assume, however, that integration <u>for the most part</u> is performed after each piece of information is elaboratively encoded. Then one can estimate the time it takes to integrate <u>and</u> decide, the integration-decision interval, by subtracting elaborative encoding time from impression formation time. An analysis performed on these intervals revealed a reliable consistency effect, namely the integration-decision interval was shorter for consistent than for inconsistent sets. Although the set-size effect approached but did not quite reach acceptable levels of significance, its direction was in marked contrast to previous analyses inasmuch as the integration-decision interval tended to be <u>greater</u> for <u>small</u> sets than for <u>large</u> ones.

In general, the findings on differential sensitivity to the quantity of the information and to its consistency support the partition of opinion formation into initial encoding, elaborative encoding, integration, and decision. At the same time there remains the problem of distinguishing between integration and decision. Once individuals deliberately integrate information, they seem automatically to proceed to make a decision. Hence, it is difficult to devise an orienting task that will cleanly separate these two operations. In Study 3 we attempt to do so.

Study 3

Time Required to Form an Opinion with Informative and Uninformative Arguments

Even though integration may not be varied independently of decision, the opposite can be attempted. To do this - to separate the effects of decision from integration - we can try to eliminate the need for integration by presenting "pre-integrated" information. Such a procedure allows individuals to decide without having deliberately to integrate prior to the decision. This is done in the present study by using a single trait (instead of the multi-trait set). The amount of information is varied by manipulating the associative structure activated by a trait, that is, its implicit information. More specifically, the traits were classified according to whether they implied a large number of other traits or only few. The former, therefore, are <u>informative</u>, the latter <u>uninformative</u>.

According to our analysis, since initial encoding is minimally concerned with semantic features, it should be insensitive to whether the trait is informative or uninformative. Also, inasmuch as the implications are accessed via the activation of a single schema (i.e., they are "pre-integrated"), the time to elaboratively encode an informative description should be no different than that for elaboratively encoding an uninformative description (Hayes-Roth, 1977; Smith, Adams, & Schorr, 1978). Integration is assumed to be bypassed since the implications of a trait are by definition already integrated. The decision operation, however, still ought to benefit from increasing amounts of information, here, implicit information, if it is a functionally distinct process. This means that the decision time for an informative description should be faster than that for an uninformative one. Since neither initial nor elaborative encoding ought be affected by the amount of implicit information associated with a trait, then differences in the impression formation latencies must be due to the effects of the amount of information on the decision operation alone.

Method

Four categories of traits were constructed from the set used in Study 1. This was done by taking 10 descriptions that were <u>above</u> the mean for the estimated number of implications (informative traits) and 10 that were <u>below</u> the mean (uninformative traits), separately for positive and negative traits.

Subjects were run under the same conditions as in Study 2 (i.e., individually, under computer control, with the same monitor and response buttons). Also, the two parts of the experiment were identical in structure of those of Study 2, except that during the impression part each trait-set contained only a single trait. The procedure for forming an impression was the same as that in Study 2. Finally, subjects rated each of the experimental traits for their importance in forming an opinion.

Results

None of the main effects or interactions in the analysis of the initial encoding latencies or the elaborative encoding latencies reached acceptable levels of significance. As expected, the analysis of the impression times revealed only one reliable effect, namely, opinions were formed faster with informative trait descriptions than with uninformative ones (see Table 4).

The lack of relationship between the affective value of a description and processing time is shown in the low correlations between direction of judgment and impression latency (rho = .01), suggesting that there is no difference in the operations performed upon positive and negative traits. This, however, does not exclude the possibility that the traits leading to an <u>extreme</u>

Table 4

Mean Latencies (in seconds) in Study 3 (error rate in parentheses) as a Function of Informativeness Under Different Operations in Opinion Formation

Operation:	Initial Encoding		Elaborative Encoding		Decision	
Trait Likability:	Negative	Positive	Negative	Positive	Negative	Positive
Informative Traits	.41(.01)	.42(.01)	.61(.07)	.60(.06)	1.35	1.31
Uninformative Traits	.41(.01)	.41(.03)	.62(.17)	.63(.13)	1.51	1.48

Note : Latencies are from correct trials in initial and elaborative encoding, and from all trials in impression formation.

impression are processed differently from those leading to a
<u>moderate</u> impression. (e.g., see Judd & Kulik, 1980). An analysis
of the relationship between extremity of the impression and informativeness indicated that only 42 % of the uninformative traits
generated extreme impressions whereas 64 % of the informative traits
did so. This raises the possibility that implicit information
had no direct effect on processing time but that these effects instead were mediated by the extremity of the impression. To remove
the contaminating effect of extremity, we performed a regression
of the impression time on extremity. This demonstrated that the
impact of informativeness cannot be explained by the extremity of
the judgment.

Finally, an analysis of the ratings of the trait descriptions
revealed that informative descriptions were perceived to be more
important in forming an opinion than uninformative ones.

The preceding studies delineate some of the operations in
opinion formation. These operations were identified empirically
on the basis of their differential sensitivity to the amount and
consistency of information in a trait description. More specifically, not only did a large trait-set hindered processing to a greater extent than a small one, but more importantly, this effect
varied with the operation being performed, namely, it was most
pronounced during initial encoding, moderately so during elaborative encoding, and least pronounced during the integration-decision
interval. Indeed, there was a tendency for the integration-decision
interval to decrease as set-size increased. Varying consistency
produced the opposite pattern of results. Although an inconsistent trait description generally hindered processing to a larger
extent than a consistent trait description, the effect was least
pronounced during initial encoding, moderately so during elaborative encoding, and most pronounced during the integration-decision interval. The quantity of information in a description
was also manipulated via the associative structure, that is, the
implicit knowledge activated by a trait (rather than set-size).
Presumably because implicit information is "pre-integrated",
an informative description did not hinder initial or elaborative
encoding any more than an uninformative one. The decision operation, however, was performed more rapidly with informative traits
than uninformative ones. This effect seems theoretically comparable to the tendency in Study 2 for the integration-decision interval to decrease as set-size increased. In any case, it strongly
suggests that once information is organized by a schema, the "richer" the representation, the easier it is to arrive at an opinion.

Study 4

The Representation of Informative and Uninformative Arguments

The final experiment is concerned with the encoding and storage of an argument as a function of its informativeness. The operations described above imply that knowledge in the memory system will be prioritized in terms of its usefulness in forming an opinion. That is to say, informative arguments will (i) undergo more elaborative processing, and thereby (ii) occupy a more central position in the representation than uninformative arguments. As a result, not only should informative arguments be more easily accessed than uninformative ones, but when both kinds of arguments are recalled, they should also be retrieved first.

Intuitively we perhaps already know that an informative argument is encoded differently than an uninformative one. For example, suppose you were asked whether someone should drive or walk to work. The argument "She wears glasses to correct near-sightedness" is by itself uninformative inasmuch as it has no direct bearing on the issue in question. Hence, this piece of information should be processed with minimal elaboration, no more than is needed to understand it as a discrete fact. The very same argument, however, can become highly informative when it appears together with another piece of information, say, "She broke her glasses last night at a party". Now, both propositions will be tightly linked and elaborated upon so that inferences are drawn based on prior knowledge about the consequences of driving without glasses (e.g., "last week, Igor, who has the same eye problem, tried to drive without and had a bad accident"), and represented within a single unified structure. There is, in fact, appreciable evidence to support this point of view. To illustrate, recent research suggests that arguments that are informative receive more attention (Fiske, 1980), are more accessible (Judd & Kulik, 1980; Lingle, Geva, Ostrom, Leippe & Baumgardner, 1980), and have greater impact on judgements than those that are uninformative (Fiske, 1980; Tyler, 1980; Vinokur & Burnstein, 1978) - or conversely, when an uninformative argument is encountered during opinion formation, it is comprehended more narrowly, with less elaboration, than an informative one.

Elaboration, of course, does not depend only on the informativeness of an argument. It is known that when thematically related arguments are encoded they will be linked by a denser network of associations than thematically unrelated arguments (Anderson, 1976; Mandler, 1979). For instance, the statement "Sue wears glasses to correct near-sightedness" should receive greater elaboration when it appears together with the argument "Sue's father is an optometrist" than when it accompanies the argument "The price of gas is really soaring". In the former case the two arguments are linked to each other via general knowledge about "glasses", "optometrists", "families", etc. In the latter case, the two propositions are more likely to be represented as discrete pieces of information.

Informativenesse, furthermore, may determine an argument's location within the knowledge structure tagged by the opinion. More specifically, informative arguments, because they are more elaborated upon, should occupy a more central position in the underlying representation than uninformative ones. According to network models of memory, when the person is able to access any one of several arguments, priority will be based on their relative centrality. Functionally, this means that a central argument, because of its position in the network, will be activated and reported before a peripheral one. 2)

It is reasonably well established that the likelihood of retrieving an argument is an increasing function of the amount of elaboration performed on it (e.g., J. Anderson, 1976; Crowder, 1976; Craik & Tulving, 1975). Therefore, our hypothesis about differences in elaboration implies that the memory for an argument will also increase with its informativeness and thematic relatedness to other arguments. Finally, our second hypothesis, that informative arguments occupy a more central position than uninformative arguments, implies that the former should be accessed and reported prior to the latter, even when differences in retrievability (i.e., the probability of recall) are controlled.

---

2) Comparable analyses demonstrating the importance of the central-peripheral distinction for characterizing informative and uninformative arguments in the area of attitude change and persuasion can be found in Peak, (1958), Rosenberg and Abelson, (1960), Wishner, (1960), and Zajonc, (1960).

Table 5

An Example of a Situation with Five Arguments

(Type of Argument in Parentheses)

	Experimental Condition		
	Informative-Related	Uninformative-Related	Uninformative-Unrelated
Situation	Should Sue drive or walk to class this morning?	Should Sue drive or walk to class this morning?	Should Sue drive or walk to class this morning?
	Sue lives about one mile from campus (I-R)	Sue lives about one mile from campus (I-NR)	Sue lives about one mile from campus (I-NR)
	It's about 30 degrees outside and the wind is blowing (I-NR)	It's about 30 degrees outside and the wind is blowing (I-NR)	It's about 30 degrees outside and the wind is blowing (I-NR)
	Her car is a blue 19/2 VW with spoked wheels (NI-NR)	Her car is a blue 19/2 VW with spoked wheels (NI-NR)	Her car is a blue 19/2 VW with spoked wheels (NI-NR)
Target	Sue wears glasses to correct near-sightedness (I-R)	Sue wears glasses to correct near-sightedness (NI-R)	Sue wears glasses to correct near-sightedness (NI-NR)
Mediating	Sue broke her glasses last night at a party (I-R)	Sue's father is an optometrist (NI-R)	The price of gas is really soaring (I-NR)

Note: Type of argument :
(I-R)   -- Informative-Related
(I-NR) -- Informative-Unrelated
(NI-R) -- Uninformative-Related
(NI-NR) -- Uninformative-Unrelated

Method

In the first part of this study subjects were presented with a series of hypothetical "situations", each of which was followed by five arguments that varied in their informativeness as well as in their thematic relatedness. They then formed an opinion of each situation on the basis of these arguments. In the second part, after having received all the situations and the arguments, subjects were given a surprise cued recall test where they were presented with the situations and were asked to recall the arguments associated with them.

More specifically subjects were presented with eighteen dilemma-like situations and four categories of arguments :

a) Arguments that were informative in regard to the decision and were thematically related to another argument (I-R type arguments);

b) Arguments that were informative but not related to another argument (I-NR type arguments);

c) Arguments that were related to another argument but uninformative in regard to the decision (NI-R type arguments);

d) Arguments that were neither informative nor related to another argument (NI-NR type arguments).
An example is shown in Table 5.

In each segment, the situation and four of the arguments associated with it were identical for all subjects. Two of these arguments were I-NR and one was NI-NR (see Table 5). The relatedness of the fourth argument (the target argument, hereafter) to the fifth argument varied between conditions as a function of the latter (the mediating argument, hereafter). The three experimental conditions differ in respect to the mediating argument, and thereby, in respect to the target argument, although the content of the latter remained the same regardless of its status. The three conditions are labeled according to the status of the target argument.

In the informative-related condition, the mediating argument was not only thematically linked to the target argument but it also made the latter informative in respect to the decision; in the uninformative-related condition, the mediating argument was related to the target argument, but the two were not relevant to the decision - they were uninformative; finally, in the uninformative-unrelated condition the mediating argument was not related to the target argument, nor was the latter informative.

The arguments in each segment were presented one at a time on a monitor. Next, the "situation" sentence along with a six-point scale was displayed. The subjects then responded by pressing one of the buttons on the response box. These responses reflected the subject's opinion on which alternative to choose. Once this part was completed, the recall test was administered.

Results and Discussion

First, we examined the accuracy with which subjects recalled the target argument. Note that this comparison is highly sensitive because it involves the identical argument with the identical retrieval cue. For each subject the accuracy with which the target argument was recalled was computed across the eight experimental segments. Analysis revealed a reliable difference between the three conditions. Subjects in the informative-related condition recalled a larger proportion of the target arguments than those in the uninformative-related condition, which in turn recalled a larger proportion than subjects in the uninformative-unrelated condition (M s = .88, .64, .50, respectively). The accessibility of an argument, therefore, is an increasing function of its informativeness.

In order to obtain further support for the hypothesis that informativeness affects elaboration, we compared the degree of association between the target and the mediating arguments under our three experimental conditions. Elaborative encoding in the present context involves the creation of associative links among the propositions in the communication as well as links between the latter and schematic knowledge. The extent to which this operation is performed, therefore, should be reflected in the strength of association between the arguments. If the two arguments are highly associated, that is, clustered in memory, then the recall of one should be accompanied by the recall of the other. In other words, either both arguments are accessed, or neither is accessed. If, however, they are not associated, the recall of one argument should be independent of the recall of the other.

An analysis revealed that the three conditions differed from each other so that when the arguments were both informative and related they were more highly associated than when they were related but not informative. Moreover, arguments were least associated when they were neither informative nor related. This suggests that the effects of informativeness and thematic relatedness together produce a more accessible representation than either separately. Thus, the hypothesis that the elaboration an argument receives increases with (i) its informativeness in respect to the opinion and (ii) its thematic relatedness to other arguments in the communication is reasonably well supported.

Not only should informative arguments be recalled better than uninformative ones, but they should also be accessed prior to uninformative arguments, even when the likelihood that an argument will be recalled is controlled. In order to test this hypothesis we compared the <u>actual</u> probability of recall of each argument in each order position to the <u>expected</u> probability derived from a model which assumes that the likelihood of retrieval of argument i in position j depends only on the marginal probabilities (for details see Schul & Burnstein, 1981). The absolute sum of differences between the observed and the expected probabilities was taken as the dependent measure. According to our hypothesis the latter should increase as the centrality of an argument increases. That is to say, when all the arguments are equally central within the representation of the "situation", no systematic deviation from the null model would be expected. However, if informative arguments are central and uninformative ones, peripheral, the former ought to be accessed prior to that predicted by the model, while the latter ought to be accessed later, and therefore, there should be large differences between the observed and expected probabilities. In fact, subjects under the informative condition (I-R) turned out to be reliably different from subjects under the two uninformative conditions (NI-R;NI-NR), while the latter did not differ from each other. This suggests that the centrality of an argument in the underlying representation is determined by its informativeness, and not by its thematic relatedness to other arguments.

General Discussion

In our formulation, implicit information was said to be "extracted" from a communication via a series of operations, namely, analysis of orthographic, grammatical, and lexical features (initial encoding) comprehension, (elaborative encoding), consolidation of the encoded information (integration), and finally, a judgement in light of this integrated knowledge (decision). The relationship between the implicit information contained in a communication and its persuasiveness was explored in the context of this processing model. Our major findings were as follows: First, an informative argument had more impact on the opinion than an uninformative argument. Second, the readiness with which such an opinion was formed depends on the consistency as well as on the quantity of information in the communication. Third, the effects of consistency and quantity varied with the operation performed on the information, that is, inconsistencies hindered integration the most, elaboration, a moderate amount, and initial encoding, the least; whereas quantity hindered initial encoding the most, elaboration, a moderate amount, and integration, the least. At the same time the decision operation seemed unaffected by inconsistencies and was actually facilitated by the quantity of information. Finally, an informative argument was stored in a more central position in the representation underlying the opinion, and thus, was more accessible than an uninformative argument.

Two major problems were anticipated in testing this formulation. First, there was the technical difficulty of separating integration and decision. In research on levels of processing (cf. Craik & Tulving, 1975) subjects are led to orient to different aspects of a statement (e.g., its phonetic versus its semantic features) by varying the response they are required to make to this material. Using this paradigm as a guide we were able to devise separate orienting tasks to distinguish the effects of recognition from comprehension. However, no equally direct method suggested itself for inducing the person to integrate several arguments without implying the function that normally follows this operation, that a judgment is forthcoming.

In Study 2 we attempted to subtract out the processing time for the decision. In Study 3 pre-integrated arguments were used, thus, eliminating integrative activity and allowing us to go directly from comprehension to decision. Fortunately, the two procedures led to congruent findings inasmuch as both indicated that increasing quantities of information, explicit or implicit, facilitated the decision process while hindering the other operations. In other words, increasing amounts of <u>unintegrated</u> information slows, whereas increasing amounts of <u>integrated</u> information expedites opinion formation. Hence, once the inconsistencies in a trait description are resolved, there is a positive relationship between the amount of information and the ease with which an impression is formed.

The second problem had to do with a tendency for trait descriptions to be automatically integrated during comprehension. Opinions about others are such a common part of everyday discourse that their component parts, trait descriptions, get routinely chunked, say, by a "person impression" schema, even when the individual merely has to understand or memorize each description as a separate piece of information (Carlston, 1980). This is not to say that trait descriptions and other naturally configurable information are inevitably integrated upon being encoded. Rather we think the "person impression" schema and similar integrative structures are activated by default, that is, when no alternative encoding operation is specified. Accordingly, integration should appear as a distinct stage when this default procedure is pre-empted. Just recently we have completed an experiment that bears on this problem (Burnstein & Schul, 1981). In this study, integrative activity vanished during comprehension when instructions indicated that the arguments could describe non-humans, a case of pre-empting the "person impression" schema. Moreover, in the final study presented here, we found that if two arguments in a loose narrative were thematically related and thus naturally configurable, they evidenced partial integration in recall even though they could be discounted as irrelevant to the opinion the person was required to form. They appeared thoroughly integrated, however, when they could not be so discounted. Both sets of findings, therefore, suggest it is possible to describe the conditions under which integration is a deliberate operation and the conditions under which it is an automatic result of elaboration.

Finally it is worth noting that implicit information is not inherently informative. Among other things, schematic elaboration is sometimes blithe or fantastic. Ideas accessed in this mode, while novel, are not useful in deciding between alternative positions, courses of action, etc. They, thus, have little impact on opinion (Vinokur & Burnstein, 1978). Under what conditions, then, is implicit information useful and, thus, persuasive ? In analyzing attitude polarization we interpreted opinion formation as a problem solving process. From this perspective an informative argument called up a satisfying solution, one that resolved the dilemma (Burnstein & Vinokur, 1977; Hoffman, 1979; Vinokur & Burnstein, 1974). Our conjecture is that the same process underlies the persuasiveness of implicit information. Whether to attend University X rather than University Y, or how someone can be both a "good person" and a "thief" represents a large class of choices in which one must take into account what <u>at first glance</u> seems like incompatible ideas - the encoding structures typically called upon in this context do not resolve these incompatibilities. Consequently, one either continues to search for a schema that does resolve matters or settles for something less. In the latter case, discounting occurs. In starkest form this requires the individual to ignore one point of view as "unthinkable", say, that "getting the best education possible should be the person's <u>only</u> concern in deciding between schools"; or, that "a good person <u>simply cannot</u> be a thief". Although discounting schemata are not at all atypical (quite the opposite), they do not resolve the matter happily because neither will still the nagging thought that the person really can "flunk out to of X" or turn out be in some sense both "good" and a "thief".

We would speculate that the most informative arguments are those that locate opposing facts within a context so that their opposition vanishes; they become, as a result, compatible or even mutually supportive. For instance, the "transfer" argument activates a system of propositions that interprets the issue as one in which the worst possible result of pursuing the uncertain course, that is, "flunking out of X", is no different than what would have transpired had the certain course been taken to begin with, that is, "graduating from Y". This schema demonstrates an underlying compatibility among the facts. An argument that calls such a schema is highly informative, and thus, highly persuasive.

REFERENCES

Abelson, R. P. Psychological implication. In R. P. Abelson et al (Eds.), Theories of Cognitive Consistency:A Sourcebook, Chicago;Rand MacNally and Co., 1968.

Anderson, J. R. Language, memory, thought. Hillsdale, N.J.: Lawrence Erlbaum Associates, 1976.

Anderson, N. H. Likableness ratings of 555 personality-trait words. Journal of Personality and Social Psychology, 1968, 9, 272-279.

Bartlett, F. C. Remembering. Cambridge, England: Cambridge University Press, 1932.

Burnstein, E. & Schul, Y. Studies on the informational Basis of Opinions; Memory for integrated and Non-integrated Trait Descriptions. Unpublished manuscript, University of Michigan, 1981.

Burnstein, E. & Vinokur, A. Persuasive argumentation and social comparison as determinants of attitude polarization. Journal of Experimental and Social Psychology, 1977, 13, 315-332.

Burnstein, E., & Vinokur, A. What a person thinks upon learning he has chosen differently from others. Nice evidence for the persuasive-arguments explanation of the choice shift. Journal of Experimental and Social Psychology, 1975, 11, 412-428.

Cacioppo, J. T., & Petty, R. E. Effects of message repetition and position on cognitive response, recall and persuasion. Journal of Personality and Social Psychology, 1979, 37, 97-109.

Carlston, D. E. The recall and use of traits and events in social inference processes. Journal of Experimental Social Psychology,

1980, 16, 303-328.

Craik, F. I. M., & Tulving, E. Depth of processing and the retention of words in episodic memory. *Journal of Experimental Psychology*, 1975, 104, 268-294.

Crowder, R. *Principles of learning and memory*. Hillsdale, N. J.: Lawrence Erlbaum Associates, 1976.

Dwyer, J. H. Analysis of variance and the magnitude of effects. *Psychological Bulletin*, 1974, 81, 731-737.

Dyer, F. N. The Stroop phenomenon and its use in study of perceptual, cognitive and response processes. *Memory & Cognition*, 1973, 1, 106-120.

Ebbesen, E. B. Cognitive Processes in understanding ongoing behavior. In R. Hastie et al (Eds.) *Person memory: The cognitive basis of social perception*. Hillsdale, N.J.: Lawrence Erlbaum, 1980.

Ebbesen, E.B., & Bowers, R.J. Proportion of risky to conservative arguments in a group discussion and choice shift. *Journal of Personality and Social Psychology*, 1974, 29, 316-327.

Friedman, A. Framing pictures: The role of knowledge in automatized encoding and memory for gist. *Journal of Experimental Psychology*, 1979, 108, 316-355.

Greenwald, A. G. Cognitive learning, cognitive response to persuasion and attitude change. In A. G. Greenwald, T.C. Brock, and T. M. Ostrom (Eds.), *Psychological Foundation of Attitudes*. New York; Academic Press, 1968.

Hayes-Roth, B. Evolution of cognitive structures and processes. *Psychological Review*, 1977, 84, 260-278.

Hayes, W. *Statistics*. New York; Holt, 1963.

Hoffman, L. R. *The group problem solving process: Studies of a valence model*. New York: Praeger, 1979.

Insko, C. A. Primacy versus recency in persuasion as a function of the timing of arguments and measures. *Journal of Abnormal and Social Psychology*, 1964, 69, 381-391.

Judd, C. M., & Kulik, J. Schematic effects of social attitudes on information processing and recall. *Journal of Personality and Social Psychology*, 1980, 38, 569-578.

Lingle, J. H., Geva, N., Ostrom, T. M., Leippe, M., & Baumgardner, M. H. Thematic effects of person judgments on impression organization. *Journal of Personality and Social Psychology*, 1979, 37, 674-687.

Mandler, G. Organization and repetition: Organizational Principles with special reference to rote learning. In L. G. Nilsson (Ed.), *Perspectives on Memory Research*, Hillsdale, N.J.: Lawrence Erlbaum Associates, 1979.

McClelland, J. L. On the time relations of mental processes: An examination of systems of processes in cascade. Psychological Review, 1979, 86, 287-330.

Meyer, D. E., & Schvaneveldt, R. W. Facilitation in recognizing pairs of words: Evidence of dependence between retrieval operations. Journal of Experimental Psychology, 1971, 90, 227-234.

Miller, N., & Campbell, D. Recency and primacy in persuasion of a function of timing of speeches and measurements. Journal of Abnormal Social Psychology, 1959, 59, 1-9.

Minsky, M. A framework for representing knowledge. In P. H. Winston (Ed.), The psychology of computer vision. New York, McGraw-Hill, 1975.

Newtson, D. A. Attribution and the unit of perception of ongoing behavior. Journal of Personality and Social Psychology, 1973, 28, 28-38.

Ostrom, T. M., Lingle, J. H., Pryor, J. B., & Geva, N. Cognitive organization of person impressions. In Hastie, R. et al (Eds.) Person memory: The cognitive basis of social perception. Hillsdale, N. J. : Lawrence Erlbaum, 1980.

Parducci, A. Range-frequency model, Psychological Review. 1965, 72.

Peak, H. Psychological structure and psychological activity. Psychological Review, 1977, 84, 231-259. 407-418.

Posner, M. I. Coordination of internal codes. In W. G. Chase (Ed.) Visual information processing. New York: Academic Press, 1972.

Posner, M. I. Chronometric exploration of mind. New York: Lawrence Erlbaum, 1978.

Posner, M. I., & Keele, S. W. Decay of visual information from a single letter. Science, 1967, 158, 137-139.

Posner, M. I., & Snyder, C. R. Attention and cognitive control. In R. L. Solso (Ed.) Information processing and cognition: The Loyola Symposium. Hillsdale, N.J.: Lawrence Erlbaum, 1975.

Rosenberg, M., & Abelson, R. An analysis of cognitive balancing. In M. Rosenberg et al. (Eds.), Attitude organization and change. New Haven; Yale University Press, 1960. in semantic memory. In S. Kornblum (Ed.) Attention and performance IV. New York; Academic Press, 1973.

Rumelhart, D. E. & Ortony, A. The representation of knowledge in memory In R. C. Anderson, R. J. Spiro, and W. E. Montague (Eds.), Schooling and the acquisition of knowledge. Hillsdale, N.J.: Lawrence Erlbaum Association, 1977.

Schank, R. C., & Abelson, R. P. Scripts, plans, goals, and understanding : An inquiry into human knowledge structures. Hillsdale, N.J.: Lawrence Erlbaum Association, 1977.

Schul, Y., & Burnstein, E. The informational basis of social judgments: Memory for informative and uninformative arguments. Unpublished manuscript. University of Michigan, 1981.

Schvaneveldt, R. W., & Meyer, D. E. Retrieval and comparison processes

Smith, E. E., Adams, N., & Schorr, D. Fact retrieval and the paradox of interference; Cognitive Psychology, 1978, 10, 438-464.

Tesser, A. Self-generated attitude change. In L. Berkowitz (Ed.), Advances in Experimental Social Psychology (Vol. II). New York: Academic Press, 1978.

Toglia, M. P., & Battig, W. F. Handbook of semantic word norms. N. J.; Lawrence Erlbaum Associates, 1978.

Tyler, T. R. Impact of directly and indirectly experienced events: The origin of crime related judgments and behaviors. Journal of Personality and Social Psychology, 1980, 39, 13-28.

Vinokur, A., & Burnstein, E. The effects of partially shared persuasive arguments on group induced shifts: A group problem solving approach. Journal of Personality and Social Psychology, 1974, 29, 305-315.

Vinokur, A., & Burnstein, E. Novel argumentation and attitude change; The case of polarization following group discussion. European Journal of Social Psychology, 1978, 8, 335-348.

Vinokur, A., Trope, Y., & Burnstein, E. A decision analysis of persuasive argumentation and the choice-shift effect. Journal of Experimental Social Psychology, 1975, 11, 127-148.

Watts, W. A., & Holt, L. E. Persistence of opinion change induced under conditions of forewarning and distraction. Journal of Personality and Social Psychology, 1979, 37, 778-798.

Watts, W. A., & McGuire, W. J. Persistency of induced opinion and retention of the inducing message contents. Journal of Abnormal and Social Psychology, 1964, 68, 233-241.

Wishner, J. Reanalysis of "impression of personality". Psychological Review, 1960, 67, 96-112.

Wyer, R. S. Cognitive organization and change : An information processing approach. Potomac, M.D.:Lawrence Erlbaum, 1974.

Zajonc, R. B. The process of cognitive tuning in communication. Journal of Abnormal and Social Psychology, 1960, 61, 159-168.

THE COMING ERA OF REPRESENTATIONS

S. Moscovici

Ecole des Hautes Etudes en Sciences Sociales, Paris.

REDISCOVERING THE SOCIAL MIND

I find myself in a peculiar situation. Here I have been advocating a social psychology focused on cognitive and linguistic phenomena for over twenty years. And now that this social psychology is taking shape under our very eyes, I am obliged to explain today what I had in mind and wanted to do in the past. And this is something that I must do not only here, for you, but for others who are challenging me and urging me to jump aboard the moving "cognitivistic" train. As though I had meanwhile climbed off that train ! As though I had abandoned my advocacy or stopped my research in my chosen direction !

During this whole period, the theory of social representations had remained an unobtrusive theory. My concept of representations was not part of the common terminology. There was certainly, since its original formulation (Moscovici, 1961), no dearth of studies spelling it out more accurately and broadening its scope (Abric, 1970; Herzlich, 1973; Flament, 1979; Chombart de Lauwe, 1979; Faucheux and Moscovici, 1968; Doise, 1978; Roqueplo, 1974; Jodelet, 1980, etc.). However, its stress on the cognitive aspect of social reality and its way of conceiving this reality were incompatible with and remained incompatible with a positivist conception of science and a behaviorist approach to reality. Only after the publication of Farr's excellent articles (1978) did it become possible to build a bridge between our studies and those being carried on elsewhere. The very fact that I can discuss all this at a Summer School represents a change in my eyes. It allows me to hope that there will be greater understanding for our ideas. But I have no great illusions.

Resistances and incomprehensions remain numerous, inasmuch as no change has taken place meanwhile in the commonly held view of science and of reality. You may perhaps contribute to the needed change.

At this juncture, the concept of representation, even social representation, has ceased to be unobtrusive. It is on the way to becoming a concept that is central and common to the social sciences. The history of mentalities, a topic which is arousing much interest, refers to it explicitly (Le Goff, 1974) and provides brilliant illustrations. It is above all in the realm of artificial intelligence, however, that it turns out to be indispensable (Bobrow and Collins, 1975). The time has come when people speak of an era of representations to characterize the new thinking to which computers and their science have given rise (Hofstadter, 1979). And I believe that this term is justified.

In view of the fact that your Summer School has been devoted to analyzing cognitive phenomena and that you have surely found out a great deal on that score, including social representations, my task will be less arduous. For that reason I shall simply try to explain to you how this concept relates to other concepts. My main objective is to show you how it fits into an evolution that makes it relevant as well as necessary, even though in many respects social psychology is not yet ready to incorporate it. In other words, we shall examine here to what extent it is present in a whole series of studies and why it solves a number of difficulties with which these studies are contending. I have particularly in mind studies on attribution and social cognition.

Let me now get somewhat ahead of myself. What has been happening in the course of the last several years is the rediscovery of the social mind. Why speak of a rediscovery, you will ask me. The reason is that we are talking about the fundamental problem of social psychology. This science was founded, in a way, to formulate the laws of the social mind. Three phases can be distinguished in the evolution taking place under our eyes, each of them characterized by a well-defined concept : social attitudes, social cognitions, and finally social representations. Each phase succeeds in solving the difficulties of the previous phase. Hence, what was peripheral in one phase becomes central in the next. I am afraid that I will not be able to go into all the details, space and time being limited. I hope nevertheless that I can tell you enough to get a clear idea of the whole evolution.

COGNITIVE SOCIAL PSYCHOLOGY. REFORM OR REVOLUTION

    We are told on all sides that we are in the midst of a cognitive revolution. 1) As you know, the word revolution tends to be bandied about too freely. It is applied carelessly to any kind of change, whether it is an important change or not. Are we justified in saying that psychology experienced as strong an intellectual shock in recent years as when Freud's or Pavlov's first writings appeared ? I do not believe so. In my opinion something else is involved here : we are reverting to a more classic conception of psychic phenomena, which gives greater scope to mental images, reasoning, and active memory. In short, psychology is once more defined as a science of the conscious mind. And this reversal has taken place less because of any exceptional discovery than because of the impetus of anthropology, linguistics, child psychology, and computer science. What we are witnessing is not a revolution but an inevitable accommodation to an altered scientific setting. The behavioral paradigm has not been rejected, but rather, it has been adapted to the new context. Just as painting has returned from abstract art to representational art, psychology has reverted from behavior to consciousness. This shift has certainly had a liberating effect and has made it possible to resume contact with the concrete manifestations of mental experiences. A step has been taken in the right direction, even if it does not go far enough.

    No matter how one evaluates what has been happening in psychology, one thing is certain : these trends should not take us by surprise. Zajonc (1980) brilliantly elucidates this point, asserting that social psychology has been cognitive for a long time. And he is not mistaken. The very term "cognitive social psychology" is a pleonasm. But what Zajonc has in mind above all is this first stage of development about which I want to talk to you, the stage in which psychologists stressed the rational character of behavior and social relations. What was their reason for this emphasis on rationality ? Was their emphasis unwarranted ? It was not. You know that the first social psychologists, who were studying crowds, influence phenomena, propaganda, gave much

---

1) I shall not discuss in this chapter what we mean by social. We could obviously define it as any information or reaction relating to a person rather than to a cat or a house, but that would be rather rudimentary. It is not the nature of the object that differentiates the social from the non-social, but one's relation to it. There are sacred cats and sacred houses, and there are

scope to emotional, affective, and unconscious factors. In fact, to irrational factors. These theories were acclaimed in reactionary and succeeded particularly in Nazi circles. It is hardly surprising that social psychologists, notably German scholars like Lewin (1951) and Asch (1952) protested against this kind of approach to behavior and social relations. Lewin dealt with primary groups, not masses; Asch substituted the rationale of influence processes in such groups to the doctrine of influence by prestige and suggestive power. Out of these studies there emerged a view of man as a rational animal. Henceforth human behavior and thought were studied in a social setting. It is easy to understand, under these circumstances, why cognitive phenomena seemed to be at the core of this new social psychology in its second home, the United States. And yet, if we look at things more closely, we can see that cognitive phenomena were already present in the former approach, in connection with attitude phenomena. And everything revolved around them.

Without wishing to take over the task of the future historians of our science, I would like to make two remarks at this juncture. On the one hand, attitudes are defined as cognitive structures ; states of mind toward values and states of readiness organized through experience. It is true that under the influence of behaviorism, this mental aspect was given short shrift, but still it did not disappear entirely. On the other hand, attitudes are the backbone of all other psychic manifestations : perceptions, judgments, and behaviors. Hence most theories (Sherif and Hovland, 1961; Osgood and Tannenbaum, 1955) deal with their structure and dynamics. And the most influential theory, cognitive dissonance theory (Festinger, 1957), which generated the most original set of studies in the history of social psychology, is, as you know, a theory of attitude changes. It states that clashes between two cognitions are the driving force in all modifications of our opinions and judgments. We seek to attenuate these conflicts and to make our attitudes consistent with our behaviors. Let us assume that I have a low opinion of dissonance theory. If I were to present it to you and say that it was a very fine theory, I would be telling a lie. But after my lecture, I would have a

---

human beings who are less than objects, for their doctor, for instance. The blurring between social and interpersonal elements casts doubt on a large part of the work being done under the heading of social cognition.

higher opinion of the theory than I did beforehand, because I would do my best to decrease the discrepancy between my statements and my beliefs.

During those years, on the other hand, whatever referred to perception, to social judgment, etc. seemed to be relegated to the background. How did it come about that these neglected phenomena again became the center of attention? During the period when social attitudes (and social influence !) claimed a central place in research, man was generally viewed as a rational animal. But dissonance theory revealed him to be a rationalizing rather than a rational creature. His changes in attitudes and cognitions reflected his efforts to bring them in line with his behaviors and subjective motives, not the converse. Whenever a conflict arises between an opinion and an action, man does not rely on reason to solve the problem. He rationalizes in order to reduce the tension between the two and extricate himself from an unpleasant condition. And the less internal vindication that he has for acting contrary to his opinion, the more painful the tension. Conversely, if the conflict has an external origin and was imposed on him by somebody else, the tension is less painful. I would for instance feel less dissonance if I had leftist opinions and were compelled by the police to cast a rightist vote than if I cast a rightist vote on my own, for an irrelevant reason, such as the fact that the candidate happens to be my neighbor.

Thus the way the source of the tension between opinions and actions, that is, relations between oneself and others, was perceived became crucial. Hence, what used to be secondary namely social perceptions became primary. There had been no good answer to the question of how we perceived and thought of those with whom we are in contact, nor how we perceived ourselves. At the same time, however, a contraction of the field of investigation to a part of the whole took place. The range of phenomena to be taken into account was narrowed. Relations between groups were replaced by relations between people, focus on the group was replaced by focus on individuals. As a result, whereas previously epistemological problems were conceived as social problems, social problems were now conceived as epistemological problems.

THE ART OF ASKING WHY : FROM LORE TO SCIENCE

> We would do nothing in this world
> if we were not guided by erroneous
> ideas. This observation by
> Fontenelle seems far from stupid
> to me.
>   Flaubert

There were probably additional reasons for the gradual decline of interest in cognitive dissonance theory. Antagonism between Gestalt and behaviorism, resistance to it by the more classically oriented social psychology, and intrinsic difficulties with the theory, not to speak of the admittedly odd fact that Festinger himself gave up on it. This marked the beginning of a second stage, in which attention was focused on social cognition. I suppose that you know more about it than I. You will excuse me, I hope, if I repeat a few familiar points here. To reduce the chance of possible misunderstandings, let me establish rapidly the basic features of the framework within which we shall be operating. Unless I am mistaken - and everything about this field is rather vague - the area of social cognition refers to the individual's perception and logical analysis of information about others, that is to say the way he characterizes other individuals and makes inferences about their covert, inner psychological life. On the one hand, therefore, everything is localized on the level of close relationships. On the other hand, man is no longer conceived only as a rational animal but as a thinking machine.

What does this imply ? Simply that, like machines, he gains knowledge by processing the informations that reach him from the outside world (Graumann and Sommer, 1981). We are dealing here with a very special sort of machine, however, a machine that does not reproduce the brain of a professional scientist but the brain of a naive scientist. In other words, this individual is envisaged as being "the man in the street", "Mr. Everybody" : sound of mind, neither too intelligent nor too stupid, neither too educated nor too ignorant. You and I, for example, when we are talking about the character of a friend or about the reason for not being appointed to a position we were seeking.

Let us investigate the inside of this peculiar machine a little more closely to see what it contains. First of all, we find a set of "implicit theories" about personality, (for instance naive concepts, fixed ideas, commonsense prejudices, etc. about human beings (Rosenberg and Sedlak, 1972). What are their functions ? Two functions are proposed : "the first concerns the role of general bias in judgments of others, and the second has to do with individual differences in perception" (Schneider, 1973, p. 294). In any case, these implicit theories are relatively impervious to each person's experience. They are heavily influenced by language and completely distinct from the corresponding scientific theories.

In the second place, this naive scientist is confronted with a bewildering variety of actions and a bewilderingly broad range of situations when he observes the behavior of other people. In trying to straighten things out and to obtain a stable view, he asks himself why such or such a thing happens and attempts to make a causal analysis of these actions and situations. As you know, in the course of this analysis he concentrates on attributing the cause of what he observes either to the person or to his setting (the situation). Let us say an unemployed friend asks for your help. You might then wonder whether he is out of work because he does not feel like working, because he is unable to work, or because economic conditions prevent him from finding work. I am sure that there is no doubt in your mind about the answer. Thus, for our naive scientist, understanding always means interpreting, <u>intelligere</u> always comes to the same thing as <u>explicare</u>.

When we look more closely at the way this thinking machine carries out an analysis, we recognize the presence of "schemata". These schemata are somewhat like pre-connections, activating organizations between perceptions and memory that sift and bring order to the unselected information stream by arranging it into appropriate patterns. In Graumann and Sommer's words : "Schemata are seen to guide the process of perception" (1981, p.20). The distinction is made between <u>causal schemata</u> and <u>event schemata</u>. The former transform every information element into the effect of a cause; we can find an enumeration of causal schemata in a famous article by Kelley (1972). The latter, which might also be considered scripts, describe a sequence of events in which we have taken part (Schank and Abelson, 1972). A summer school script, for instance, would represent what has happened since your arrival here. It would cover your laboratory work, your seminars, and all the rest, up to this **morning's** lecture.

What purpose do these scripts, 2) these accumulations of

---

2) From the point of view of this discussion, scripts are perceptual schemas and programs that define a sequence of actions. They are built in accordance with the behavioristic model, which

mental habits actually serve ? What they do is to bring back to mind a prior situation and suggest to us a behavior fitting the present situation. They act as models or blueprints to a certain extent : the present copies the past and thus excludes surprise and imaginary elements. Before coming here, for instance, I prepared my lecture with the idea that you would remain nicely seated and listen to me. But if you had all gotten up when you saw me come in, had held hands and begun to dance in a circle, it would have come as a surprise to me. The picture you would be giving me of a summer school would certainly not correspond to the script I had in mind.

In the third place, once the analysis has been completed, the machine offers its answer, that is, the appropriate reaction toward the individual under observation. Obviously, this reaction will be different if we think that what somebody does or says is internally or externally motivated. As you can see, we are not very far removed from a purely behaviorist cycle, which begins with a stimulus, pauses for a moment in a properly equipped black box, and ends with a response. I can imagine what you will ask : but in what respect is this naive scientist naive ? How does this lay epistemology differ from a scientific epistemology ?

It is not enough to state that the naive scientist has no Ph.D. ; neither did Edison nor Faraday. Nor that he is trying to make sense of the everyday world. So does every scientist. Nobody would claim that these are valid criteria. The American school, to which most social psychologists belong, would offer the following answer : the naive scientist does not think logically, he has systematic biases, and he makes a large number of errors. He therefore does a poor job of processing the available informa-

---

gives priority to stimuli and learning. According to Schank and Abelson, in order to understand what happens in a given situation, one must have been exposed to the actions determined by the situation. And deviations from the standard pattern are handled with some difficulty (Schank and Abelson, p. 67). This is obviously not what happens with social representations. These tend to take the place of specific situations, redefine them, and go beyond them. Social representations are "systems" of preconceptions, images, and values, which have their own cultural meaning and persist independently of individual experiences; they automatically include some prediction of possible deviations. So do scientific theories, as a matter of fact. The concept of "implicit" theories is just a stratagem making it possible to treat linked information as though it were free information.

tion. This is not just an unsupported assertion. Ingenious experiments have been carried out to confirm it.

I am sure that nobody will be surprised by this new version of the outworn notion that the man in the street is not very smart. And yet this seems a shaky conclusion to me. It underscores the fallacies in which one is trapped when one neglects social representations. Here I must stop for a moment to be more specific, as we have reached the locus of all the impasses with respect to social cognitions.

If one wished to describe the features of this lay epistemology on the basis of the experiments made so far, one would concentrate on three of them : imperviousness to information, behavioral confirmation, and personalism. Let us describe them schematically one after the other.

(1) The main problem in social cognition lies in matching the objective information with an appropriate causal schema. This might seem an odd problem, since one might imagine that this was a matter of course. The importance of the problem becomes clear, however, if one raises the question : what is the central concern of social psychologists ? The answer to that is : determining how a new piece of information is influenced by previously acquired knowledge. A set of experiments has revealed a highly interesting state of affairs. In one of these experiments (Snyder and Swann, 1978), subjects are asked to gather information about a person. Some of the subjects are told beforehand that this person is an extrovert, while other subjects are told that the person is an introvert. The subjects are thus prompted by being given some sort of "hypothesis" about this fictitious person. What do we observe ? Well, those subjects who start out with the idea of meeting an extrovert ask questions that are somehow related to extroversion, while those who believe that they are meeting an introvert ask questions relating to introversion. Each group, one might say, tries to verify its hypotheses, the implicit "theory" that has been instilled in it. We can conclude from this, as well as from other experiments, that we are looking for information that confirms our views, disregarding any that might invalidate them (Lord et al., 1979). What we do is to use the evidence at our disposal to support our "stereotypes" (Snyder and Cantor, 1979).

And that is not all. Once we have formed an opinion, we tend to stick to it. Suppose that I come and tell you that a person you know has done something unfair toward you and has displayed envy and jealousy with respect to you. You now develop a certain way of thinking about that person. Suppose that I later come and tell you : "You know, what I told you about that person is incorrect. I lied to you." I thereby discredit and disavow the information that I gave to you earlier. I might expect you to change your mind as a result. In truth, that is not what happens, as everyday and laboratory experiences prove. People maintain the judgment they have formed on the strength of such information, which still seems plausible to them, since they have meanwhile constructed an explanation that is consistent with it. This phenomenon underlies the most common illusions of social life. Chapman and Chapman (1967) assert that we -and this "we" includes clinical and social psychologists as well - all establish correlations between events that have no correlation in reality. Or whose correlation might even be in the opposite direction from the one mentioned. "These systematic errors, they write, persist both under repeated exposure to the stimulus materials and under conditions designed to maximize both motivation and opportunity to observe accurately" (p. 203).

We have had ample opportunity to confirm this fact in practice, for instance with a spelling or typing error that one keeps repeating stubbornly, as though the wrong spelling had left an indelible mnemonic trace. And all educators know how perilous it is to draw students' attention to an erroneous construction, which then remains in their memory despite all efforts to correct it.

All these findings show that there exists a certain <u>imperviousness to information</u>, which is very widespread and which manifests itself under different circumstances. As "naive scientists", people tend to resist facts and knowledge that does not conform with their implicit theories. They tend to shut out such information and at the same time attribute little importance to it. It almost seems that a genuinely universal principle is at work : every belief or theory retains any information that confirms it and gets rid of any information that invalidates it. Striking historical instances of this principle are easy to find : Stalin's disregarding reports of an imminent German attack, Dayan disregarding reports warning him of an Egyptian attack, etc. 3)

---

3) These laboratory discoveries are part of the common stock of knowledge of anyone who has studied social reality. "Political beliefs and perceptions are not based upon empirical observations or, indeed, upon information at all. More than that, non-empirically based cognitions are the most resistant to revision upon the

(2) If we have a notion or representation as to what the other person is supposed to be like, we try to confirm it by all means at our disposal. More specifically, we shape relations, manipulate the situation in such a way as to stimulate behaviors that fit our beliefs about others 4). That is what anti-Semites do : they create conditions around Jews that make them seem miserly, timid, or deviant. All social interactions are generally channelled so as to lead the individuals who are the target of such beliefs to furnish behavioral confirmation of the perceiver's beliefs. There is an elegant experiment illustrating this point. Pairs of subjects who have not previously known each other (a male perceiver and a female target) interacted in a getting-acquainted situation. The men were supposed to interact with women whom they had been led to think as attractive or unattractive on the basis of prior information. The actual behavior of the target was then analyzed to see whether it conformed to the perceiver's stereotype. The results are striking. As it turned out, when a female target was perceived (unknown to her) as physically seductive, she reacted with an amiable and sociable behavior. Conversely, if the man assumed her to be without attraction, she showed herself in an unfriendly and unsociable light (Snyder et al., 1977). It should be added, however, that these behaviors were evident only in those areas where men believed that physical charm and personal characteristics were somehow interconnected. An analogous phenomenon was observed where subjects believed that certain persons were generally hostile or friendly in their disposition (Snyder and Swann, 1978). It would seem, therefore, that individuals tend to create closed worlds. Each of us, living in a closed world, tries to generate behaviors in others that will confirm the preestablished ideas we have about them. In truth, we create this information, Once this information manifests itself, it confirms

---

observation of the world, and accordingly they have the most patent influence upon which empirical observations and social cues are taken into consideration and which ignored". M. Edelman, Politics as Symbolic Action, Academic Press, New York, 1971, p.31.

4) Behavioral confirmation is a term applied to a phenomenon widely observed by many social psychologists. People try to play criminal or sick roles to rationalize their deviant conduct and to justify the professional diagnosis and prescriptions.

the initial data of our individual world and perpetuates this world. The often-heard expression "I told you so !" is a perfect illustration of this vicious circle where reality reflects the image that the individual has of it.

(3) In looking for an explanation about a person's behavior, the "naive scientist", as you know, can choose between attributing the cause of this behavior either to the person and his dispositions (character traits, motivations, etc.) or to the circumstances. Professional scientists are exactly in the same situation, of course, (They might attribute it to God or fate, but that is not part of the theory !). But all those who have studied how these attributions are usually made have been struck by one thing : that personal causes are generally preferred. It is more natural to blame individuals than circumstances. The American social psychologist Ross (1977) calls this the <u>fundamental error</u>. There is an impressive collection of results corroborating the fact that an individual who is put in the position to make a judgment about somebody, disregards everything relating to the circumstances (Nisbett and Ross, 1980) and notices mainly things that concern the person, overemphasizing his share in the action. The motives of this action and the relations deriving from it are personalized (Batson, 1975; Snyder, 1977; Snyder et al., 1977; Leyens, 1980).

In view of the regularity of these observations, it is easy to imagine that a kind of spontaneous philosophy is at work. This is what we understand by personalism, which organizes the world around individuals, their values, and their responsibilities. Personalism leads to errors of judgment and to isolating oneself from objective reality. I believe that Nisbett correctly summarizes a widely accepted opinion : "And as three generations of social psychologists have observed, the strong preference for personal dispositions as a basis for predictions is likely to defeat people from attending to those factors that can serve as a useful guide for predictions. That is, to situational factors, or as Lewin put it the field of forces operating at the time the behavior takes place (Nisbett, 1980, p.114).

If I were not afraid of giving offense to certain positivist ears, I would say that "Mr. Everybody" tends to ask spontaneously : Who is to blame ? And like Hercule Poirot in Agatha Christie's novels, he wants to know who benefits from the crime. Once the criminal has been arrested, it is up to the lawyers to look into the real causes of the crime, the conditions of his social and economic life. This is intended to impress the jury and to excuse the crime. The truth of the matter is that in human affairs, we try to find causes; we do not deal neutrally with information : we are building up a case. But I am afraid these points are irrelevant here.

The naive scientist is therefore a poor scientist 5). He is impervious to information, limits himself to <u>confirming his theories</u> instead of <u>falsifying theories</u>, and explains everything he observes on the basis of personal causes. What makes him display such indifference, one might go so far as to say such an aversion to reality ? Why should he be so reluctant to correct his systematic errors and biases when wanting to be on guard against them is, in our eyes, a natural and almost constant occupation of the human mind ? It would seem that the trouble lies with his ignorance of the rules of logic and his lack of training in clear thinking. That is why he offers a danger. And students in English-speaking universities are beginning to be taught about the "perils of the intuitive scientist" (Gergen, 1981). How could humanity have survived for millions of years on the strength of theories and explanations presented by such weak thinkers ? How were they able to invent agriculture and chemistry and even discover America ? One wonders. Especially when one sees professional scientists who have their methods all worked out and are perfectly sure about their causes, capable of destroying this work in a few hours. With nothing but an atomic bomb.

---

5) Kruglanski is right in noting that professional scientists are not immune to the mistakes of naive scientists. But that does not alter the situation in the least. The main thing is to know whether "logical" mistakes were made in the processing of information or whether the mistakes were of a "theoretical"nature and involved the deductions made and the information created. There is a peculiar asymmetry in scientific epistemology : nobody would ever contend that such and such a scientist, for instance Lorentz or Poincarré, was guilty of a mistake in reasoning in refusing the theory of relativity, whereas those who investigate lay epistemology insist that the "man in the street" is guilty of it in refusing to attribute causality to situations and not to persons. It seems to me that it is as difficult to go along with Kruglanski and accept that there is no difference between the two types of scientists as it is to define their differences on a scale of perfection as logical beings. We ask the wrong question when we say : "Who thinks better ?" The social psychologists' self-congratulatory answer : "we do !" is as unsatisfactory as Kruglanski's "nobody does".

FROM SOCIAL COGNITIONS TO SOCIAL REPRESENTATIONS

> How much truth is man able to bear ?
> Nietzsche

Studies on this subject have already become numerous, and their specialization is such that no student can hope to master them all. The general material and monographs range all the way from social psychology to child psychology and clinical psychology. There are studies on all or nearly all aspects of lay epistemology and causal attribution. How can one then initiate a fruitful discussion, especially one along general, theoretical lines ? I will nevertheless take up the challenge. Let me preface my discussion with the observation that, despite its abundance, the literature, with some rare exceptions, tends to be inconclusive. The factual evidence makes the task of scientific analysis a very hazardous proposition. On the other hand, you must admit that its conclusions seem hardly surprising. They were already familiar to you, even without experiments, as premises of classical social psychology, which was founded, after all, to answer the question : "What accounts for people's thinking and reasoning being so often faulty ?" Pioneers in the field then divided into two opposing schools of thought, one side insisting that emotions are responsible for clouding people's minds, the other stressing prejudices and mechanisms triggered by group situations. I am actually impressed by their foresight. Reading the book by Nisbett and Ross (1980), I almost thought I was rereading passages from Le Bon, McDougall, and Bechterew.

It is true, however, that we are ahead of them in one respect. We do have a sufficiently vast amount of facts at our disposal to have the right to discuss the matter freely, without succumbing to idle speculation. Each of the lines of investigation I have just described is valuable. Taken as a whole, they provide an indispensable documentation for sociological and psychological intuition. Still, if we wish to obtain a consistent overview of the phenomenon under investigation, we must look for it at a much deeper level. None of the logical or psychosociological models offered up to this point can explain certain striking features of lay epistemology, so that the field of social cognition is undergoing a difficult phase.

In my opinion, social cognition was headed for this impasse from the start, since cognition was limited to a single aspect, perception. At the same time, reality, the source of the information in question, was viewed as neutral, non-social, presumably objective. (We will never get anywhere if we exclude the imaginary, the symbolic, the illusory, from thinking : these are its most crucial constituents !). On the contrary, one of the most striking results that these experiments have forced us to recognize is the fact that the information coming to us from the outside world is shaped not by neutral reality but by implicit theories and preconceptions, and that these in turn shape this world for us. This is what is the conclusion of someone who has not by any means been concerned with social representations : "Not only are our images of the social world a reflection of events in the social world, but the very events in the social world themselves may be reflections and products of our images of the social world" (Snyder and Swann, 1978, p.160).

This recalls Faust pondering over the origin of all knowledge. What came first : words, power, or deeds ? No, first came the image !

If the facts are such that this reversal is required, we are compelled to redirect the spotlight of research, which until now has been fixed to explore the nature of information, and focus it on implicit theories, typical preconceptions, images, and so on. What do all these have in common ? Two main features : first of all they have a collective character. They are incapable of accounting for individual differences, but only for differences between groups. And secondly, they are all mixtures of concepts, images, and perceptions. These are the very features that, in the main, characterize the category of social representations. We must therefore focus the spotlight of research on representations. Representations alone can channel the give-and-take between us and the reality we face. They are shared by a large number of persons, passed on from one generation to the next, and imposed on each of us without our conscious assent. You will tell me : "But all you are doing is changing the wrapping, The marchandise is still the same". No, it is not. As you could see, we have already made some change by assigning them a determining role. In addition, the reversal entails consequences that are far from negligible. For instance, in the theory of social cognitions, these representations are used to explain observed biases and errors. From our perspective, however, biases and errors are irrelevant or at best secondary. Let me invoke Heider's authority on this score : "An explanation of this (social) behavior, therefore, must deal with common-sense psychology regardless of whether its assumptions and principles prove valid under scientific scrutiny. If a person believes that the lines in his palms fortell his fortune, this belief must be taken into account in explaining certain of his expectations and actions" (1958, p.5). In other words, the content and the structure of these intellectual constructs are all that matter.

But let us not pause here too long. Suffice it to note that a number of researchers working in the field of social cognition have already been led to carry out genuine experiments on social representations. Do you need to be convinced ? Let me give you a few examples. In studying the social representation of psychoanalysis, I described two basic types of representation of the psyche - the mechanistic and the vitalist type - both of which are widespread. These types reappear in experiments carried out on the other side of the Atlantic. Langer and Abelson (1974) for instance had their subjects listen to the recording of an interview with a person who was presented in half the cases as a job applicant and in the other half of the cases as a patient. The subjects were specially trained in psychiatry and psychology. Half of them had been given psychoanalytic training, the other half had been exposed to behaviorist training. They were asked to judge the affective equilibrium of the person whose interview they had just heard. These were the results ; the behaviorists thought that the persons were equally well adjusted in both experimental situations. The psychoanalysts, for their part, thought the same individual to be much more maladjusted when he was presented as a patient than when he was supposed to be a job applicant. The reason for this difference is obvious. And the results convince us that our representation of the psychic mechanism affects the way we interpret the information we receive about people and how we evaluate them.

Even more striking conclusions result from another relatively recent group of studies. The authors, Fischer and Farina (1979) and Farina et al. (1978) set about teaching their students two representations of mental illness, each of which is widely held in our culture. According to one representation, which stresses the organic approach, mental illness is seen as genetic in origin, is considered difficult to predict, and responsive only to drug therapy. According to the other representation, illness is viewed basically as a learning disturbance, which can be remedied if new habits are adopted and the environment is altered. The first representation treats illness as a mechanical and external phenomenon, while the second representation deals with it as a dynamic and internal phenomenon. (The stoics long ago already differentiated between what does and what does not depend on ourselves !). At the end of this indoctrination, the students were asked how they reacted to various troubles they had had to face. Those who had an organic representation of illness naturally were less inclined to ask for personal help to surmount their problems, relying instead on all kinds of drugs. The students with a more clinical social representation, on the other hand, thought of themselves as therapists for their own problems and were less likely to use drugs or alcohol to cope with their discomforts.

We might say, then, that whenever we acquire or change a social representation, we will simultaneously alter a number of other- and self-directed behaviors. One can see here in its purest form how the public and psychologists share one and the same overall view. One can also see the potential consequences of social representations once a certain well-defined image of personality, illness, and so on is propagated socially. This image leaves its mark on thinking, on human relations, and on language and behavior (Moscovici, 1961). My moving from example to example will lay me open to your criticism that I am just skimming the surface, but I do believe that it made some sense to broach the preliminary question of the reversal in the relations between social representation and social information. I do admit, however, that the time has come to take up the main point. Let us proceed.

The hypotheses and postulates of social cognition theories assume first of all that the individual is the seat of psychic reality, while the rest, including the group, is derivative. They therefore assume that a given human intelligence - or a thinking machine - is always and everywhere identical to itself. This means that individuals must follow the same mental and logical laws under all circumstances. Scientists are the highest and most highly perfected expression of this deal. Differences in judgment and interpretation currently observed among us ordinary people must therefore be attributed to the incorrect application of these laws in the various strata of society. This entails imperviousness to information, causal attribution errors, and all the rest. Without spelling it out, all the articles cited earlier convey this message : the naive scientist is inferior to us professional scientists, the logic of the man in the street is utterly worthless compared to that of the man at the blackboard. Chapman and Chapman (1967), in fact, are not afraid to hint as much : "Much stronger views are often expressed privately by experimental psychologists who contend that clinicians are inferior as scientists because they are unresponsive to evidence" (p.204).

Evidence of what and for what ? You can rest assured that the same conclusion will always be reached and will always lead to the same impasse about an inferior and faulty thinking process as against a superior and valid one as long as the problem is stated in the same terms : does the ordinary, so-called naive person give a correct explanation about a psychological and social fact ?

The mistake lies in stating the problem this way, assuming as it does that this person proceeds exactly like the professional scientist, equipped with the same technical tools and traditions : theories and informations except for his incapacity to think clearly and apply logical rules. It is assumed that this person is responsive only to data, observes facts, gestures, and words by other individuals in a disinterested way, and then explains them on the basis of causal schemata. While in fact this person might well view these facts, gestures, or words from a completely different angle, absorb them in a much more passionate way and automatically impose on them the group's framework. And have a folk representation of them.

After all, by stating the problem this way, the layman's cognitive activity is <u>a priori</u> interpreted as a rudimentary version of the scientist's, and is thus considered as almost abnormal or even pathological. A noted cognitive therapist, Ellis, contended (1977)that his patients' disturbances are neurotic because their thinking does not abide by the rules of logic. They also lack experience. In short, they do not think like scientists. Like a number of his colleagues in cognitive therapy, Ellis considers it his duty to rectify his patients' reasoning so as to bring it in line with the laws of scientific thinking, the highest model of human thought. Social psychologists have adopted a somewhat similar attitude. Both of them act like the members of the Royal Art Society who find fault with primitive painting for not abiding by the laws of perspective.

If we take social representations as our point of departure, however, this thought process seems perfectly normal and even appropriate. Please be a little patient, and I will try to illustrate it by a concrete example : personalism. According to the American school of thought, personalism is the fundamental mistake, the dividing line between naive and scientific thinking. We must therefore ask the following question : is personalism the result of misapplying the "laws of thinking" in the causal analysis of reality or does it on the contrary result from the correct application of these laws, taking a mistaken, because personalist, representation of social reality as a starting point ? Which, you must admit, does not amount to the same thing. In the first case we are dealing with a real mistake, in the second the problem lies in the maladaptation of the "concepts" to the "facts". As matters stand, there are many factors in our society, notably ideological and linguistic in nature, which induce us to personalize. Take a common phenomenon : highway accidents. The very word accident suggests that it involves seeking out a victim and a perpetrator, both of whom can be isolated from the stream of cars. The word is manifestly inappropriate. In truth, automobile collisions on the freeway, with the dead and wounded they entail, are as regular and predictable a phenomenon as the collision of atoms in an accelerator. The regularity and the frequency of each of these occurrences can be predicted with equal ease. All that we do not know is which car will crash into which other car, as we cannot predict which atom will collide with which other atom.

In the face of such a predictable event, it is as nonsensical to speak of automobile accidents as it is to speak of atomic particle accidents. But by doing so, we imply that somebody was at fault and proceed to designate that individual. Take the legal system. In civil and criminal law, only Mr. So-and-so or Mr. So-and-so can be held responsible. Our entire social system, from the structure of language to the structure of law, leads to a search for a personal cause, to the "human factor", as it is called. Within this system, a whole representation of the world of accidents is built up and receives reinforcement from religious, political and economic authorities. Here is the Archbishop of Marseilles stating indignantly : "It is not true that automobile traffic must take its toll in human lives; the killer is not the vehicle but the driver". And Roland Barthes, the noted literary critic (who has meanwhile died from the sequelae of an automobile accident), reflects the same view : "In my eyes the automobile problem lies in the hands of psychoanalysis". All these ideas have been internalized and automobile drivers see things the same way. If asked what is the greatest obstacle to the reduction of automobile accidents, 78 % will tell you : the drivers' behavior (Barjonet, 1980). In the last analysis, personalizing under these circumstances is not a matter of erroneous reasoning, but a matter of drawing a logical conclusion from the commonly accepted system of representations.

I could prove the same thing about the material in the various experiments to which I referred earlier. To the extent that they involve a naive (or clinical) psychology, the automatic implication is that individual causal factors are sought behind the situational factors. I would go so far as to say that in these cases no other choice is possible, since a mechanical or impersonal cause would be unacceptable. To be more rigorous, I will even say that personalism is a fundamental feature of any ideology that can be qualified as laissez-faire, capitalistic, or individualistic. One of its effects is that workers attribute their failure to continue their studies to personal incapacity : "It was my own fault, "they all repeat, to explain their dropping out of the school system (Fremontier, 1980). Long before all these studies were undertaken, the sociologist Gabel (1974) wrote : "One of the characteristic features of ideological causality is overemphasis of this "individualistic-comprehensive" tendency; that is, to claim to explain collective behaviors by motivations that have individual validity. This phenomenon is characteristic of the idelogy of the American Right" (p.71).

You can see the point I want to make. One can more easily understand causal attribution to individuals as a consequence of our representations about human beings and social groups than as an analytic error of our naive scientist. The representations themselves can be wrong, no doubt, but that is not a matter of logic or psychology, but of the history and interpretation of our culture 6). I might possibly concede the correctness of the currently fashionable theories on one score, though I feel that the differences they describe originate elsewhere. What distinguishes science from social representations or myths, I believe, is how frequently the question "why" is asked, but not whether the question is answered by : a person or a situation. Scientific thinking does tend to discourage and limit the search for an explanation, while popular thought encourages and multiplies it. The anthropologist Marcel Mauss wrote long ago that magic is "a gigantic variation on the theme of the causality principle". And the philosopher Wittgenstein echoed this thought with : "Superstition is the belief in a relation of cause and effect".

Any generalization in this field is suspect, but there is no way to avoid it. In truth, we would have to give up the individualist hypothesis and postulate to reverse the procedure. Psychological laws and the rules of logical information are not what determines the interpretation of behaviors, feelings, and words.

---

6) It is easy to see how certain social representations lead to personalism from the following passage : "Americans are taught at home, in the school, and in persuasive political rhetoric that America is the land of equal opportunity. Given such opportunity, those who are poor are inclined to attribute their unhappy condition to their own failings and inadequacy. Poor people are bound to be troubled by this logical inference and widely held belief. They are reinforced in their feelings of guilt by the affluent and their legislative representatives , who attribute their own success and others' failure to personal worth or lack of it". Edelman, op.cit., p.55.

It is quite apparent that both of them play only a minor role. The major role is played by social representation, whose effect is "also well established in the consensus information literature which shows that people's attributions are often influenced by their normative expectations rather than by actual, sample-based information". (Kassin, 1981, p.186).

The only way out of the predicament is to start out with social representations, to take them as the given data which must serve as the point of departure for scientific research. By no longer relating them to an isolated individual and seeking to grasp their mechanisms within the cultural setting, the possibility exists for understanding their laws. Undoubtedly this will not lead all at once to "theories" that are as simple and as well suited for laboratory manipulations as those of our American colleagues. Social representations have their own properties, which can only be discovered by studying their relations with social groups, just as the laws of the animal world must be studied on the basis of groups of animals rather than animals in isolation. Only by knowing these properties can we shed light on the genesis of our analytical categories in terms of persons or situations and of logical rules. For in mental life, beyond the simple responses of our senses, everything is necessarily social in nature. By this approach we shall reach a more accurate view of things than by dividing us into the "naive" and the "scientific", into men in the street and men in their studies. It will then become obvious that most of us think badly "because we think differently, according to a different social"theory".

These observations must be spelled out more specifically, and I hope to do so shortly. For the moment, all I wanted to do was to indicate that we have reached a point of no-return. The models are not very helpful for us, and if we wish to proceed further on our path, we must build new models. With this purpose in mind, I would like to add a more personal comment. What seems most questionable and even artificial in all that has been written about social cognition is not so much the reduction of the collective world into the ivory tower of the laboratory. It is its terrible simplification of the mental life of human beings in society. I must admit that I fail to understand how a discussion about the definition of social cognition or the viability of causal attributions can disregard the fact that human beings are governed by a genuine curiosity, religious or philosophical beliefs and some kind of ethical commitment. In laboratories, we are dealing with an a-cultural, agnostic, non-ethical and, needless to say, isolated individual. Or else this cultural aspect has been eliminated by throwing it all into the catch-all of prejudices and stereotypes. In my opinion, any cognition theory, any analysis of our mental life which does not assign a pivotal role to studying the modes of culture which create language, which has no interest in the type of relations between people or in the attitudes toward knowledge and institutions, any such theory seems irrelevant to me. Only by grasping the phenomena of social representation can relevance be restored. All those who have worked toward this goal will confirm the truth of this observation 7).

WHO IS THE REAL NAIVE PSYCHOLOGIST ?

Quite possibly, many aspects of my arguments will turn out to be wrong or exaggerated. We will have to wait for a more searching discussion to find it out. Meanwhile, let me go even further in my speculations. In their early stages, the research on social cognitions and social representations both dealt with the same object : naive or popular psychology. They even started out from a comparable hypothesis. Heider had expressed it as follows : "Since common-sense psychology guides our behaviour toward other people, it is an essential part of the phenomena in which we are interested. We interpret other people's actions and we predict what they will do under certain circumstances. Though these ideas are usually not formulated, they often function adequately. They achieve in some measure what a science is supposed to achieve : an adequate description of the subject matter which makes prediction possible" (1958, p.5).

While selecting the same object and the same hypothesis, however, these studies have gone off in two opposite directions. By describing the contrasts between them, I hope to give you a better understanding about the problem which the study of social representation addresses. To differentiate these two perspectives, I shall associate one of them with the name of Hercule

---

7) In child psychology a comparable evolution can be observed. At first children were studied in isolation, then their social cognition (interpersonal knowledge, attributions, etc.) became the focus of interest. Currently interest is shifting to children's social representations about money, government, the cultural setting, etc. See for instance the chapter on "Issues in Childhood Development" in H. McGurk (ed.), Psychology in Progress, Methuen, London, 1978.

Poirot, Agatha Christie's leading character, and the other with Bouvard and Pécuchet, the two characters created by Flaubert. According to the first approach, naive psychology is based on the common sense of naive psychologists, on which scientists rely in turn to extract its theoretical and authentic core. This common sense has its origin within the family, in the relations between spouses or friends, in daily life, and it makes it possible to interpret the mysteries in the relations between two people. The naive psychologist, like Hercule Poirot, has seen just about everything. He has acquired a great deal of experience with different situations and people. He has evolved his own little philosophy about them and thinks he knows what makes them steal and kill or love and help each other. In the absence of any particular schooling, his knowledge stems from observing other people's behavior, the most varied deeds and situations. To interpret them, he tries to collect the most accurate information and to verify it. He attempts to analyze each person's behavior causally. We find many of his implicit theories in Agatha Christie. He uses these theories only to sift the information he has obtained and indicate the stage setting in which the actual interactions will take place. These theories determine the main lines of the naive psychology underlying each novel.

Heider suggests in some way that all of us behave more or less like Hercule Poirot in solving the enigmas of our existence and in improving our relations with others in society. In short, I would say that each of us wonders on the one hand what is the function of this psychology and on the other wants to know how it affects each individual's behavior. In this context, understanding means a process whereby "ordinary" people match what they see and hear with pre-stored frames of actions to which they have already been exposed. What we are dealing with here, up to a point, is a natural perceptive process in which the untutored subject perceives the world from a certain distance, under the most varied circumstances. Like the industrious bee, the scientist then secures the pollen that has been gathered and distills it into honey.

According to the second perspective, in today's society everything that is viewed as naive and commonsensical is derived from science. Which is itself in a constant state of flux. Scientific discoveries, which constitute real events, force people to assimilate these new findings and confront them with their own ideas and experiences. This is just as true for physics as it is for psychology. In that case the best strategy was to study how and why a scientific theory, such as psychoanalysis, becomes a commonsense psychology, creating new ways of classifying individuals, explaining their behaviors, and of speaking about and with them. That is exactly the course I took. I set out to investigate a cultural shock, not a shock caused by reality. The layman is not a "naive scientist", this monster whose existence has never been verified, but an "amateur scientist", a human and intellectual type that actually had a place in science (Moscovici, 1961) and continues to exist in some branches of science even today. This amateur scientist is stimulated by previously elaborated knowledge and then proceeds to adapt it to his personal interests. Thanks to this knowledge, he creates informations that allow him to understand the world in which he lives. Like Nietzsche, he rejects the "dogma of untutored perception".

Flaubert has immortalized one variant of this type of person in his novel Bouvard et Pécuchet. According to Barbey d'Aurevilly, Flaubert's purpose was to show "how to become intelligent and learned human beings without compulsory education". The two figures meet and come together for the very purpose of studying the various sciences and in order to compare their theories and apply them to the familial universe. What is involved here, undoubtedly, is a copy, as attested by the former profession of the two cronies, and also by the fact that there are two of them. An inaccurate copy, of course. The novelist gives a subtle description of the way in which the concepts of anatomy, history, etc. are metamorphosed in their hands and how they seep into the everyday preoccupations of the village where Bouvard and Pécuchet live. The cronies even become amateur psychologists, trying to validate or invalidate certain ideas about phrenology. "Gall is mistaken, and I challenge you to confirm his doctrine by randomly picking three persons in the shop". The first happened to be a peasant woman with big blue eyes. Pécuchet said, observing her :
- She has a very good memory. Her husband confirmed this fact and offered himself as a subject for investigation.
- Oh ! you, my good fellow, it's hard to make you do things. From what I hear, nobody in the world is as stubborn as you. etc."(1979, p.250).

You can visualize what comic effects Flaubert derives from these situations. Woody Allen has obtained comparable effects in his films, juggling with psychoanalytic vocabulary and explanations applied to the most incongruous situations. Without wishing to offend you, I must admit that from this point of view the amateur psychologist is not that fictitious man in the street but Heider himself, checking through novels, plays, and psychology books in order to come up with a fairly systematic version of interpersonal relations. And Kelley, Jones, Ross, Nisbett, and others would be scientific psychologists.

Let us return to the motives of our two amateur scientists. Their purpose in trying to incorporate science into the realm of everyday experience is not only utilitarian or practical, to insure the survival of the species or to fulfil a duty. Flaubert stresses their disinterestedness. But their true motives are also delight, mental energy, and social venturesomeness. For them, a personal contact with science means being in touch with what has the greatest force of truth and action in the human sphere.

I shall use an example to elucidate the contrast between Hercule Poirot's method and that of Bouvard and Pécuchet. Imagine that you have in front of you a portion of cheese on a plate. It has a distinctive shape, color, odor, and texture; Poirot knows what he is talking about : it is a camembert. When he puts his knife in it and tastes it, the flavor of the cheese confirms his judgment of identifying it. It is neither a roquefort, nor a chester, nor a munster but a camembert. This is a flawless piece of information, and the detective will then wonder about the choice of this cheese, will inquire with the merchant about when it was purchased, etc.

Now place the same camembert on Bouvard and Pécuchet's table. Put a glass of red wine next to it. "How typically French", one of our two heroes will say. And they will bring up chemical and then historical theories, they will recall the landscapes of Normandy, talk of cows and meadows in bloom, and they will hum the famous song "J'irai revoir ma Normandie". They will feel a thrill of patriotism. And as with Proust's famous madeleine, the characteristic qualities of the cheese will recede and all that will be left behind will be the emblem of a nation and the representation of a country.

We have broached this field of research by studying the <u>genesis</u> of naive psychology, not within an individual but within a cultural context. We have at the same time pinpointed what seems to me the task of social psychology in this cognitive realm : to study what happens when there are <u>transformations from one way of knowing things to another way</u> - for instance from science to common sense - and what effect these transformations have on <u>communication and action</u>. In each of the cases, concepts, language, images, etc. are presented again (represented) in a new context. And that is precisely what happens when we shift from oral to written communication or vice-versa, when a novel is changed into a play or a film scenario. And the same might even be happening when we teach the theoretical ideas we conceive to our students. In short, social representations emerge during such a set of transformations in which new contents are generated.

Let me just say a word on the subject of information. During these metamorphoses, things are not only modified, but they are seen in a new light as well. People thus become receptive to manifestations that had previously escaped them. And, like Bouvard and Pécuchet, they try to produce these informations in order to bring the world into harmony with their new ideas. One might draw the conclusion that on the basis of new representations, information is created that connects directly with them. And this information did not exist beforehand. Thus, when commonsense psychology became impregnated with psychoanalysis, people began to explore their surroundings in order to try to discern signs of such and such a complex or Freudian slips on the part of close relatives and observe their behavior toward parents, children, etc. They processed this information, which they had largely provoked and even created themselves.

All the things that strike us in the world around us are as much the effect of our shared representations as the cause of these representations. That is why I feel that we must distinguish in our discussions and theories between <u>free information</u>, which comes to us unsolicited, and <u>linked information</u>, which depends on our prior mental connections and often results therefrom. I guess that general psychologists and computer scientists usually deal with the former kind of information, while we social psychologists always deal with the latter. That is why it is not possible to transpose concepts from one field to the other. We do it anyway, but it is of course a mistake.

To this I must add another point. Many people make the generous-minded mistake of believing that by injecting a goodly amount of correct and free information, one can dispel the effects of "implicit theories", prejudices, and stereotypes prevailing in a group. This is the enlightenment philosophy in the laboratory ! The truth of the matter is that only linked information can have a compelling effect on most of us amateur scientists. Galileo's telescope taught and made visible new phenomena only to the proponents of the heliocentric representation of the world. All the others who maintained the geocentric representation, could see nothing but strange appearances - and the reason was not that they were catholic or obtuse. To make someone responsive to new information, there is no need to overwhelm him with large quantities of it nor to "rectify" his thinking. All that is needed is to connect it by modifying the representation of the object to which the information is related. Despite everything, psychoanalysis has colored common sense, and more than common sense, without offering any measurable data, without any confirmed fact. Facts were gathered only after the theory had gained acceptance, in order to persuade oneself and others of its correctness.

In other words, "prejudices" are not dispelled and stereotypes are not weakened : they are overthrown. To paraphrase Leibnitz, one might say that there is nothing in representation that is not in reality, except the representation itself. Whether we like it or not, whether we agree with it or not. This way of thinking is a fact that has existed far too long for us simply to disregard it. We are neither moralists nor priests whose function it is to judge human nature. We are scientists. Our vocation is to analyse human nature and to tell the truth about it. All that has been written about personalism, about imperviousness to information, contains too much moralizing and not enough analytic insight in my opinion. We cannot escape reality, and I have tried to present this reality to you. We are dealing not only with a logical but with an anthropological problem here. We have neither invented it nor are we right to reduce it in size to make it more palatable to the preconceptions of social psychology. It is at the heart of culture and of such practices as scientific vulgarization, education, psychotherapy, mass media, and so forth.

WAITING FOR GODOT

Are we about to enter a third stage ? Are we in the process of overcoming a crisis ? Will the hypotheses about social cognition which have been the keystone for so much research, be dismantled in turn ? This has recently become a serious possibility (Hewstone and Jaspars, 1981). In any case, we already have the matrix for new solutions.

We must undertake additional research, particularly theoretical research, before we can determine whether existing difficulties can be overcome by taking social representations into account. More facts alone are not the answer; as it is, we are overwhelmed by facts. There are several steps to take, if we wish to progress along this path.

Our first step must be to shift our investigations and interest from the individual to the collective plane. Instead of concentrating on understanding what it means to be an "individual who is engaged in thinking", we must try to understand what constitutes a "group or society engaged in thinking". There are of course several ways of dealing with this question. Most persons concerned with social representations would probably interpret it in the following way. They would first of all view this question as an indication that a shift has been made from the interpersonal to the social and cultural level. (This is quite natural; after all, most so-called "popular" notions are part of the cultural sphere). When we think of society, we do not have in mind an entity that merely serves as a backdrop for the individual, but as an entity sui generis. You must keep in mind that social psychology was established specifically to answer this kind of question. By refusing to deal with this question, we are relegating social psychology to the role of a minor science, which must turn to general psychology or even computer science for its solution.

It means, furthermore, giving priority to intersubjective and social links rather than to links with the object. In other words, the link to the object is an intrinsic part of the social link and must therefore be interpreted within that context. Our common representations thus seem to determine the nature of our behaviors and informations. Social cognition theories are based on the opposite view, in which the distinctive characteristics of the social element are lost. Simon is perfectly justified in writing : "When the processes underlying the social phenomena are identified, as they are in the chapters of this book, particularly those of the second and third part, they turn out to be the same information processes we encounter in non-social cognitions" (Carroll and Payne, 1976, p. 254).

This is a rather disquieting conclusion. Either the social realm exists in its own right and has its own dynamics, which must produce certain effects, or else it is a foolish thing for us to study these information processes. In that case it would be better to leave the matter to other sciences, instead of deluding ourselves with the idea that we have easier access to the mental life of human beings in society ! We cannot have it both ways. For my part, I fully subscribe to the following contention of the philosopher Merleau-Ponty, whose approach is perfectly adapted to our needs : "The mere fact that one practices social psychology means that one must transcend objectivist ontology. To stay within it would necessarily limit one's vision of one's chosen "object" and thereby damage one's research.

Objectivist ideology in this area directly impedes the development of new knowledge. For the person shaped by western objective knowledge, for instance, it was perfectly obvious that magic or myth had no intrinsic truth, that the effects of magic and mythic and ritual ways of life must be explained by "objective" causes and the rest attributed to subjectivist illusions. If social psychology really wants to see our society as it is, it cannot take this postulate as its point of departure, since the postulate itself is part of western psychology, and by adopting it, we would be left with nothing but foregone conclusions" (Merleau-Ponty, 1969, p.43).

The second step would be to put an end to the separation between the processes and the content of social thinking. This separation has been made a matter of principle (Kassin, 1981; Kruglanski, 1979) and a precondition for the scientific character of our research. Its implicit justification is the following. Thought processes are general and invariant, while their contents are particular and variable. The former are culture-free and the latter are culture-bound, the former are independent of the latter. Hence the laws of inference are valid for any topics and events. "Attribution theory, writes Kassin, emphasizes the stimulus parameters that give rise to the perception or inference of a causal relation between two events" (1981, p.170). Consequently, social cognition research becomes laboratory research in logic 8).

---

8) It might be added that the concept of social cognition implies a conscious and logical process. This is not true of social representations. These are based on conventions and symbols and comprise both conscious and unconscious, rational and irrational, aspects. The result is that the term "cognitive" is not accurate when it is applied to social phenomena. It would be more appropriate to use the word "symbolic", which is not the same thing. It is therefore erroneous to state that social representations are cognitive representations. Social psychologists tend to confuse the cognitive and the symbolic. If, as it is claimed, their cognitive revolution lies behind them, their symbolic revolution still lies ahead of them, and the same applies to psychologists in general. In the absence of such a revolution, social representations would have little to contribute. A further argument is the fact that there is no way to deal with inferences unless we deal with the concomitant representations, just as logical operations are inseparable from representational operations. Of particular interest on this score

There is no question that, for whatever reason, one can always conceptually separate process from contents, so that the former refers to general coordination, rules or systems and the latter to particular instances. That does not solve the problem whether this separation should be made everywhere and above all whether it is legitimate to make it in our own field. Let us leave aside some of the evidence. The rules of logic are tied specifically to a given culture and a given mental activity. The law of non-contradiction, which is of greatest importance in western logic and thinking, seems to play a secondary role in Chinese science and thinking, as it does in the realm of symbolic thinking. On the other hand, there are many themes, images, and maxims hence contents, that enjoy an extraordinary permanence and universality. There is the theme of the hero, for example, the theme of a primary community, of a just world existing somewhere (Lerner and Miller, 1978), the theme of longing for such a just world, and so on. Our social representations are shaped and given coherence by themes of this kind. Flament (1979) has shown how Heider's principle of balance is by no means purely a matter of logic. It has an ideological content as well. The same ideological content appears in Taoist philosophy and runs through the philosophy of Rousseau. Since the French Revolution, this philosophy has enjoyed considerable popularity. Once we penetrate a little below the outer layer, we soon notice that psychological laws are the condensed version of a whole sociology (Moscovici, 1981).

And the matter does not rest there. In the epistemology of science, theories and their logic, causality relations and physical or biological concepts are treated as a single unit. Why limit ourselves to logic and causality in dealing with lay epistemology, disregarding the underlying "theories" or "representations ?" By dissociating what is really an organic entity -for every thought is a thought about something- our research tends to lose a good deal of its importance and relevance, and even its pertinence for society at large. It is only by analyzing themes, utterances, images, and their combinations that we can root our studies in the culture to which we belong and understand this culture. Only then are we in a position to ask pointed questions and give meaningful answers (Gilligan, 1977). You can

---

is Ph.N. Johnson-Laird and M. Steedman, "The psychology of syllogism", Cognition Psychology, 10 (1978), p. 64-99.

guess my feelings. Cognitive social psychology, if you will forgive the pleonasm, has no business imitating computer science or general psychology. Its concern is not with hardware but with software, not with the application of programs and languages, but with their creation : the generation of cognitions.

In any case, as far as social representations are concerned, we should follow the example of anthropology and psychoanalysis, which elucidate mechanisms by looking at the content resulting from these mechanisms and deduce the contents on the basis of the mechanisms. I have already developed these ideas, which are by no means original, on several occasions. The objection raised against them is that they are metaphysical. In my eyes this in no way diminishes their relevance, on the contrary. They even converge with certain ideas expressed by the man who is considered the pioneer of cognitive psychology : Neisser. Let me quote him at some length. After expressing his regret about cognitive psychology's retreat to the laboratory and the fact that its interests have become "disappointingly narrow", he warns against the sterility of a theory conceived by specialists for specialists, shielded from any contamination by culture. He writes : "A seminal psychological theory can change the beliefs of a whole society, as psychoanalysis, for example, has surely done. This can only happen, however, if the theory has something to say about what people do in real, culturally significant situations. What it says must not be trivial, and it must make some kind of sense to participants in those situations themselves. If a theory lacks these qualities - if it does not have what is nowadays called "ecological validity" - it will be abandoned sooner or later" (Neisser, 1978, p.2). These are the qualities that a theory of social representations must set as its goal. In their absence, it will lack depth and will not bring any enlightenment to the people for whom it should be of interest.

The third step is to reverse the role of the laboratory and the role of observation. If we take social representations as our basic data, as the phenomena to be analyzed, we can grasp them only in their own context. If we isolate them and separate them from one another and from their institutions, we will be left with nothing but shreds of a devitalized reality, reduced to its most simplified expression. Studying them in the laboratory as non-social data is tantamount to studying nonsense syllables : human meaning is then simply replaced by physical signs (Von Cranach et al., 1980).

On the other hand, analysis of social representations must by definition be comparative : it involves comparison between groups, comparison between cultures, and comparison between mentalities or ideologies. Today we are making an artificial comparison between the representations of scientists and those of the man in the street. To the extent that it is artificial, it cannot help but be arbitrary. Hence let us concern ourselves with reality, so we can draw on reliable data and put the conclusions of scientific analysis to a valid test. All considered, the optimal method is to return to a blend of observation and comparison, an approach that is in keeping with our traditions. The laboratory can then take up the task of analyzing certain processes that have been isolated from the whole and validating specific hypotheses with respect to them. The question arises : was it ever different ? The answer is less straightforward than current discussions would suggest (Harré and Secord, 1972). Each researcher certainly takes accumulated observations into account before tailoring them for an experiment. These observations were implicit and conceived for other purposes. We must now transform them into as explicit data as possible and conceive them as basic data. Our knowledge in this area is rudimentary, despite pioneering studies ranging from field observations to laboratory experiments.

The ideas I have outlined here are relatively incomplete, not to say simplistic. There are far more complex issues waiting in the wings. These issues must wait for a discussion on the basic aspects of social psychology and its object. In such a discussion, the sides taken would be clear and the participants easy to choose. Whether such a discussion will take place and be carried to its conclusion remains to be seen.

REFERENCES

Abric, J.C. Images de la tâche, image du partenaire et coopération en situation de jeu. <u>Cahiers de Psychologie</u>,1970, <u>13</u>, 71-82.

Asch, S.E. <u>Social Psychology</u>. Englewood Cliffs, N.J. : Prentice Hall, 1952.

Barjonet, P.E. L'influence sociale et les représentations des causes de l'accident de la route. <u>Le Travail Humain</u>, 1980,

Batson, C.D. Attribution as a mediator of bias in helping. <u>Journal of Personality and Social Psychology</u>, 1975, <u>32</u>, 455-466.

Bobrow, D.,& Collins, A. <u>Representation and understanding : Studies in cognitive science.</u> New York : Academic Press, 1976.

Chapman,L.J.,& Chapman, J.P. Genesis of popular but erroneous psychodiagnostic observations. <u>Journal of Abnormal Psychology</u>, 1967, <u>72</u>, 193-204.

Chombart de Lauwe, M.J. <u>Un monde autre : l'enfance</u>. Paris : Payot, 1979.

Codol, J.P. Représentation et comportement dans les groupes restreints. Document non publié, Université de Aix-en-Provence, 1972.

Doise, W. <u>Groups and individuals</u>. Cambridge : Cambridge University Press, 1978.

Ellis, A. Rational emotional therapy. <u>The consulting Psychologist</u>, 1977, <u>7</u>, 2-42.

Farina, A., Fisher, J.D., Getter, H. & Fisher, E.H. Some consequences of changing people's views regarding the nature of mental illness. <u>Journal of Abnormal Psychology,</u> 1978, <u>87</u>, 272-279.

Farr, R. On the varieties of social psychology : An essay on the relationships between psychology and other social sciences. <u>Social Science Information</u>, 1978, <u>17</u>, 503-525.

Faucheux, C. & Moscovici, S. Self-esteem and exploitative behavior in a game against chance and nature. <u>Journal of Personality and Social Psychology</u>, 1968, <u>8</u>, 83-88.

Festinger, L. <u>A theory of cognitive dissonance</u>. Stanford, Ca : Stanford University Press, 1957.

Fisher, J.D. & Farina, A. Consequences of beliefs about the nature of mental disorders. <u>Journal of Abnormal Psychology</u>, 1979, <u>88</u>, 320-327.

Flament, C. Représentation dans une situation conflictuelle. <u>Psychologie Française</u>, 1967, <u>12</u>, 297-304.

Flament, C. Modèle d'équilibre et représentation sociale. Paper presented at the Colloquium on Social Representations, Paris, 1979.

Flaubert, G. Bouvard et Pécuchet. Paris : Gallimard, 1979.
Fremontier, J. La vie en bleu. Paris : Fayart, 1980.
Gabel, N.Y. Idéologies. Paris : Anthropos, 1974.
Gergen, K. & Gergen, M. Social Psychology. New York : Harcourt Brace, 1981.
Gilligan, C. In a different voice : women's conception of self and morality. Harvard Educational Review, 1977, 4, 481-517.
Graumann, C.I. & Sommer, M. Schema and inference. Document non publié, Université de Heidelberg, 1981.
Harré, R. & Secord, P. The explanation of social behavior. Oxford : Blackwells, 1972.
Heider, F. The psychology of interpersonal relations. New York : Wiley, 1958.
Herzlich, C. Health and illness : A social psychology analysis. London : Academic Press, 1973.
Hewstone, M. & Jaspars, J. Intergroup relations and attribution processes. In H. Tajfel (Ed.), Social identity conflict and stereotypes : Studies in intergroup behaviour. Cambridge : Cambridge University Press, 1981.
Hofstadter, D.R. Gödel, Bach. Hassock, Sussex : Harvester Press, 1979.
Jodelet, D. La représentation du corps. Unpublished doctoral dissertation. Ecole des Hautes Etudes en Sciences Sociales, Paris, 1980.
Kassin, S.M. From lay-child to lay-man : developmental causal attribution. In S. Brehm, S.M. Kassin & F.X. Gibbons (Eds.), Developmental social psychology. New York : Oxford University Press, 1981.
Kelley, H.H. Causal schemata and the attribution process. In E.E. Jones, D. Kanouse, H.H. Kelley, R.E. Nisbett, S. Valins & B. Weiner (Eds.), Attribution : Perceiving the causes of behavior. Morristown : General Learning Press, 1972.
Kruglanski, A.W. Lay epistemo-logic process and contents : another look at attribution theory. Psychological Review, 1980, 87, 70-87.
Langer, E.J. & Abelson, R.P. A patient by any other name...; clinician group differences in labeling bias. Journal of Consulting and Clinical Psychology, 1974, 42, 4-9.
Le Bon, G. La psychologie des foules. Paris : Flammarion, 1895.
Le Goff. Les mentalités. In Le Goff & P. Nora (Eds.), Faire de l'histoire. Vol. 3. Paris : Gallimard, 1974.
Lerner, M.J., Miller, D.T. & Holmes, J.G. Deserving and the emergence of forms of justice. In L. Berkowitz and E. Walster (Eds.), Advances in experimental social psychology. Vol. 9. New York : Academic Press, 1976.

Lewin, K. Field theories in Social sciences. New York : Harper and Row, 1951.
Leyens, J.Ph. Recherche de stabilité et d'invariance chez les psychologues. Paper presented at the Colloquium : Mudança y Psicologia social, Lisbonne, 1980.
Lord, C., Ross, L.D. & Lepper, M.R. Biased assimilation and attitude polarization. The effects of prior theories on subsequently considered evidence. Journal of Personality and Social Psychology, 1979, 37, 2098-2109.
Mauss, M. Sociologie et anthropologie. Paris : P.U.F., 1950.
Merleau-Ponty, M. Le visible et l'invisible. Paris : Gallimard, 1964.
Moscovici, S. La psychanalyse, son image, son public. Paris : P.U.F., 1961.
Neisser, V. Cognition and reality. San Francisco : Freeman, 1976.
Nisbett, R.E. The trait construct in lay and professional psychology. In L. Festinger (Ed.), Retrospections on social psychology. New York : Oxford University Press, 1980.
Nisbett, R.E. & Ross, L.D. Human inference : Strategies and shortcomings of social judgment. Englewood Cliffs, N.J. : Prentice Hall, 1980.
Osgood, C.E. & Tannenbaum, P.H. The principle of congruity in the prediction of attitude change. Psychological Review, 1955, 62, 42-55.
Proust, M. A la recherche du temps perdu. Paris : Gallimard, 1954.
Roqueplot. Le partage du savoir. Paris : Le Seuil, 1974.
Rosenberg, S. & Sedlak, A. Structural representations of implicit personality theory. In L. Berkowitz (Ed.), Advances in experimental social psychology. Vol. 6. New York : Academic Press, 1972.
Ross, L.D. The intuitive psychologist and his shortcomings. In L. Berkowitz (Ed.), Advances in experimental social psychology. Vol. 10. New York : Academic Press, 1977.
Schank, R.C. & Abelson, R.P. Scripts, plans, goals and understanding : An inquiry into human knowledge structure. Hillsdale, N.J. : Erlbaum, 1977.
Schneider, D.J. Implicit personality theory. Psychological Bulletin, 1973, 79, 294-309.
Sherif, M. & Hovland, C.I. Social judgment : assimilation and contrast effects in communications and attitude changes. New Haven, Connect. : Yale University Press, 1961.

Snyder, M., Tanke, E.D. & Berscheid, E. Social perception and interpersonal behavior : On the self-fulfilling nature of social stereotypes. <u>Journal of Personality and Social Psychology</u>, 1977, <u>35</u>, 656-666.

Snyder, C.R., Schenkel, R.J. & Lowery, C.R. Acceptance of personality interpretations. The Barnum effect and beyond. <u>Journal of Consulting and Clinical Psychology</u>, 1977, <u>45</u>, 104-114.

Snyder, M., & Swann, W.B.Jr. Behavioral confirmation in social interaction: From social perception to social reality. <u>Journal of Experimental Social Psychology</u>, 1978, <u>14</u>, 148-162.

Snyder, M. & Cantor, N. Testing hypotheses about other people : the use of historical knowledge. <u>Journal of Experimental Social Psychology</u>, 1979, <u>15</u>, 330-342.

Von Cranach, M., Kalber Matten, U., Indermuhle, K. & Gugter, B. <u>Zielgerichtetes Handeln</u>. Bern : Haus Hubov, 1980.

Zajonc, R.B. Cognition and social cognition : a historical perspective. In L. Festinger (Ed.), <u>Retrospections on social psychology</u>. New York : Oxford University Press, 1980.

DU BIAIS D'EQUILIBRE STRUCTURAL A LA REPRESENTATION DU GROUPE

C. Flament

Département de Psychologie, Université de Provence,
Aix en Provence

INTRODUCTION

La théorie de l'équilibre structural de Heider (1946) est bien connue, ainsi que le remarque Zajonc (1968, p.353) constatant "le fait désolant que 20 ans après l'énoncé original du principe de l'équilibre, pratiquement aucune recherche sur l'équilibre n'a fait plus que simplement tenter de démontrer la validité de la définition fondamentale".

Depuis dix ans, nous avons, comme bien d'autres, essayé d'expliquer pourquoi la définition était valide. Pour ce faire, nous nous sommes placé dans la perspective de l'étude expérimentale des représentations sociales, en nous appuyant sur la mathématisation de l'équilibre par la théorie des graphes (cf.Flament, 1970).

Lorsque Heider considère que l'équilibre est un principe d'organisation cognitive, relevant de la psychologie naïve, cela peut être traduit : le principe d'équilibre organise la représentation des relations interpersonnelles positives et négatives.

Plus prudents, certains auteurs, et Zajonc notamment, préfèrent parler de "biais" organisant les réponses obtenues dans certaines situations expérimentales.

Avant de proposer quelques observations sur les rapports possibles entre biais et représentation, rappelons que ces réponses sont celles de sujets à qui on a demandé d'apprendre, de construire, de modifier, de compléter ou de choisir des structures de relation d'amitié entre des personnes fictives. Dans de telles situations de "vide social", et si les sujets ne répondent pas au hasard, on peut penser que les sujets se réfèrent à un modèle social (une représentation) - il faut alors dire quel modèle, et pourquoi c'est lui qui est évoqué - ou bien, on peut supposer que les sujets utilisent des règles purement formelles dont l'utilité n'est que de permettre de répondre avec un sentiment de rigueur à des questions qui n'ont guère de sens. C'est ce que, pour l'essentiel, affirme Léonard (1972), qui a, avec un certain succès, tenté de retrouver l'équilibre avec un matériel non social (on évoque les pièces d'un jeu de construction, dont on dit seulement qu'"elles s'emboîtent" ou "ne s'emboîtent pas"). De nouveaux résultats, plus fins obtenus par Léonard (communication personnelle) nous semblent rompre trop fortement l'analogie pour que cette hypothèse puisse être retenue, et nous nous contenterons de rechercher une représentation sociale derrière l'équilibre structural.

BIAIS, SCHEMES ET REPRESENTATION

Lorsqu'on veut étudier une représentation, on pose des questions, précises ou non, auxquelles les sujets répondent : cela peut aller du choix entre deux mots codés à l'expression la plus libre. Si on n'observe aucune structure dans les réponses, ce peut être pour trois raisons : 1) on n'a pas su mettre en évidence une structure qui reste cachée; 2) on n'a pas su trouver les questions mettant en oeuvre la représentation visée; 3) la représentation visée n'existe pas.

Si on observe une structure dans les réponses, on parle de biais (par exemple, le biais d'équilibre); nous donnons à ce terme un sens purement technique de déviation systématique des réponses par rapport à une norme (par exemple : réponses correctes dans une expérience d'apprentissage; réponses aléatoires dans une expérience de complétion de structures - pour prendre des exemples classiques dans l'étude de l'équilibre).

Le fait qu'on trouve un biais lorsqu'on recherche une représentation, peut conduire à confondre les deux. Cela provient sans doute d'une conception trop simple de la représentation. Structure cognitive relativement stable, une même représentation peut se manifester différemment en diverses situations (en réponse à diverses questions). Il convient donc, pour expliquer le biais observé, et connaître la représentation visée, de rechercher les mécanismes structurant les réponses en fonction des échos que les questions ont évoqués dans le champ de la représentation. Nous utiliserons le mot : schème, pour désigner de tels opérateurs cognitifs.

Si on s'efforce de bien distinguer les schèmes des représentations, on s'apercevra qu'il n'y a pas de schème spécifique ne jouant que pour une représentation particulière - tout au moins nous en faisons l'hypothèse. Ces schèmes, relativement généraux, sont normalement étudiés en dehors des recherches sur les représentations : schèmes logiques, du genre de ceux qu'étudie Piaget; schèmes rhétoriques (analogie, métaphore...); schèmes psychanalytiques...

Il n'est pas suffisant d'identifier un schème susceptible de produire un biais; encore faut-il expliquer pourquoi ce schème général est appelé à fonctionner dans ce cas particulier. Dans le biais d'équilibre, on peut isoler un biais de transitivité de l'amitié ("les amis de mes amis sont mes amis"); le schème de transitivité est connu des piagétiens (Bullinger, 1973); il nous faudra montrer que c'est bien ce schème qui est effectivement responsable du biais, et expliquer pourquoi la représentation de l'amitié (ou de quelque chose d'autre) mobilise ce schème logique pour structurer les réponses.

Et c'est en répondant à cette question, en identifiant ce en quoi la représentation a à faire avec le schème logique - qu'on découvrira des aspects importants de la représentation.

Nous sommes parti, proche de Heider, en considérant que le biais d'équilibre traduisait la structure des relations interpersonnelles, positives et négatives dans leur représentation. Existe-t-il un schème d'équilibre ? Harary (1953) a défini la théorie des graphes équilibrés avant d'avoir entendu parler de l'équilibre heidérien. Les physiciens ont, en ferromagnétisme, une théorie, dite "des triangles frustrants", isomorphe à la théorie de Harary. Et il faut dire que certaines présentations de ces théories évoquent un schéma de pensée qui semble naturel, au point qu'on ferait volontiers l'hypothèse qu'il existe un schème psychologique de l'équilibre.

Nous n'avons pas eu à nous poser la question trop longtemps : des résultats expérimentaux suggèrent que, en ce qui concerne les relations interpersonnelles, on doit décomposer le biais d'équilibre en deux, et donc, rechercher plusieurs mécanismes explicatifs. Ce faisant, il n'est pas évident qu'il s'agit d'une étude de la représentation des relations interpersonnelles, et un de nos problèmes sera de trouver l'objet dont la représentation se traduit par les biais observés.

DECOMPOSITION DU SCHEME D'EQUILIBRE

Bien des recherches analysent les structures triangle par triangle. On sait que les huit triangles possibles se regroupent en quatre cas, comme le montre le tableau I :

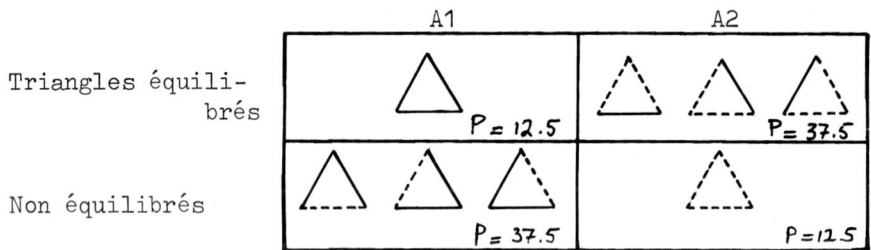

Tableau I - Les huit triangles possibles

Quatre des triangles sont équilibrés; la signification des colonnes A1 et A2 apparaîtra dans un instant. On a désigné par P le pourcentage d'apparition de chacun des quatre cas dans l'hypothèse d'équiprobabilité des réponses positives et négatives. Les relations positives sont en traits pleins, les relations négatives, en tirets.

En examinant attentivement le détail des résultats expérimentaux (lorsque c'est possible), on constate que, si le triangle équilibré de type A1 (trois positifs) a toujours et massivement, les faveurs des sujets, il est loin d'en être de même des triangles équilibrés de type A2 (deux négatifs et un positif). (Ce fait, au niveau de valeurs brutes, peut être masqué par la probabilité du second cas, qui est triple de celle du premier).

Dans une expérience dont nous reparlerons, Pichevin et Poitou (1974) sont amenés à calculer un rang moyen de préférence des huit triangles (tableau II).

	A1	A2
Triangles équilibrés	1,9	5,5
Non équilibrés	4,4	4,4

Tableau II - Rang moyen de préférence des quatre types de triangles

Seul, le triangle équilibré de type A1 a un rang moyen s'écartant significativement du rang moyen résultant du hasard (4,5).

De tels résultats suggèrent que les réponses obtenues dans les expériences sur l'équilibre, ne sont pas organisées par un seul biais, celui de l'équilibre, mais supposent l'existence de deux processus psychologiquement distincts.

Pour aider à la recherche de ces processus, il est commode de s'appuyer sur une formalisation proposant deux axiomes au lieu d'un (Flament, 1968 et 1975).

Dans les cas expérimentaux qui nous intéressent (graphes complets), il suffit de poser les axiomes suivants :
A1 - Si un triangle a deux côtés positifs, le troisième côté est positif;
A2 - Si un triangle a deux côtés négatifs, le troisième côté est positif.
On voit alors que, dans le tableau I, les colonnes notées A1 et A2 regroupent les triangles pour lesquels les axiomes A1 et A2, respectivement, peuvent s'appliquer; dans la ligne "triangles équilibrés" figurent les triangles où l'axiome concerné est vérifié; et dans la ligne "triangles non équilibrés" figurent les triangles ou l'axiome concerné, au contraire, n'est pas vérifié.

Une généralisation aux graphes quelconques a été proposée (Flament, 1975) :
A'1 - Aucun cycle n'a exactement une arête négative.
A'2 - Tout cycle de longueur impair a au moins une arête positive.

L'axiome A'1 est l'axiome de groupage (clustering) de Davis (1967); nous avons proposé de nommer A'2, axiome de parcimonie. En effet, dans un graphe vérifiant A'1, on a un nombre quelconque de groupes d'amis, chacun sans hostilité interne; si, de plus, A'2 est vérifié, il y a équilibre, et le nombre de groupes d'amis est alors d'au moins deux. Cette remarque est essentielle pour comprendre le lien entre cet axiome de parcimonie et l'hypothèse psychologique que nous allons faire.

AXIOME DE PARCIMONIE ET SITUATION DE STRESS

On sait que les situations de stress modifient les structures cognitives, généralement dans le sens d'une simplification ou d'une extrémisation. Ce processus, appliqué à une représentation des relations interpersonnelles vérifiant l'axiome de groupage (un nombre qui peut être grand, de groupes d'amis), conduit à une représentation simplifiée ("parcimonieuse") comportant un groupe, au plus deux : l'axiome de parcimonie tend alors à être vérifié, et la représentation est équilibrée - sans qu'on suppose l'action d'un éventuel schème d'équilibre.

Nous faisons donc l'hypothèse suivante : soit deux situations ne se différenciant que par le fait que l'une est sous stress, l'autre étant (relativement) normale; les réponses des sujets vérifieront toujours l'axiome A1, mais vérifieront l'axiome A2 plus en situation de stress qu'en situation normale.

Pour vérifier cette hypothèse, Rossignol et Flament (1975) ont manipulé le stress de deux façons :

1. "Réussite-échec" : avant le questionnaire d'équilibre, les sujets passent un test d'intelligence (truqué) : certains réussissent, d'autres échouent, massivement et publiquement. On notera R ou E.
2. "Préférence-vérité" : c'est une variable dans la consigne du questionnaire d'équilibre : "Répondez rapidement, sans réfléchir; ... dites ce que vous préférez le plus"; "Dites ce qui vous paraît vrai..., réfléchissez bien". Cette deuxième consigne est supposée plus stressante que la première. On notera P ou V.

On a donc quatre situations : la plus normale est R-P; la plus stressante est E-V; entre, se trouvent R-V et E-P, sur l'ordre desquelles on ne fait pas d'hypothèse particulière.

Les huit triangles possibles sont présentés aux sujets par les huit phrases du type : "Les amis de mes ennemis sont mes amis"..., que les sujets notent de 0 à 5. A partir des réponses, on calcule deux scores d'acceptation, un par axiome. Nous présentons (tableau III) les résultats en faisant varier les scores de - 2,5 à + 2,5, zéro étant le point neutre.

	R.P.	E.P.	R.V.	E.V.
Axiome 1	1,67	1,41	1,30	1,25
Axiome 2	0,07	0,64	0,71	0,82

Tableau III - Scores d'acceptation des axiomes

Pour l'essentiel, les résultats confirment l'hypothèse : l'axiome A1 est toujours bien accepté (même si, dans les trois situations de stress, il y a une légère baisse de l'acceptation, que nous ne nous expliquons pas très bien); l'axiome A2 n'est accepté qu'en situation de stress. On notera que les trois situations de stress sont à peine différenciées, et ceci pour les deux axiomes.

L'expérience a été répliquée (Pichevin et Rossignol, 1976), en utilisant des structures plus complexes que des triangles (relations entre cinq personnes); les résultats sont moins clairs, mais, après formalisation précise de la parcimonie (Flament, 1975), les tendances apparaissent identiques.

Nous sommes donc porté à conclure :

1. Le schème d'équilibre n'a pas de réalité psychologique.
2. Si les représentations des relations interpersonnelles positives et négatives vérifient parfois l'axiome de parcimonie, c'est pour des raisons psychologiques fort générales (action du stress sur les structures cognitives), qui ne nous intéressent pas ici.

On peut penser que la situation de stress modifie la représentation elle-même; il est plus satisfaisant de penser qu'il existe un schème modifiant l'expression de la représentation; un tel schème, de nature psychanalytique, est étudié par Rossignol et Houel (1976).

Il nous reste à identifier le schème psychologique qui entraîne la vérification de l'axiome 1 - et c'est là qu'apparaîtra la représentation du groupe, et non plus la représentation des relations interpersonnelles.

AXIOME DE GROUPAGE ET SCHEME D'EQUIVALENCE

Formellement, l'axiome A1 exprime simplement que la relation d'amitié est transitive (sous la forme A'1, la transitivité peut ne pas être totale). Cette transitivité ("les amis de mes amis sont mes amis") est ce que nous devons expliquer, directement ou indirectement.

Tous les auteurs admettent que l'amitié est pensée comme symétrique (biais de réciprocité). De plus, on peut convenir que l'amitié est une relation réflexive (chacun est l'ami de lui-même - bien que cela ait peu de sens).

Donc, formellement, l'amitié est perçue comme ayant les propriétés d'une relation d'équivalence. Ce qui suggère que la représentation de l'amitié est peut-être gouvernée par le schème de l'équivalence formelle :
1) La relation d'amitié est pensée comme un cas particulier de relation d'équivalence;
2) Toute relation d'équivalence, maîtrisée en tant que telle, est transitive;
3) Donc, la relation d'amitié est pensée comme transitive, et l'axiome A1 est vérifié.

Si le point 1 est admis, on aura remplacé le problème qui semblait s'imposer (Pourquoi l'amitié est-elle transitive ?), par cette nouvelle question : pourquoi l'amitié est-elle considérée comme une équivalence ?

Mais il faut d'abord établir le point 1. Pour ce faire, Flament et Bullinger (1977) ont étudié les réponses d'enfants de 5 à 10 ans; une grande partie de ces enfants ne maîtrise pas, ou pas complètement, le schème formel de l'équivalence. On peut donc, en les interrogeant selon les techniques de l'école de Piaget, espérer enregistrer des raisonnements différenciés selon les âges (mais l'aspect génétique ne nous intéresse pas). Il faudra alors vérifier si chaque enfant utilise le même mode de raisonnement dans une épreuve formelle (égalité de grandeurs) et dans une épreuve sociale (amitié).

Epreuve formelle (Disques) : on utilise des disques de bois, de même diamètre (mais de couleurs différentes); ces disques sont alignés sur une planchette, et ne peuvent être comparés, par superposition, que de proche en proche; les questions portent sur l'équivalence de grandeur de disques non voisins.

Epreuve sociale (Poupées) : on dispose des poupées alignées devant l'enfant; les sentiments (amitié ou hostilité) entre poupées voisines, sont affirmées par l'expérimentateur; les questions portent sur les sentiments entre poupées non voisines.

Chaque enfant est soumis aux deux épreuves.

L'analyse de leurs réponses permet de dégager, de la même façon dans chaque épreuve, trois types de raisonnement :

- Traitement classificatoire : l'attribution de propriétés aux objets (disques, ou poupées) permet à l'enfant de partager l'ensemble de ces objets en classes d'équivalence (éventuellement de façon floue, si plusieurs interfèrent). On rencontre ce traitement surtout chez les plus jeunes enfants.
- Traitement relationnel : les relations entre les objets des diverses paires sont considérées comme appartenant à un champ relationnel unique, et peuvent donc se composer (par exemple, pour donner un raisonnement de transitivité). On rencontre ce traitement surtout chez les enfants âgés.
- Traitement pas oscillations : entre le classificatoire et le relationnel, l'enfant effectue des mises en relation locales fondées, pour différentes paires d'objets, sur différentes propriétés de ces objets.

Le tableau IV montre que 70 % des enfants traitent identiquement disques et poupées; pour les autres, le décalage génétique est minimum.

POUPEES

	Classif.	Oscillat.	Relat.	
DISQUES Classif.	4 (6;5)	2 (7;3)		6 (6;8)
Oscillat.	3 (7;5)	6 (9;4)	1 (10;1)	10 (8;10)
Relat.		4 (8;9)	13 (9;2)	17 (9;0)
	7 (6;10)	12 (8;9)	14 (9;2)	

Tableau IV - Répartition des 33 enfants selon leurs traitements dans les deux situations (entre parenthèses, l'âge moyen)

Nous concluons donc que la relation d'amitié est pensée selon le schème de l'équivalence formelle, ce qui entraîne la transitivité (Axiome A1). Il n'est donc pas nécessaire d'expliquer cette transitivité, mais d'expliquer pourquoi l'amitié est vue comme une équivalence sociale.

AMITIE ET HIERARCHIE

Qu'amitié et équivalence aillent ensemble peut sembler naturel : pour être amis, il faut se ressembler, avoir les mêmes goûts, être de même niveau... N'est-ce pas d'une psychologie par trop naïve ?

Nous avons étudié les rapports entre amitié et égalité hiérarchique (Flament, 1971; Flament et Monnier, 1971 a et b). Par exemple, on décrivait une hiérarchie et on demandait, si, entre tel et tel individu de la hiérarchie, les relations étaient "plutôt amicales" ou "plutôt hostiles". Le tableau V donne les résultats pour trois enquêtes parallèles (I : sujets : étudiants aixois; hiérarchie : entre étudiants dans une situation de travail; II : sujets : étudiants aixois; hiérarchie : entre personnels d'une administration: III : sujets : lycéens genévois; hiérarchie : entre lycéens).

	Egalité hiérarchique			Inégalité hiérarchique	
	Niveau supérieur	Niveau moyen	Niveau inférieur	Niveaux consécutifs	Niveaux non conséc.
I	25	40	51	70	40
II	45	49	68	57	40
III	26	37	31	78	30

Tableau V - Pourcentage de réponses "plutôt amis" concernant des paires d'individus situés hiérarchiquement.

On voit qu'on imagine les relations entre égaux comme plutôt négatives, sauf lorsqu'il s'agit d'individus également au niveau inférieur d'une hiérarchie administrative; au contraire, des individus situés inégalement mais consécutivement dans une hiérarchie (relation hiérarchique directe) sont vus comme étant facilement amis.

Inversément, nous avons présenté (Flament et Monnier, 1971b) des paires d'individus amis ou hostiles, en demandant s'ils étaient "à égalité" ou non dans une hiérarchie (sujets : lycéens genévois; structures : entre lycéens).

	Egalité	Inégalité	
Amis	55	45	100
Ennemis	53	47	100

Tableau VI - Pourcentage de réponses "à égalité", ou non, concernant des paires d'individus, amis ou non.

Les différences de pourcentages dans les résultats (tableau VI) seraient peut-être intéressantes à commenter si elles n'étaient négligeables.

De ces résultats, on peut conclure qu'il n'y a pas automatiquement, loin de là, corrélation entre amitié et égalité. Ce qui peut sembler en contradiction avec la conclusion de la section précédente. Mais alors, nous étudiions le raisonnement d'enfants traitant, indépendamment, d'amitié et d'équivalence formelle;

ici, nous avons étudié les rapports entre amitié et structures hiérarchiques, dans lesquelles l'égalité sociale, bien particulière, ne peut être réduite aux aspects formels de l'équivalence. Dans une hiérarchie, ce sont l'inégalité, la dépendance, qui caractérisent la situation. Et on peut se demander si, dans une telle situation, l'amitié évoquée est de même nature que celle qu'on étudie dans les expériences classiques sur l'équilibre : notons que les résultats du tableau V excluent la transitivité de l'amitié (l'amitié entre niveaux consécutifs devrait entraîner, par transitivité, l'amitié entre niveaux non consécutifs); et c'est d'un type bien particulier d'amitié dont parlent nos sujets, lorsqu'ils donnent ce genre de commentaires : "Dans une administration, il est bon de se faire certains amis"...

Le "vide social" dans lequel se font les expériences d'équilibre, peut laisser penser que c'est l'image de l'amitié en général qui y est à l'oeuvre; nos résultats suggèrent qu'une telle image générale n'a sans doute pas d'existence et il nous faut trouver quelque chose de plus consistant. Nous allons voir que l'image du groupe amical et égalitaire peut très bien répondre à notre quête.

LE GROUPE EGALITAIRE

L'amitié et l'égalité sont liées dans l'image du groupe, telle que nos étudiants la présentent lorsqu'au début d'un cours, on leur demande une définition de la notion de groupe : un groupe est un ensemble d'individus ayant des relations affectives positives (les relations négatives ne sont jamais mentionnées); ils ont des activités, des buts, des idées, des attitudes..., en commun; ils ne sont pas différenciés, sauf peut-être dans l'organisation d'une activité efficace, et alors, l'égalité est recouvrée par le biais de l'équité; ils ne sont pas hiérarchisés (sauf dans les réponses des élèves d'une école militaire !).

Cette image du groupe, tirée de notre expérience pédagogique, est confirmée par une étude systématique de Poitou (1978, chap.VI).

Poitou montre (chap. IV), que la notion de groupe telle qu'on la trouve dans les théories de la psychologie sociale (qui se veut) scientifique, n'est que cette image, infiniment plus nuancée, articulée et argumentée ! ... Cette convergence de la psychologie naïve et de la psychologie universitaire est, pour Poitou (chap.V), de nature idéologique (au sens marxiste du terme). L'histoire de cette notion idéologique peut nous dévoiler son fonctionnement actuel, et suggérer des expériences de vérification.

Les penseurs de l'époque des Lumières, frayant la voie à la révolution industrielle, affirmaient que la Société devait être libre, égalitaire et fraternelle, comme le proclame toujours la devise de la République Française. La liberté et l'égalité (essentiellement juridiques) permettaient l'établissement d'un marché du travail salarié; la fraternité devait conduire à l'équité en palliant les éventuelles inégalités pouvant résulter de la dissymétrie des protagonistes sur ce marché du travail.

Ecrivant après les nombreuses crises révolutionnaires du 19ème siècle, Durkheim (1893, 1898) ne peut plus penser qu'une société harmonieuse puisse résulter de ces grands principes régissant directement les rapports entre individus au sein de la société. Il reporte l'analyse au niveau du groupe - du groupe de travail, notamment, qui a "le pouvoir moral capable de contenir les égoïsmes individuels, d'entretenir dans le coeur des travailleurs un plus vif sentiment de leur solidarité commune, d'empêcher la loi du plus fort de s'appliquer aussi brutalement"... (Durkheim, 1893, p. XII).

Ces considérations ne sont pas restées dans les dissertations universitaires; on les retrouve, depuis le début du siècle, dans de nombreux textes, d'origine bourgeoise, relatifs aux relations dans l'Entreprise; par exemple, dans les journaux (patronaux) d'entreprise, qui exaltent la "grande famille" et l'"esprit Maison".

Pour Poitou, le rôle idéologique de la notion de groupe est donc clair : affirmant la solidarité de tous les membres de l'entreprise, elle permet de nier tout antagonisme entre classes sociales, entre ouvriers et patrons. La mutation industrielle du milieu du siècle (importance sans cesse croissante des "petits cadres", des salariés en col blanc) a très largement développé l'efficacité de ce rôle idéologique : en effet, ces "cols blancs", issus en grand nombre de familles de travailleurs indépendants sont, de par cette origine, et de par la nature de leur insertion dans l'entreprise, particulièrement sensibles à l'image de cette entreprise comme groupe égalitaire et fraternel. C'est alors que s'est particulièrement développée la théorie - et la pratique - de la Dynamique des Groupes.

Mais il nous semble que ce n'est pas là toute l'histoire de la notion de groupe égalitaire et fraternel. On doit aussi évoquer bien des courants millénaires de la sensibilité sociale occidentale : christianisme utopisme socialisant... Ce qui est nouveau, dans la philosophie des Lumières, c'est l'affirmation d'une

égalité universelle; avant, l'égalité était restreinte à des catégories de personnes (citoyens romains, chrétiens...).
Ainsi, Spinoza (XVIIe siècle), dont Heider (1975) s'est largement inspiré, énonce (Ethique, Livre III) des propositions tout à fait semblables à celles de l'équilibre heiderien, mais souvent en en limitant le jeu entre gens "de même classe et de même nation".

Il nous semble alors que l'apport de l'idéologie bourgeoise, en ce qui concerne notre problème, est qu'elle autorise, et même, pousse, à penser le groupe égalitaire et fraternel comme pouvant être composé d'individus quelconques, et notamment, d'individus en relation d'antagonisme social.

Nous pouvons donc nous attendre à ce que, si les structures d'amitié que nous demandons à nos sujets portent sur des individus différenciés, le schème d'équivalence fonctionne uniquement sur chaque sous-structure dont les membres sont indifférenciés.

En fait, les individus fictifs évoqués dans les expériences sont toujours différenciés, ne serait-ce que par les prénoms. On doit donc s'interroger sur le seuil de différenciation, et/ou sur les critères pertinents de différenciation, au delà de quoi la structure n'est plus un groupe unique.

IMAGE DU GROUPE ET DIFFERENCIATION

Les expériences, mentionnées plus haut, sur les rapports entre amitié et hiérarchie, montrent qu'insister sur les aspects hiérarchiques suffit à supprimer la référence au groupe égalitaire et fraternel. A défaut d'informations particulières sur le fonctionnement de ces groupes hiérarchisés, la différenciation hiérarchique n'a pas de raison d'être compensée en équité, et l'image du groupe ne peut s'appliquer totalement à la structure.

L'analyse de Poitou montre que le rôle idéologique de cette image est de masquer, non pas les différences hiérarchiques au sein de l'entreprise, mais les antagonismes de classes qui coupent la hiérarchie en deux (ouvriers et cadres). On peut donc s'attendre à voir réapparaître l'image du groupe fraternel si on présente une hiérarchie explicitement située dans une entreprise - ceci, tout au moins lorsqu'on interroge les individus les plus sensibles, selon Poitou, à l'influence de l'idéologie dominante dans ce domaine, à savoir, les cadres moyens de l'entreprise.

Aloisio (1970) a, dans une même entreprise, interrogé, d'une part, les chefs de service (cadres moyens), d'autre part, des agents d'exécution (ouvriers); utilisant cinq niveaux hiérarchiques attestés dans l'entreprise (agent d'exécution, agent de maîtrise, chef de service, sous-directeur, directeur), on demande si, "dans une entreprise comme la vôtre", les relations entre deux personnes, désignées uniquement par leurs grades, étaient plutôt amicales ou plutôt hostiles. Pour les deux populations, les sous-directeurs n'ont guère de liens positifs, ni entre eux, ni avec les autres : ce qui semble refléter une situation réelle de conflit dans l'entreprise dont font partie les sujets. A part cela, les deux populations donnent des images très différentes de l'entreprise : pour les chefs de service, des conflits existent (entre les sous-directeurs; entre agents d'exécution et agents de maîtrise, deux niveaux "cols bleus" en rivalité), mais, pour l'essentiel, il n'y a pas de coupure entre le haut et le bas de la hiérarchie, des liens amicaux reliant tout le monde, au moins indirectement : en passant par les chefs de services eux-mêmes, qui assurent ainsi la cohésion de la famille qu'est l'entreprise. Au contraire, pour les agents d'exécution, deux groupes s'opposent : les manuels (agents d'exécution et de maîtrise, tous amis) et les cadres.

Poitou insiste sur le rôle essentiel de l'image du groupe égalitaire et fraternel, dans le masquage des antagonismes socio-économiques fondamentaux, et une expérience de Pichevin et Poitou (1974) le met en évidence, d'une façon qui demande à être discutée. Les sujets sont amenés, par une technique de construction de structures, à ordonner les huit triangles possibles selon leurs préférences. On a trois situations : - situation contrôle : les trois sujets fictifs sont désignés par des prénoms; - situation "différenciation par l'âge" : en plus des prénoms, on indique que l'un a 40 ans, les deux autres, 20 ans; - situation "différenciation par la classe sociale" : en plus des prénoms, on indique que l'un est patron, les deux autres ouvriers. On interroge des étudiants français, et des étudiants africains poursuivant leurs études en France (les prénoms utilisés étant français pour les sujets français, africains pour les sujets africains).

En situation contrôle, le groupe amical (triangle entièrement positif) a, pour rang moyen de préférence : 1,9 chez les étudiants français, et 2,3 chez les étudiants africains, toutes les autres structures ayant un rang voisin de 4,5 ce qui peut réaliser du hasard (voir les résultats des français au tableau II). Le tableau VII donne les résultats pour les situations de différenciation.

Différenciation Sujets	par l'âge Français	Africains	par la classe Français	Africains
△ (sommet *)	3,0	4,5	4,7	4,0
△ (sommet * pointillé)	3,2	2,1	1,2	2,0
Meilleur rang parmi les autres structures	3,6	3,8	4,3	4,3

✱ = 40 ans, ou patron;
■ = 20 ans, ou ouvriers.

Tableau VII - Rang moyen de préférence

L'opposition de classe patron-ouvriers est sans doute aussi (superficiellement) connue des étudiants africains que français. Par contre, l'opposition par l'âge n'a pas le même sens pour les deux populations : pour les Français, il s'agit du phénomène, très prégnant, de "conflit de générations"; pour les Africains, c'est une trace encore très vivace de l'organisation des sociétés africaines précapitalistes où les différences de génération sont indicatives des places dans les rapports sociaux. Dans la perspective de Poitou, on ne s'étonne donc pas que la structure "40 ans contre 20 ans" soit préférée par les Africains au même titre que la structure "patron contre ouvriers", et qu'il n'en soit pas de même chez les Français.

Mais il faut noter (ce que ne font pas Pichevin et Poitou) que la différenciation par l'âge joue chez les Français : la structure toute positive n'est qu'à 3,0; et la structure "40 ans contre 20 ans" est à 3,2, alors que les deux autres structures comportant deux négatifs et un positif sont à 6,1 et 5,4...

On doit donc conclure, en opposition à l'analyse de Pichevin et Poitou, que la différenciation par l'âge est efficace chez les Français comme chez les Africains. La différence entre les réponses de ces populations vient de ce que la différence d'âge renvoie, pour les Africains, à un modèle général de société en classes d'âge antagonistes - alors que pour les Français, elle ne renvoie à aucun modèle général (de société ou de famille...).

Ces quelques résultats permettent de conclure que c'est bien, dans les expériences sur l'équilibre structural, l'image du groupe égalitaire qui se manifeste.

De plus, ces expériences enregistrent l'image d'une société multigroupale antagoniste, lorsque des différenciations sont pertinentes pour une population.

Une reprise partielle de l'expérience précédente donne quelques aperçus sur les modèles de situation unigroupale ou multigroupale (Audierne, 1973). On a travaillé avec des sujets français seulement, dans les conditions de contrôle (sans différenciation) et avec différenciation de classe (il est regrettable que la différenciation par l'âge n'ait pas été reprise). On observe les mêmes tendances que chez Pichevin et Poitou. Mais, de plus, on avait demandé aux sujets de commenter chaque structure en décrivant une situation concrète où elle était susceptible de se rencontrer.

En condition contrôle, la structure toute positive (qui est dominante) est considérée comme "normale" et est peu commentée; les autres structures sont commentées en faisant appel à des traits de caractère des protagonistes.

En condition de différenciation, la structure dominante (patron contre ouvriers) est "normale". Le plus intéressant réside dans les commentaires sur la structure où patron et ouvriers sont amis :
- c'est la Société Idéale (environ 10 %)
- c'est dans une petite entreprise, une entreprise familiale, une entreprise artisanale (environ 40 %)
- les trois hommes se connaissent en dehors de l'entreprise (école, service militaire, club sportif...) (environ 50 %).

CONCLUSION

Dans cette suite de recherches à partir de l'analyse du biais d'équilibre, nous nous sommes centré sur l'explication du biais de transitivité de l'amitié. Après avoir montré que le schème d'équivalence formelle est responsable de ce biais, nous nous sommes arrêté sur cette thèse : amitié et égalité ne vont pas ensemble en général, mais essentiellement dans la représentation du groupe égalitaire et fraternel.

Cette représentation se projette, suivant les cas, dans la totalité de la structure sous étude, ou dans plusieurs sous-structures de cette structure. Bien que ce ne soit pas notre problème ici, on doit évoquer la représentation d'une société multigroupale dont chaque segment, suffisamment homogène, permet le jeu de l'image du groupe égalitaire. L'analyse de Poitou suggère que ces segments se définissent par rapport aux antagonismes de classes. Il apparaît que ces antagonismes jouent un grand rôle, mais peut-être plus en proposant aux sujets un modèle commun de segmentation. D'autres segmentations peuvent n'être prégnantes que pour une partie des sujets.

L'étude de ces représentations multigroupales reste à faire.

BIBLIOGRAPHIE

Aloisio, R. Image des relations amicales dans une entreprise hiérarchisée, Mémoire de maîtrise, Université de Provence, 1970.

Audierne, J.F. Nature et place du biais d'équilibre dans les représentations de structures sociales, Mémoire de maîtrise, Université de Provence, 1973.

Bullinger, A. Comparaison, mesure et transitivité. Archives de Psychologie, Monographie n° 1, 1973.

Davis, J.A. Clustering and structural balance in graphs. Human Relations, 1967, 20, 181-187.

Durkheim, E. De la division du travail social. Paris : P.U.F., 1967.

Durkheim, E. Leçons de sociologie : Physique des moeurs et du droit. Paris : P.U.F., 1950.

Flament, C. Théories in structural balance. In Algebraïc models in psychologie, Leiden, University of Leiden, 1968.

Flament, C. Equilibre d'un graphe : quelques résultats algébriques, Mathématiques et Sciences Humaines, 1970, 8, 5-10.

Flament, C. Image des relations amicales dans des groupes hiérarchisés, Année Psychologique, 1971, 71, 117-125.

Flament, C. Independent generalizations of balance. Paper presented at the Advanced Research Symposium on Social Networks, Dartmouth, 1975.

Flament, C. et Bullinger, A. Représentation de l'amitié et équivalence formelle, Bulletin de Psychologie, 1977, 30, 198-205.

Flament, C. et Monnier, C. Schèmes d'équilibre et de congruence dans la représentation de structures sociales multirelationnelles, Archives de Psychologie, 1971a, 41, 71-88.
Flament, C. et Monnier, C. Rapports entre amitié et hiérarchie dans la représentation de groupe, Cahiers de Psychologie, 1971b, 14, 209-218.
Harary, F. On the notion of balance of a signed graph, Michigan Mathematical Journal, 1953, 2, 143-146.
Heider, F. Attitude and cognitive organization, Journal of Psychology, 1946, 21, 107-112.
Heider, F. On balance and attribution. Paper presented at the Advanced Research Symposium on Social Networks, Dartmouth, 1975.
Leonard, F. Un modèle du sujet : l'équilibre de Heider. In S. Moscovici (Ed.), Introduction à la psychologie sociale, tome 1, Paris : Larousse, 1972.
Pichevin, M.F. et Poitou, J.P. Le "biais d'équilibre" : un exemple de consigne implicite, Cahiers de Psychologie, 1974, 17, 111-118.
Pichevin, M.F. et Rossignol, C. Représentation du groupe, structure du sujet et équilibre structural, Bulletin de Psychologie, 1976, 29, 724-734.
Poitou, J.P. La dynamique des groupes, une idéologie au travail. Marseille-Paris : Ed. C.N.R.S., 1978. Traduction anglaise : Group dynamics : an ideology at work. London : Academic Press (à paraître).
Rossignol, C. et Flament, C. Décomposition de l'équilibre structural : aspects de la représentation du groupe, Année Psychologique, 1975, 75, 417-425.
Rossignol, C. et Houel, C. Analyse des composantes imaginaires de la représentation du groupe, Cahiers de Psychologie, 1976, 19, 55-69.
Zajonc, R.B. Cognitive theories in social psychology. In G. Lindzey and Aronson, E. (Eds.), Handbook of social psychology, Readings (Mass.) : Addison Wesley, 1968.

IMPLICATIONS DES THEORIES IMPLICITES DE PERSONNALITE POUR
LE DIAGNOSTIC PSYCHOLOGIQUE

J.P. Leyens

Université de Louvain
Louvain-la-Neuve - Belgique

Comme si cela faisait partie intégrante de la définition
de leur profession, la plupart des psychologues se veulent non
seulement des agents de changement, mais surtout des agents
de changement social. Même si cette volonté n'est pas toujours
prise au sérieux par une frange du public qui considère la psychologie comme un objet de consommation de luxe sans véritable
impact sur la société, il n'empêche que l'on peut trouver des
institutions qui la prennent au pied de la lettre. C'est ainsi
que certains régimes politiques ont interdit le rang universitaire aux études de Psychologie : ce fut le cas au Portugal avant le
25 avril 1974, et ce l'eût été encore récemment dans un pays
scandinave si les électeurs avaient suivi les propositions d'un
candidat politique d'extrême droite. De même, certains ordres
religieux empêchent leurs prêtres et séminaristes d'entreprendre
les études de psychologie parce que, à tort ou à raison, celles-ci risquent d'ébranler l'orthodoxie instituée.

Les psychologues se veulent et se prétendent donc des agents
de changement social. Loin de vouloir nier ce désir auquel j'adhère d'ailleurs pleinement, je voudrais montrer que certaines de
nos habitudes de travail les plus ancrées, parfois élevées au rang
de théories, contrecarrent radicalement cette volonté. Sans doute
n'est-il pas original de constater que les travaux des psychologues respectent en général l'idéologie dominante, c'est-à-dire
l'ordre établi ? De nombreux auteurs ont dénoncé ce fait qui est
particulièrement évident dans le cas de l'orientation scolaire
lorsqu'on s'aperçoit que les conseils des psychologues ne font
qu'accentuer les différences de classes socio-économiques

existantes (Billiet & Nizet, 1974). Il n'y a pas longtemps encore, mais dans un autre domaine, Moscovici (1979) a fustigé le biais envers le conformisme dans les études sur l'influence sociale : tout se passerait pour le psychologue comme si l'idéal humain correspondait à une sujétion de l'individu aux normes actuelles, intangibles, sacrées, de la société.

1. LES THEORIES IMPLICITES DE PERSONNALITE

Une chose est de constater ces faits, une autre est de les expliquer; c'est pourtant cette dernière gageure que nous voudrions entreprendre. Sans du tout vouloir prétendre à l'exhaustivité, nous préférons aborder ce problème par une voie que nous estimons heuristique : celle des théories implicites de personnalité. L'expression : "théories, implicites ou naïves, de personnalité" a été créée, il y a plus de 20 ans, par Bruner et Tagiuri (1954) dans le cadre des études de perception sociale [1]. Jusqu'il y a peu, cette création ne devait guère avoir de retentissement. Ce n'est que tout récemment qu'elle s'est imposée à l'attention des psychologues sociaux. J'entrevois deux raisons à cet intérêt subit pour un concept presqu'oublié. D'une part, il y a eu l'explosion de la psychologie cognitive et son rapprochement avec la psychologie sociale, dans le chef notamment des théories de l'attribution. D'autre part, la notion de personnalité a été attaquée de façon tellement vigoureuse par Mischel (1968) qu'elle a failli en perdre son statut scientifique au profit d'une construction mythique, "implicite" à la plupart des gens.

Mais que faut-il entendre par cette expression : "théories implicites de personnalité" ? Tout d'abord le fait qu'à partir de la connaissance de certains traits de personnalité, ou de certaines caractéristiques physiques, nous inférons aussitôt d'autres traits de personnalité; d'une personne qualifiée d'intelligente et chaleureuse, nous dirons immédiatement qu'elle est généreuse; d'une autre, que nous jugeons jolie, nous ajouterons qu'elle est également d'humeur agréable. Tout se passe comme si nous transportions en nous une matrice de corrélations entre traits qui nous serait disponible à volonté. Les théories

---

[1] Employé par ces auteurs pour rendre compte des inexactitudes de perception sociale, le concept était dans l'air du temps (cfr. Schneider, 1973).

implicites de personnalité se réfèrent également à ces croyances
générales que nous entretenons à propos du genre humain; pour
compléter l'image du statisticien profane, commencée avec la
matrice de corrélations, on pourrait dire que chacun de nous a
une idée bien précise de la moyenne et de la variabilité de certaines caractéristiques humaines que l'on peut rencontrer. S'ils
ont tellement insisté sur le conformisme, sans doute est-ce parce
que les chercheurs partageaient l'idée que le membre idéal d'un
groupe était celui qui épousait toutes ses normes et valeurs.
Si les psychologues scolaires orientent les enfants de milieux
peu privilégiés vers des études professionnelles plutôt qu'universitaires, c'est probablement parce qu'ils estiment que dans
ces milieux, l'intelligence abstraite et la motivation envers
les études théoriques sont peu fréquentes.

Si nous voulons fonctionner avec rapidité, économie et sou-
plesse, le recours aux théories implicites de personnalité est
inévitable, si pas indispensable. En effet, notre environnement
est à ce point riche en informations, et notre capacité à traiter
indépendamment chacune de ces informations à ce point limitée,
que nous devons avoir recours à des systèmes de classification
stables et signifiants. Lorsque nous interagissons avec quelqu'un
qui effectue un comportement déterminé, il serait aberrant de notre
part de vouloir tester toutes les hypothèses susceptibles d'expliquer ce comportement : nous n'aurions plus d'interlocuteur.
Il est souvent tout aussi aberrant de n'avoir aucune hypothèse.
C'est à ce niveau que les théories implicites nous sont d'une
aide inestimable : elles constituent des grilles de lecture facilement accessibles de la personne et du comportement d'autrui
autant que de nous-mêmes.

Si le recours aux théories implicites de personnalité (TIP)
présente des avantages évidents, il comporte aussi des risques
d'erreurs. D'une part, les TIP assurent ordre, stabilité et significations dans nos interactions, et donc efficacité, prévision
et contrôle, mais, d'autre part, elles peuvent aussi être erron-
nées et ne pas du tout correspondre à la réalité. Dans ce cas,
elles sont extrêmement pernicieuses, dans la mesure où nous avons
une foi presque totale en elles, que nous n'estimons pas pouvoir
nous tromper et que nous plions dès lors la réalité à nos désirs
jusqu'au moment où elle correspond effectivement à ces désirs et
donc qu'elle valide nos théories implicites. En d'autres mots,
nous nous arrangeons toujours pour que nos théories implicites
de personnalité soient vérifiées, ce qui ne veut pas dire que
cette stratégie soit consciente, ou même inconsciente au sens
psychanalytique.

Dans ce chapitre, c'est sur l'aspect erroné des TIP que nous voudrions plus particulièrement insister, notamment lorsqu'elles sont employées par des psychologues. Avant d'aborder mon raisonnement, cependant, je voudrais rappeler une démonstration admirable, et devenue classique, de l'existence de TIP chez les psychologues professionnels comme chez les non-psychologues : il s'agit des recherches de Loren et Jean Chapman (1967) concernant l'illusion de corrélation. Ces recherches nous serviront ultérieurement pour souligner certaines conséquences de l'emploi de TIP erronées par les psychologues. De quoi s'agit-il ?

Selon Machover (1949), l'inventeur du test du "dessin d'une personne", il serait possible de déterminer la personnalité du dessinateur d'après les caractéristiques de son dessin d'un personnage quelconque. Or, ce test est absolument dépourvu de valeur diagnostique : plusieurs revues de la question sont unanimes à ce propos. Comment expliquer dès lors que l'on fasse encore tellement appel à ce test et que les utilisateurs soient d'accord pour attribuer certaines caractéristiques du dessin à des troubles déterminés de la personnalité ?

Les Chapman ont envoyé à des spécialistes de renom, utilisant le test du dessin d'une personne, des questionnaires leur demandant les caractéristiques des dessins de personnes présentant des symptômes particuliers; par exemple, un homme préoccupé de sa masculinité ou de son intelligence, ou encore un autre qui est soupçonneux à l'égard des gens, etc. Les réponses envoyées indiquent un très grand consensus. C'est ainsi que le dessin d'un homme préoccupé par sa masculinité se caractériserait par une musculature développée et de larges épaules; celui de quelqu'un ayant des problèmes au niveau de l'intelligence aurait une grosse tête; celui d'un soupçonneux montrerait des particularités au niveau des yeux ou des oreilles, etc.

En possession de ces données de spécialistes, Chapman et Chapman ont voulu voir comment réagiraient des gens n'ayant aucune expérience du test. Pour ce faire, ils ont choisi des étudiants à qui ils ont montré une série de dessins. Chaque dessin était prétendûment l'oeuvre d'un homme présentant 2 symptômes inscrits dans un coin de la page. Il y avait en tout 6 symptômes, les mêmes que ceux qui figuraient sur les questionnaires envoyés aux experts : 1. Préoccupation au niveau de la masculinité; 2. au niveau de l'intelligence; 3. problème d'impuissance sexuelle; 4. préoccupation du fait d'être bien nourri et soigné; 5. du fait que les autres disent du mal de sa personne; 6. et suspicion généralisée. Le point important à noter ici est que les symptômes avaient été appariés aux dessins de telle façon qu'il y avait une absence totale de corrélation entre un symptôme donné et un type particulier de dessin, caractéristique de ce symptôme selon l'avis des spécialistes.

Après que les étudiants eurent examiné tous les dessins, les Chapman leur demandèrent comment se caractérisaient ceux de personnes ayant, chacune, un des six symptômes en question. Puisque, par construction expérimentale, il n'y avait aucune relation entre les dessins et les symptômes, le consensus des sujets aurait dû être inexistant, et ce d'autant plus que ces sujets étaient inexpérimentés par rapport à la pratique d'un tel test. Ce fut loin d'être le cas : le degré d'accord fut très élevé et il reproduisit presqu'exactement l'avis des experts.

On se trouve donc ici devant une illusion de corrélation. Comment l'expliquer ? Peut-être les étudiants, tout comme les experts d'ailleurs, sont-ils victimes de la force associative entre un symptôme et une caractéristique de dessin ? En effet, dans la vie courante, pour ne prendre qu'un exemple, nous avons souvent tendance à associer la masculinité à une musculature développée. Pour vérifier la plausibilité de cette hypothèse, les Chapman ont demandé à d'autres étudiants de donner, en l'absence de tout dessin, les caractéristiques qui seraient, selon eux, associées à divers symptômes particuliers. Les résultats furent spectaculaires. Non seulement le consensus des étudiants fut extraordinairement élevé mais il correspondait à celui des sujets qui avaient pu manipuler des protocoles.

A des fins de démonstration, j'ai moi-même refait cette expérience avec toutes sortes de populations : des psychologues professionnels, des étudiants de psychologie et de criminologie, des non-psychologues, etc. Toujours, les résultats ont été identiques [2]).

---

2) Les Chapman (1969) ont également travaillé avec un test autre que celui de Machover, à savoir le Rorschach. A l'inverse du précédent, celui-ci donne lieu à certaines réponses qui sont des indicateurs valides d'une symptomatologie particulière. En ce qui concerne les tendances homosexuelles, par exemple, certains signes se sont révélés avoir une valeur diagnostique : il s'agit de réponses mi-animales, mi-bêtes, ou monstres à la carte 4, et de réponses animal humanisé à la carte 5. Ces signes valides ne sont cependant pas les plus populaires, aussi bien chez les prétendus experts, que chez des personnes absolument étrangères à la

Nous reviendrons plus tard sur la suite qui a été donnée à ces recherches. Contentons-nous, pour l'instant, de noter la force de certaines TIP et d'imaginer leurs conséquences éventuelles lorsqu'elles sont employées par des experts en psychologie, auréolés de prestige, qui sont confrontés non plus aux dessins de personnes hypothétiques mais à ceux de leurs clients.

2. L'ERREUR FONDAMENTALE

Puisque, pour interagir "valablement", nous avons besoin de croire que notre univers est doté d'une structure stable de significations, il n'est pas étonnant que les chercheurs qui s'intéressaient aux causes que nous attribuons à un comportement donné, l'aient fait en termes dichotomiques : stable-instable, ou en d'autres termes : dispositionnel-situationnel. En effet, si les comportements dépendent uniquement des circonstances, ils varieront comme celles-ci, girouettes apparentes qui tournent avec un vent imprévisible; par contre, s'ils sont déterminés par des dispositions, immuables par définition, ils seront également stables, et donc aisés à prédire. Il se fait aussi que beaucoup d'études ont démontré que les observateurs d'un acte d'autrui avaient tendance à l'interpréter en termes dispositionnels plutôt que situationnels alors que tous les indices sont pourtant présents pour l'attribuer aux circonstances. Il s'agirait là d'une erreur à ce point fréquente que Ross (1977) l'a dénommée : erreur fondamentale 3).

Les premières démonstrations de cette erreur fondamentale reviennent à l'école de Jones (1979). Imaginez la situation suivante : on demande à des étudiants américains - dont on sait par ailleurs qu'ils sont opposés au régime de Fidel Castro - de juger l'obédience castriste d'un autre sujet d'après la dissertation qu'il vient de rédiger à propos du régime cubain actuel.

---

pratique du Rorschach; les uns comme les autres accordent plus de foi à des signes non valides, mais populaires parce que généralement associés avec l'idée d'homosexualité (par exemple : confusion de sexe ou sexe incertain) qu'aux signes valides, mais non-populaires. Encore une fois, l'illusion se rencontre chez des experts tout comme chez des étudiants naïfs à qui on a donné un matériel manifestant une absence de corrélation ou même une corrélation inverse.

3) Nous ne sommes pas d'accord avec Harvey, Town et Yarkin (1981) qui n'y voient qu'un biais. Contrairement à ces auteurs, il nous semble que suffisamment de recherches ont été accumulées

Selon les conditions expérimentales, les étudiants sont avertis qu'ils liront un essai en faveur ou en défaveur de Castro et que l'orientation de celui-ci reflète les vues de l'auteur ou, au contraire, qu'elle a été imposée par l'expérimentateur. Puisque tous les étudiants croyaient que le reste de l'Amérique était également contre Castro, il n'y a rien d'étonnant à ce qu'ils jugent les dissertations anti-castristes - c'est-à-dire en faveur du consensus général- comme réellement anti-castristes, que celles-ci aient été spontanées ou non. Il n'y a rien de surprenant non plus à ce qu'ils considèrent un essai spontanément rédigé en faveur de Castro - donc en dehors des normes habituelles - comme reflétant effectivement un penchant pro-castriste. Ce qui est beaucoup plus curieux pour des gens qui croient que tout le monde adopte leur point de vue anti-Castro est le fait qu'ils jugent une dissertation favorable à Castro, mais imposée par l'expérimentateur, comme traduisant l'orientation véritable de son auteur. Dans cette dernière condition expérimentale, les sujets négligeaient donc les facteurs circonstanciels. Confrontés à ce résultat inattendu d'après la théorie (Jones et Davis, 1965), les auteurs se demandèrent s'il ne s'agissait pas d'un artefact de procédure. En effet, le hasard faisant bien - ou mal - les choses, la dissertation obligatoirement anti-castriste pouvait être à ce point bien rédigée et convaincante qu'elle aurait pu ne provenir que d'un adepte du régime cubain. Dans les expériences ultérieures on essaya donc de corriger la chose : le temps évoluant de même que les opinions vis-à-vis de Castro, les chercheurs américains choisirent d'autres thèmes à propos desquels ils étaient sûrs de connaître l'avis général des étudiants; c'est ainsi que l'auteur présumé qui avait été obligé de disserter contre l'emploi de marijuana ne faisait, soi-disant, que reproduire des arguments qui lui avaient été dictés par l'expérimentateur. Malgré cette insistance sur les facteurs situationnels, les sujets estimaient qu'il devait y avoir une disposition, une caractéristique dispositionnelle explicative, chez l'auteur de la dissertation.

Les études de l'équipe de Jones ne constituent qu'<u>une</u> illustration de cette erreur fondamentale qui nous fait oublier la situation au profit de la personnalité. Il en existe bien d'autres, utilisant des paradigmes différents, qui montrent la même négligence (cfr. notamment Ross, 1977).

---

pour montrer que le biais en faveur des dispositions peut constituer également une erreur.

Mes questions sont dès lors les suivantes :

a. Les psychologues, plus que d'autres, manifestent-ils un biais en faveur d'une explication en termes de personnalité ? De par leur profession, n'ont-ils pas davantage tendance à recourir à des explications en termes dispositionnels plutôt que situationnels ?
b. En deuxième lieu, pour autant que les psychologues manifestent cette tendance, s'agit-il nécessairement d'une erreur ? Somme toute, dans le cadre particulier de leur profession, les psychologues pourraient avoir raison d'utiliser de manière préférentielle, des explications en termes de personnalité.
c. Enfin, qu'il s'agisse ou non d'une erreur, s'il y a une tendance définie, quelles en sont ses conséquences ? A-t-elle seulement des conséquences particulières ?

3. POURQUOI LES PSYCHOLOGUES SONT DAVANTAGE SENSIBLES A LA PERSONNALITE ?

Il y a plusieurs raisons qui nous font croire que des explications personnelles seront plus fréquentes en psychologie que dans d'autres types de profession.

a. Différence entre acteur et observateur

De par la nature de sa profession, lorsqu'il est à l'écoute de son client, le psychologue est sans doute davantage dans le rôle d'un observateur que d'un acteur, pour reprendre les termes d'une dichotomie maintenant classique dans les théories de l'attribution. Or, lorsqu'il s'agit de faire des inférences concernant son propre comportement ou celui d'autrui, l'acteur et l'observateur ne disposent pas de la même quantité d'informations et ils ne traitent pas une même information de manière identique. L'acteur sait l'effort qu'il investit, connaît sa conduite antérieure et il est éventuellement conscient de l'effet qu'il veut produire auprès des gens; ce n'est pas toujours le cas de l'observateur. D'autre part, ce qui est important aux yeux de l'acteur ne l'est pas nécessairement à ceux de l'observateur : l'acteur fera donc surtout attention à l'environnement, à la situation, tandis que l'observateur concentrera son intérêt sur le comportement de l'acteur. A cette différence quantitative d'informations s'ajoute un traitement différent de l'information : acteur et observateur assimilent l'information de leur point de vue propre, et ce d'autant plus que l'information disponible n'a pas la même pertinence pour les deux. L'acteur est davantage enclin à utiliser une échelle de référence idiosynchrasique : l'action est jugée par rapport à d'autres actions qu'il a lui-même effectuées dans le passé et non par rapport aux actes d'autres personnes. D'un autre côté, l'observateur est, quant à lui, normatif, nomothétique : il compare l'acteur avec d'autres et lui-même, et cette comparaison l'amène à faire des attributions concernant cet acteur. Jones et Nisbett (1972), les auteurs à l'origine de cette thèse, ont donc émis l'hypothèse que l'acteur, plus que l'observateur, sera porté à donner des attributions situationnelles et qu'inversément, l'observateur, plus que l'acteur, donnera des attributions dispositionnelles. Depuis lors, de nombreuses démonstrations expérimentales sont venues vérifier cette hypothèse. Il s'ensuit que si l'on accepte l'idée que les psychologues occupent davantage un rôle d'observateur que d'acteur, ils devraient privilégier les attributions de personnalité, de disposition, au détriment des attributions de situation, de circonstances. Il existe encore d'autres raisons susceptibles de rendre compte de cette tendance préférentielle.

b. Les conceptions théoriques du psychologue

De tous temps, l'humanité a été divisée en quelques traits de personnalité et il est étonnant de prendre connaissance du consensus diachronique qui a toujours régné à ce propos. Eysenck en est fier : son modèle est une amélioration de ceux imaginés par Hippocrate, Galien, Kant et Wundt; en d'autres mots, cela signifie que sous d'autres étiquettes et avec, bien sûr, une explication différente, son modèle reproduit à quelques nuances près celui qu'avait établi Hippocrate 24 siècles avant lui. Consistance de la personnalité et/ou excellentes observations de nos ancêtres ? Faut-il se réjouir de ce que les outils sophistiqués - notamment l'analyse factorielle - de Eysenck ait permis d'accorder un statut scientifique à quelques intuitions fulgurantes ?

La réponse est importante parce que, qu'ils le veuillent ou non, et sans nécessairement le savoir, tous les psychologues sont d'accord, au niveau descriptif, avec le système d'Eysenck. Il n'y a pas que les psychologues d'ailleurs : à peu près n'importe qui peut reproduire ce système ainsi qu'en témoigne une série de recherches extrêmement intéressantes menées par Gün Semin et ses collaborateurs.

Dans l'étude de Semin, Rosch et Krolage (sous presse), 33 sujets, non psychologues, devaient juger la similitude de signification existant entre 31 traits de personnalité. Ces traits étaient en fait repris au modèle proposé par Eysenck pour rendre compte de la compatibilité de sa solution avec les modèles proposés par Galien, Kant et Wundt; ces traits se répartissaient en quadrants de tempérament : mélancolique, colérique, sanguin et flegmatique. La représentation à laquelle aboutirent les sujets est extraordinairement proche du modèle théorique 4).

A 78 autres étudiants, non familiers avec la psychologie, Semin, Rosch et Chassein (1981) ont demandé d'énumérer des comportements caractéristiques soit d'une personne extravertie, soit d'une personne introvertie. Ils arrivèrent ainsi à une liste de 58 comportements seulement et une vingtaine d'étudiants aurait suffi tant l'information qu'ils donnaient était stéréotypée. 40 étudiants, toujours étrangers à la psychologie, durent alors juger dans quelle mesure chacun de ces 58 comportements était typique soit de l'extraversion, soit de l'introversion. Les 12 items les plus caractéristiques de chaque catégorie servirent à établir un questionnaire qui fut donné à remplir à 33 autres étudiants, sans connaissances particulières en psychologie. Les mêmes étudiants répondirent à une des formes du questionnaire classique d'extraversion-introversion mis au point par Eysenck. La corrélation entre les résultats des deux questionnaires est .51 et elle est significative à .001.

Cela veut-il dire que les théories scientifiques et les instruments de mesure auxquels elles ont donné naissance ne sont que d'ésotériques transpositions de croyances populaires, ou que la psychologie a influencé le public à un point tel qu'il peut reproduire les découvertes scientifiques, ou encore qu'un modèle comme celui d'Eysenck a transcendé la sagesse populaire en lui conférant un statut scientifique ? La réponse est prématurée.

Pour notre propos, il suffit de noter que la structure des traits de personnalité - pas seulement leur existence et leur emploi - est chose acquise par tout le monde... mais les psychologues sont peut-être les seuls à lui accorder un statut scientifique. Pourquoi donc, alors, n'y auraient-ils pas recours de manière privilégiée ?

La psychométrie n'est pas la seule à proposer un modèle "scientifique" de la personnalité. La psychiatrie et la psychanalyse ont fait de même et, avec la société ambiante (par exemple, Moscovici, 1961), les psychologues ont assimilé ces nouveaux

---

4) Comme pour les expériences de Chapman et Chapman (1967), j'ai moi-même reproduit cette expérience lors de cours, à des fins de démonstration. Les résultats sont extrêmement fiables.

modèles qui renforçaient leurs croyances. Des psychiatres, ils ont appris une taxonomie des maladies mentales, une sorte de bestiaire qui leur permet ordre et prédiction. Des psychanalystes, en plus d'une logique à inventer, ils ont appris que le destin d'un homme se résumait à quelques stades de développement sexuel. Toujours, la priorité est donnée à la personnalité, même si les traits font place à des états (par exemple, une névrose obsessionnelle) ou à des camouflages (par exemple, des formations réactionnelles).

c. Accessibilité et fonction des traits de personnalité

Les traits de personnalité abondent dans le langage commun. A ma connaissance, il n'existe aucun comptage de ceux-ci dans la langue française mais la chose a été réalisée pour la langue anglaise. Allport et Odbert (1936) ont trouvé 18.000 termes s'appliquant à la personnalité et plus de 4.000 d'entre-eux renvoient à des traits relativement stables.

Or, différents travaux récents ont montré que l'accessibilité d'un mot détermine en partie son emploi; c'est ainsi que si le mot "hostilité" nous est plus accessible que le terme "gentillesse" nous aurons davantage tendance à l'utiliser pour interpréter un fait ambigu; l'inverse se produira face au même fait si c'est le terme "gentillesse" qui est plus accessible que celui d'"hostilité" (Srull et Wyer, 1980).

Puisque, comme nous venons de le voir, les théories "scientifiques" sur lesquelles s'appuient les pratiques psychologiques reposent essentiellement sur des traits de personnalité, il est raisonnable de faire l'hypothèse que de tels termes seront particulièrement accessibles aux psychologues et donc, qu'ils y auront fréquemment recours dans leurs interprétations de comportements.

Très souvent, la tâche des psychologues, telle que ceux-ci eux-mêmes se la définissent, consiste à se former une impression des gens, à comparer les personnes entre-elles, et à émettre des prédictions concernant leur comportement futur. Dans quelle mesure une tâche ainsi conçue n'induit-elle pas également un biais en faveur d'explications dispositionnelles ? En effet, de par l'existence même des TIP, les traits de personnalité sont insérés dans des réseaux sémantiques associatifs très développés : ils conviennent donc bien pour se former une impression de quelqu'un. De plus, ils sont riches en connotations évaluatives et devraient donc permettre des comparaisons aisées entre différentes personnes. Enfin, puisqu'ils sont relativement stables par définition, on devrait y avoir recours pour faire des projections sur le futur.

Ce raisonnement a été très récemment testé par Hoffman, Mischel et Mazze (1981). Mis au courant des traits de personnalité et des objectifs sous-tendant les comportements d'une personne donnée 5), les sujets qui avaient pour consigne de se forger une impression de cette personne ou de prédire son comportement dans cinq ans, catégorisaient les informations disponibles davantage en termes de personnalité que d'objectifs et ce de manière très significative. L'inverse se produisait pour ceux qui avaient la tâche de mémoriser les informations ou de faire preuve d'empathie envers la personne décrite; une organisation en termes de personnalité détériorait même la mémorisation. De leur côté, Cohen et Ebbesen (1979) ont montré que l'on fait davantage appel aux TIP (ici dans le sens d'un réseau stéréotypé de relations entre traits) lorsqu'on décrit quelqu'un en ayant reçu la directive de s'en faire une impression plutôt que celle de mémoriser l'information, c'est-à-dire les comportements effectués par cette personne.

On le voit, la tâche même du psychologue peut l'amener à favoriser un certain type d'attribution plutôt qu'un autre 6).

---

5) Dans les quelques conditions expérimentales auxquelles je me réfère dans ce résumé, les sujets étaient explicitement mis au courant des buts poursuivis; les traits de personnalité étaient, eux, implicites mais très facilement décelables. Lorsque les buts ne sont pas explicites mais implicites et peu décelables, l'effet se renforce pour les sujets qui travaillent dans une optique "impression" et "prédiction"; les sujets dans la condition "mémorisation", quant à eux, sont à la recherche d'un fil conducteur et le moins qu'on puisse dire est qu'ils ne favorisent pas les traits de personnalité.

6) On laissera de côté ici la question de savoir si, effectivement, les traits de personnalité permettent une formation d'impression ou une prédiction plus efficaces que d'autres critères comme, par exemple, les objectifs poursuivis dans l'accomplissement de certains comportements.

d. Le cadre de travail du psychologue

    Il est très probable qu'un boucher ne partage pas la même conception de la nature humaine qu'un inspecteur des Eaux et Forêts; il en va de même aussi sans doute pour un médecin généraliste et pour un dermatologue. Pourquoi ne serait-ce pas le cas également du psychologue qui travaille habituellement dans un cadre très spécifique ? Il reçoit des clients qui viennent le consulter pour des problèmes dont ils ne situent pas toujours clairement l'origine mais qui ont généralement trait à leur personne, c'est-à-dire leurs études, leur santé mentale, etc. Il rencontre ces personnes dans un lieu fixe, toujours le même; lors de ses entretiens, il suit quelques règles qui varient peu en fonction du client et, s'il fait passer des tests, ceux-ci sont introduits par des instructions standardisées. Notez que je n'ai rien contre la standardisation mais tout cela s'inscrit dans une dualité de rôles inamovibles : d'une part le psychologue-guérisseur, d'autre part la personne qui a des problèmes. En d'autres mots, peut-être paradoxaux, c'est tout l'environnement de travail du psychologue qui va le conduire à considérer ses clients comme des êtres asituationnels, c'est-à-dire comme des traits immuables de personnalité. Sans cette uniformité de l'environnement, le problème serait probablement très différent; que l'on imagine à cet égard le psychologue qui travaillerait comme un assistant social, qui recevrait dans son bureau mais irait également rencontrer la famille, qui discuterait avec les collègues et le supérieur de son client, etc. L'image qu'il aurait de ce dernier serait-elle la même que celle obtenue lorsqu'il reste confiné à son bureau de consultations ?

    Il y a beaucoup de chances que non.

    Ces quatre raisonnements théoriques, basés sur des démonstrations empiriques, sont convergents : davantage que le commun des mortels, les psychologues auraient tendance à privilégier des explications en termes de personnalité. S'agit-il cependant d'une erreur ?

4. S'AGIT-IL D'UNE ERREUR CHEZ LES PSYCHOLOGUES ?

L'étude la plus spectaculaire pour notre propos et, sans doute, la plus controversée (Crown, 1975; Farber, 1975; Millon, 1975; Rosenhan, 1975; Spitzer, 1975; Weiner, 1975) est celle de David Rosenhan (1973). Ce chercheur s'est présenté dans différents hôpitaux psychiatriques et a demandé d'y être admis parce que, disait-il, depuis plusieurs semaines il entendait des voix qui lui parlaient de "vide", de "creux". Plusieurs de ses amis firent la même chose. Au total, douze admissions, dans douze hôpitaux différents, furent demandées. Toutes furent acceptées, onze avec le diagnostic de schizophrénie, et une avec l'étiquette de psychose maniaco-dépressive. Dès qu'ils furent admis dans l'institution, Rosenhan et ses collaborateurs se comportèrent "normalement" dans la mesure où ils insistèrent sur le fait qu'ils n'entendaient plus de voix, qu'ils désiraient quitter l'établissement et que, par ailleurs, ils se conduisaient comme n'importe quel citoyen soucieux des règles en usage dans un cadre déterminé.

Les séjours dans les hôpitaux psychiatriques varièrent suivant les "cas" : en fait, ils s'étalèrent de 7 à 52 jours avec une moyenne de 19. Tous sortaient avec la fiche : schizophrénie (dans 11 cas) ou psychose maniaco-dépressive (un cas) <u>en rémission</u>. En d'autres termes, tous avaient reçu un diagnostic personnel, un stigma, sur base de symptômes incongrus 7), et ce dernier a été maintenu en dépit de l'évidence contraire.

Rosenhan a également montré que tout le monde n'était pas dupe de la supercherie : beaucoup de "vrais" patients exprimèrent leurs suspicions. Voyant les pseudopatients prendre continuellement des notes, ils leur disaient : "Vous n'êtes pas fou. Vous êtes un journaliste ou un professeur. Vous faites une enquête sur l'hôpital". Aux yeux du personnel de l'hôpital, par contre, le même comportement -prendre des notes- était souvent considéré comme pathologique alors que personne ne prit jamais la peine de vérifier ce qui était écrit. Il est vrai que les personnes "saines" évitent le contact avec les "malades mentaux"; ainsi que l'a encore montré Rosenhan, on sera davantage prévenant avec vous si, dans un hôpital, vous êtes à la recherche d'un inter-

---

7) Ce que disaient les "voix", inconnues des pseudopatients mais de même sexe qu'eux, avait été choisi à dessein : "creux", "vide". En effet, il n'existait aucun cas de psychose existentielle dans la littérature psychiatrique.

niste que d'un psychiatre.

Par cette série de petites recherches impressionnistes, Rosenhan met en cause plusieurs choses : la valeur du diagnostic psychiatrique, l'institution psychiatrique, l'utilité et les conséquences d'une étiquette psychiatrique. Les réactions seront vives. Un des critiques (Spitzer, 1975) écrira :"<u>Etre sain dans des places malsaines</u> de Rosenhan est de la pseudoscience présentée comme science. Tout comme ses pseudopatients furent diagnostiqués à la sortie : 'schizophrénie en rémission', un examen attentif des méthodes, des résultats et de la conclusion de cette étude conduit à un diagnostic de 'logique en rémission'" ! Quoi d'étonnant à ce que des acteurs motivés aient pu tromper la vigilance des psychiatres ? D'ailleurs, ces acteurs ne se comportèrent pas comme des personnes normales : une fois admise dans l'institution psychiatrique, plutôt que de faire semblant de prendre ses médicaments et d'attendre qu'on veuille bien reconnaître qu'elle n'a plus de symptômes pathologiques, une personne normale aurait dévoilé sa supercherie et exigé qu'on la libère. Quoi d'étonnant aussi à ce qu'il ait fallu plusieurs jours pour "libérer" les pseudopatients ? Les hallucinations auditives sont intermittentes : ce n'est pas parce qu'elles ne se manifestent pas pendant deux jours qu'elles ne réapparaîtront pas la troisième journée. Pourquoi accuser le fait que les pseudopatients aient été renvoyés avec un diagnostic <u>en rémission</u> ? Etant donné l'extrême rareté de ce diagnostic (<u>tolérant</u>), il est, au contraire, absolument remarquable que les 12 cas en aient bénéficié ! etc.

Chargé d'établir la synthèse des critiques adressées à Rosenhan, Farber (1975) se penche longuement sur la question que Rosenhan (1973, p. 251) avait formulée de la façon suivante : "les caractéristiques saillantes qui conduisent aux diagnostics résident-elles dans les patients eux-mêmes ou dans les environnements et les contextes dans lesquels les observateurs se trouvent ?" Rosenhan donnait lui-même la réponse : les psychiatres croient que ces caractéristiques sont inhérentes aux patients alors qu'elles sont redevables de l'institution dans laquelle ils officient; c'est pourquoi ils ne peuvent différencier des pseudopatients de vrais patients. Donc, les psychiatres commettent l'<u>erreur</u> fondamentale. Farber fait remarquer à ce propos que si la primauté qui est donnée soit à l'environnement soit aux causes intraorganiques est souvent matière de goûts théoriques personnels, il n'y a pas lieu de poser la question sous la forme d'une alternative. Et l'environnement et le concept de personnalité peuvent <u>à priori</u> être utiles pour la compréhension d'un comportement donné dans un cadre déterminé. Seulement, Rosenhan s'y est mal pris pour tester sa question.

> "...le test le plus efficace serait d'introduire des cliniciens dans un service composé paritairement de non-patients et de patients réels, et de leur donner pour tâche de renvoyer environ la moitié des patients du service sur la base de leur apparente normalité. Seules les données comportementales et d'interviews seraient disponibles, et les non-patients seraient contraints de ne pas révéler directement leur pseudo-statut au personnel; à part cela, tous agiraient comme ils le font normalement. Le pourcentage de renvois incorrects servirait à jauger la validité de la thèse" (Millon, 1975, pp.457-548).

Depuis l'étude de Rosenhan, plusieurs expériences de laboratoire, plus modestes sans doute et moins spectaculaires, mais davantage rigoureuses, ont tenté de répondre à la même question.

Dans une recherche publiée en 1975, Batson a demandé à ses sujets d'écouter l'interview de 9 personnes venues demander de l'aide dans un service de consultation pour étudiants. Seules 6 interviews importaient pour les résultats, les trois autres étant simplement destinées à camoufler les manipulations. Chacune des 6 personnes qui venaient demander de l'aide présentait son problème comme étant dû à la situation : non seulement elle n'avait jamais été confrontée avec ce type de problème auparavant (par exemple, difficulté d'étudier) mais la cause invoquée (par exemple, le comportement perturbateur d'un co-locataire) était décrite comme provoquant les mêmes problèmes chez d'autres personnes. Dans la moitié des cas, le consultant était présenté comme hautement crédible; dans l'autre moitié, comme peu crédible (il était manipulateur et peu porté à réfléchir sur sa personne). La seconde variable qui distinguait les interviews avait trait à l'information diagnostique dont disposait prétendûment le centre de consultation : pour deux personnes, on n'avait pas d'autre information que le contenu de l'interview; pour deux personnes, un psychiatre avait suggéré des tendances psychotiques dépressives; pour les deux dernières personnes, enfin, on laissait entendre que le problème pouvait être lié à l'emploi de drogues.

Après l'audition de chaque interview, les sujets devaient noter si le problème était dû à la situation ou à la personne du consultant et proposer une solution d'aide parmi 6 possibles qui variaient sur la dimension : protection de la société (et changement de la personne) - protection de la personne (et changement de la situation).

Ces deux auteurs ont présenté à leurs sujets un enregistrement magnétoscopique de l'interview d'une personne qui, dans la moitié des cas, était présentée comme un candidat pour un travail quelconque et, dans l'autre moitié, comme un "patient" - sans autre qualificatif -. Langer et Abelson avaient soigneusement recruté leurs sujets : tous étaient spécialisés en psychologie ou en psychiatrie mais la moitié d'entre-eux avait suivi une formation psychodynamique alors que l'autre était constituée de thérapeutes behavioristes. La tâche de chacun était de juger le degré d'ajustement émotionnel de l'individu dont ils venaient de voir l'interview. Quels furent les résultats ?

Lorsque le sujet interviewé était un postulant à un travail quelconque, psychodynamiciens et behavioristes s'accordèrent pour dire qu'il était plutôt bien ajusté émotionnellement. Quand le même personnage fut présenté comme "patient", les behavioristes le jugèrent tout aussi bien adapté que lorsqu'il se présentait à un travail; ce ne fut pas du tout le cas des psychodynamiciens: maintenant que cet individu devenait un "patient", il était soudainement considéré comme mal adapté émotionnellement (cfr. fig.2). Alors que l'interview restait identique et que seul changeait le label, celui-ci suffisait à faire basculer une personne saine d'esprit dans le cloaque institutionnel des malades mentaux. En effet, à la suite de Langer et Abelson, un autre chercheur Snyder (1976), a montré que l'étiquette de "patient" entraînait plus d'attributions causales en termes de dispositions que de situations, et que les premières menaient à des diagnostics plus sévères que les dernières.

Personnellement, je considère que les psychodynamiciens 9) de l'expérience de Langer et Abelson sont tombés dans le piège de l'erreur fondamentale quand ils ont jugé le "patient" 10).

---

9) Pour des raisons de simplicité d'exposition, j'ai présenté les deux groupes de sujets comme homogènes. En fait, ce n'était le cas que des behavioristes qui provenaient de la même université. Le groupe des psychodynamiciens, lui, venait de deux universités avec des formations quelque peu différentes : l'une était plus proche de l'orthodoxie psychanalytique que l'autre; c'est elle aussi qui était la plus sensible à l'erreur fondamentale.

10) A moins, bien sûr, de considérer qu'ils se sont trompés en jugeant le candidat au travail et que les behavioristes se sont trompés sur toute la ligne : vis-à-vis du candidat au travail et vis-à-vis du patient. Cette hypothèse me semble bien peu plausible; c'est également l'opinion de Langer et Abelson : la personne

Batson et Marz (1979) ont repris l'examen de cette question avec un plan expérimental plus simple mais une procédure plus réaliste. Ces auteurs ont demandé à des étudiants débutants ainsi qu'à d'autres qui terminaient une spécialisation en psychologie clinique de conduire l'interview de prétendus patients - des comparses dûment préparés à ce rôle - qui, selon les conditions expérimentales, présentaient des problèmes d'origine manifestement situationnelle (voir procédure précédente) ou, au contraire, dispositionnelle (ils avaient déjà connu ce genre de problème auparavant alors que leur entourage n'y était pas sensible). Quelle que fut cette origine, les spécialistes insistèrent davantage que les non-professionnels sur le fait que les problèmes relevaient de la personnalité. A nouveau, toutefois, ce résultat ne signifie pas qu'il s'agit là nécessairement d'une erreur de la part des psychologues professionnels. En effet, si ceux-ci favorisent une explication personnelle, ils sont cependant sensibles à l'impact d'autres facteurs telle que la situation. On se rappellera que certains patients présentaient un problème essentiellement dispositionnel. Dans les deux cas, les professionnels insistèrent sur la personnalité, mais, tout comme les débutants, ils le firent davantage lorsque le problème était manifestement un trouble de personnalité que lorsqu'il était présenté comme la conséquence d'une situation déficiente (cfr. figure 1 et note 8). On pourrait donc être tenté de conclure que les psychologues exagèrent l'importance de la personnalité alors que les non-psychologues surestiment l'impact de l'environnement, des circonstances historiques, de la société dans laquelle ils vivent, ou encore qu'ils se trompent tous les deux !

Dans l'expérience de Batson et Marz (1979), les psychologues entraînés avaient tous été recrutés dans la même faculté. Plus que probablement, ils avaient reçu la même formation et je soupçonne fort celle-ci d'être d'orientation behavioriste, c'est-à-dire très sensible aux facteurs situationnels. Or, les psychologues ne constituent pas une catégorie unique homogène et la propension à l'erreur fondamentale dépendra du système théorique auquel ils souscrivent. Langer et Abelson (1974) ont fourni une admirable démonstration de cette proposition.

---

8) La figure N°1 pourrait faire penser à une interaction entre expérience professionnelle et proposition de changement. Cette interaction n'est cependant pas significative et, pour une autre variable dépendante très semblable, la tendance à l'interaction joue en sens opposé.

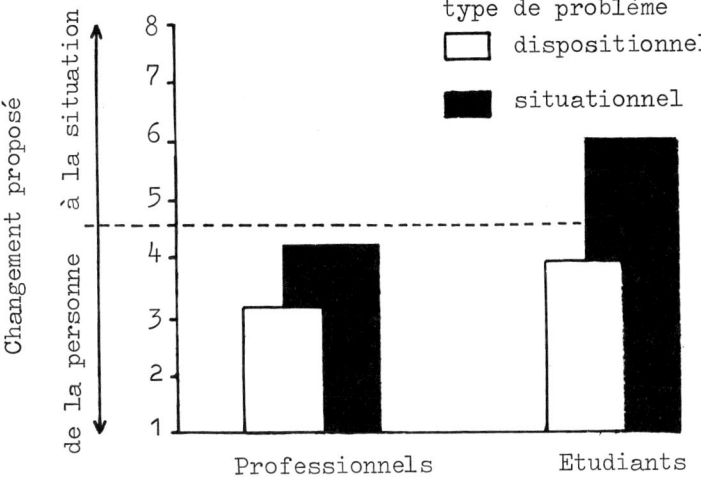

Fig.n° 1 : Mesure selon laquelle les étudiants et les psychologues professionnels proposent un changement de la situation sociale du consultant.

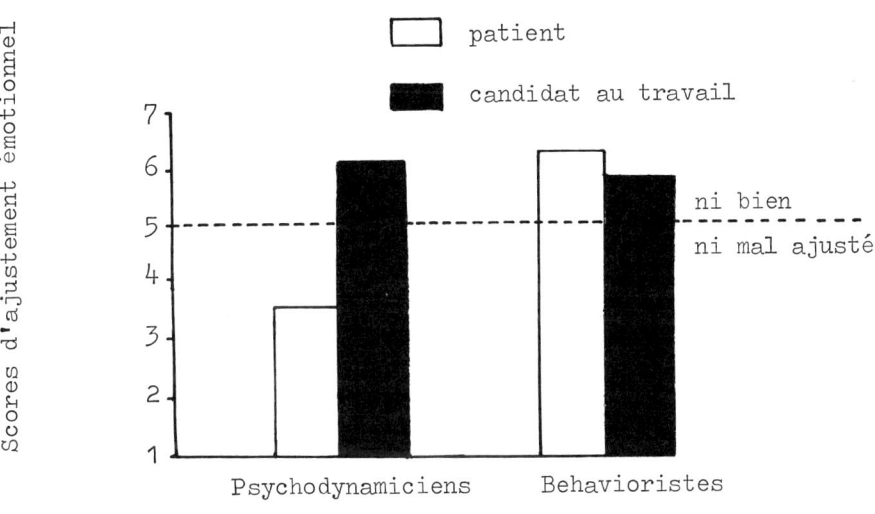

Fig. n° 2 : Scores d'ajustement émotionnel donnés par des psychodynamiciens et des behavioristes à un "patient" ou à un "candidat au travail".

Deux types de sujets ont participé à cette étude. D'une part, de jeunes étudiants universitaires, et d'autre part, des séminaristes ayant déjà une expérience considérable de la relation d'aide. Pour notre propos général, il est amusant de constater que Batson a choisi ce second type de population comme représentant des "aidants professionnels" parce que "le contexte de leur expérience n'était pas de ceux qui les prédisposeraient automatiquement à percevoir les problèmes comme ayant leur origine à l'intérieur de l'individu" ! (p. 458).

Quels sont les résultats ? Alors que chaque consultant présentait très explicitement son problème comme étant dû à la situation, 31 % seulement des sujets lui reconnaissent une telle origine. Comme on pouvait s'y attendre, l'information diagnostique a de l'importance pour l'attribution des causes : 43 % des sujets admettent une cause situationnelle lorsqu'aucune information n'est donnée, contre 26 % dans le cas d'un diagnostic probable de drogue et 24 % dans le cas de tendances psychotiques. Le résultat le plus important pour notre propos immédiat concerne les différences de population des sujets : les "aidants professionnels" sont moins enclins à recourir à une explication situationnelle (23 %) que les "non-professionnels" (40 %); la différence est significative à .05. Ajoutons immédiatement que ces attributions différentielles ont des implications pour la "thérapie" proposée : plus on juge que le problème relève de facteurs personnels, plus on a tendance à orienter le consultant vers des thérapies lourdes (vers un hôpital psychiatrique, par exemple, plutôt que vers un service social) ($r = .57, p < .01$).

Ces résultats signifient-ils que, dans cette expérience, les "aidants professionnels" ont commis une erreur en privilégiant plus que les "non-professionnels" les facteurs dispositionnels ? Pas nécessairement car quel est le critère d'exactitude ? N'est-il pas fréquent que lorsqu'on a un problème personnel à dévoiler, on cherche à se présenter sous le jour le plus favorable et donc, à charger les circonstances (atténuantes !) plutôt que sa propre personne ? Si ce raisonnement fut suivi par les sujets de l'expérience de Batson, on devrait s'attendre à ce qu'ils admettent plus facilement une cause situationnelle chez le consultant hautement crédible que chez celui qui était présenté comme peu crédible; c'est, de fait, le cas (39 % contre 24 %, $p < .02$). Il se pourrait très bien que les "aidants professionnels" aient été davantage que les autres conscients de ce problème et qu'ils aient eu raison par rapport à ce qui se passe dans un véritable centre de consultation.

Lorsque les behavioristes devaient décrire la personne qu'ils avaient vue (candidat au travail ou patient), beaucoup disaient qu'elle était "réaliste", "manquant de tranchant", "plaisante", relativement intelligente", etc. Pour les psychodynamiciens, le candidat au travail apparaissait "sympathique", "d'apparence conventionnelle", "probablement de classe moyenne", etc. Affublé de l'étiquette de "patient", le même individu, de la même interview, devenait "tendu", "défensif","dépendant", "en conflit avec l'homosexualité", "effrayé de ses pulsions agressives", etc.

5. LES CONSEQUENCES DE L'ERREUR FONDAMENTALE CHEZ LES PSYCHOLOGUES

De façon allusive, dans la section précédente, nous avons fait état de la conséquence majeure de l'erreur fondamentale chez les psychologues : la solution thérapeutique envisagée sera plus lourde. Il s'agira de changer son client plutôt que d'intervenir sur la situation perturbante et, ce faisant, de le rendre peut-être inapte à s'adapter à d'autres situations moins inadéquates ! Quand on connaît la puissance de l'effet Pygmalion, cette conséquence est loin d'être innocente.

---

interviewée n'était pas un patient et se montrait capable de s'adapter à l'environnement. Batson et Marz (1979) de même que Millon (1975) sont moins affirmatifs quant à la conclusion d'une erreur fondamentale. Selon eux, la personne interviewée a pu prononcer des phrases qui témoignaient d'un réel mal-ajustement émotionnel... et qui sont passées inaperçues chez le candidat au travail jugé par les psychodynamiciens (selon ce raisonnement, les behavioristes étaient à tout le moins consistants dans leur cécité). En toute rigueur de termes, ils ont raison, mais il n'empêche que la raison invoquée manque d'impact persuasif. Le poids de la démonstration étant en leur défaveur, c'est à eux donc de montrer qu'il n'y avait <u>pas</u> d'erreur fondamentale !

Valins et Nisbett (1972) rapportent le cas d'un patient qui avait demandé une consultation psychologique parce que ses relations sexuelles étaient insatisfaisantes et qu'il avait peur d'être homosexuel : dans la rue son regard se portait automatiquement sur les zones génitales masculines. Il ajoutait qu'il souffrait d'avoir une verge très petite. Dans ce cas, le mérite du thérapeute fut de vouloir vérifier lui-même la prétendue anormalité de la verge : sans être spécialement développée, elle n'était manifestement pas très petite. Et le thérapeute de supposer que l'insatisfaction sexuelle et la hantise de l'homosexualité n'étaient que des épiphénomènes produits par la conviction d'avoir une verge anormalement petite. Il essaya donc de corriger la perception de son client; il lui expliqua les lois d'optique à savoir qu'un objet vu de haut en bas dans un même plan apparaît plus petit qu'en réalité, il le fit s'admirer dans un miroir, etc. Le client s'en retourna persuadé de sa normalité virile et les autres symptômes disparurent en même temps. Manifestement, le thérapeute avait fait, et à bon droit semble-t-il, une attribution personnelle : il y avait erreur d'attribution chez le patient lui-même. On peut cependant imaginer ce que fut devenu ce patient aux mains (!) d'un psychothérapeute convaincu d'une homosexualité latente, refoulée, et que sais-je encore ?

Beaucoup d'études ont comparé l'efficacité thérapeutique de professionnels (psychologues et psychiatres) et de non-professionnels (aides psychiatriques, étudiants, médecins généralistes, bénévoles, etc.). Il en ressort très nettement qu'en cas de supériorité d'un groupe sur l'autre, elle se manifeste chez les paraprofessionnels (Durlak, 1979) ! De multiples raisons sont indubitablement à l'origine de cette différence d'efficacité. Je n'en suggérerai qu'une seule. Dans quelle mesure l'erreur fondamentale, reposant sur l'omnipotence des TIP, n'est-elle pas responsable ? Dans quelle mesure les thérapeutes professionnels n'enferment-ils pas leurs clients dans des catégories a priori et abusives ? Ce faisant, ne déterminent-ils pas eux-mêmes quels sont les vrais problèmes, les souffrances réelles, de leurs clients ? Imposant leur prisme personnel de vision, ils deviennent aveugles à la spécificité de leur interlocuteur et ne peuvent donc être d'une grande aide.

Assurément, au vu des nombreuses ramifications qu'il suggère, le domaine des conséquences de l'erreur fondamentale mériterait de plus amples recherches.

Pour terminer cette section, je voudrais faire remarquer que les conséquences des théories implicites de personnalité ne sont pas le seul fait des thérapeutes. Leurs clients, ou patients, sont également responsables et ceux-ci baignant dans une société déterminée, cette dernière n'est elle-même pas innocente. A la limite, on pourrait dire qu'une société donnée a les clients et les psychologues qu'elle mérite.

Dans plusieurs études récentes, Farina et Fisher corroborent mes affirmations. Leurs recherches, en laboratoire et sur le terrain, montrent que les "patients" se conforment à certaines théories concernant la maladie mentale, théories véhiculées par la société ou induites par le thérapeute. Voici le résumé d'une de leurs études (Fisher et Farina, 1979) qui fut menée sur le terrain.

Dans le cadre d'un cours de psychologie pathologique, deux professeurs enseignent à deux groupes d'étudiants différents leur conception de la maladie mentale; pour l'un, celle-ci doit être considérée comme une maladie organique, plutôt avilissante; elle a sans doute des bases génétiques; le pronostic n'est guère optimiste et le meilleur remède revient à prendre des médicaments. Pour l'autre, la maladie mentale est essentiellement fonction de troubles d'apprentissage; il s'agit donc moins de prendre des médicaments que d'adopter de nouvelles habitudes, d'estimer que l'on peut surmonter soi-même les difficultés, et de changer éventuellement d'environnement.

Les deux cours étant terminés à la fin d'un semestre, Fisher et Farina demandèrent aux étudiants qui les avaient suivis comment ils avaient réagi en face de difficultés diverses. Les résultats sont surprenants dans leur limpidité. Par rapport à ceux qui avaient eu une formation basée sur l'apprentissage social, ceux qui avaient reçu une induction biologique avaient moins envie de chercher de l'aide pour venir à bout de leurs troubles qu'ils considéraient presque comme une maladie organique dont il importe peu de connaître et la cause et la solution. Inversément, les étudiants de l'apprentissage social s'estimaient de meilleurs thérapeutes de leurs propres troubles et avaient donc moins recours à l'alcool et aux drogues pour résoudre leurs problèmes.

Sans doute pourrait-on objecter aux résultats de cette étude qu'ils dépendent essentiellement de la personne des deux enseignants ? L'objection a peu de poids, cependant, étant donné que les mêmes résultats ont été obtenus dans une expérience de laboratoire (Farina, Fisher, Getter, et Fisher, 1978) avec une induction beaucoup moins contraignante.

Ces constatations montrent de façon lumineuse que le public et les psychologues participent à une même dynamique de théories implicites. Ils signalent aussi toute l'attention qu'il faut porter aux conséquences éventuelles de ces théories lorsqu'on veut introduire dans une société donnée une image particulière de la santé ou de la maladie mentale. En effet, une fois cette théorie acceptée, il y a peu de chances qu'elle change, et nous voici prêts à aborder la dernière section de ce chapitre.

6. QUELS REMEDES ENVISAGER ?

Les gens sont très réticents à modifier leurs TIP. C'est une réaction normale étant donné leurs fonctions. Si, vraiment, elles servent à nous mouvoir avec économie dans un monde où elles apportent stabilité, structure et significations, il serait aberrant de les changer constamment. Cependant, de même que la ténacité est une vertu et l'entêtement un défaut, la persistance de certaines TIP peut dépasser le seuil du raisonnable. Beaucoup de personnes préfèrent assimiler les faits à leurs TIP favorites plutôt que d'accommoder celles-ci aux faits.

Au début de ce chapitre, et pour illustrer le concept de TIP, nous avons fait appel aux recherches des Chapman sur l'illusion de corrélation. Ces mêmes études sont suggestives de la difficulté qu'il peut y avoir de changer certaines TIP erronées. En effet, les Chapman et d'autres auteurs à leur suite (par exemple, Golding et Rorer, 1972) ont essayé par toutes sortes de moyens de réduire cette illusion de corrélation : en augmentant la motivation des sujets, en leur laissant tout le temps voulu pour examiner le matériel, en construisant celui-ci de façon à ce qu'existe une corrélation inverse à celle qui est perçue spontanément, etc. Peine perdue : si l'illusion de corrélation diminue dans certains cas, c'est dans une mesure infime.

Le fait que l'illusion de corrélation apparaisse et persiste, indépendamment des conditions, chez des étudiants inexpérimentés, ayant tout loisir de comparer les réponses de plusieurs individus possédant quelques symptômes bien précisés, rend cette persistance d'illusion bien plus plausible encore chez des praticiens qui travaillent dans des conditions moins optimales. Ils partagent un consensus qui ne peut que les renforcer; généralement, ils n'ont pas l'occasion de confronter directement plusieurs protocoles; et les symptômes, qu'ils doivent d'ailleurs trouver eux-mêmes, ne sont absolument pas limités.

Psychologues ou non, nous avons tous à notre disposition un arsenal de stratégies pour maintenir l'existence intacte de nos TIP (cfr. Kassin, 1979; Nisbett et Ross, 1980) : nier l'existence des faits contradictoires, les oublier, les taxer de non-valables, etc. Un haut magistrat belge citait Proust à ce propos dans un procès célèbre et récent : le procès dit Graindorge : "Les faits n'entrent pas dans le monde de nos croyances. Il ne les ont pas fait naître, ils ne les détruiront pas" (Le Soir, 8-12-79). Je n'illustrerai ici qu'une seule de ces stratégies parce que ses conséquences ne s'arrêtent pas au seul maintien des TIP mais font en sorte que ces TIP créent un environnement qui, finalement, les valide : il s'agit du biais en faveur de la confirmation, plutôt que de l'infirmation, qui produit l'effet Pygmalion ou l'auto-réalisation de la prophétie que nous avons déjà plusieurs fois évoquée.

Ce biais, spécialement mis en évidence par la psychologie cognitive, a des implications toutes particulières pour les psychologues qui disposent souvent de peu d'informations concernant la personne qu'ils rencontrent et qui doivent néanmoins prendre à son sujet des décisions importantes.

Snyder et Swann (1978) ont demandé à leurs sujets d'en interviewer un autre afin, disait-on à la moitié, de voir si l'interlocuteur était extraverti ou, disait-on à l'autre moitié, s'il était introverti. Les sujets n'étaient toutefois pas libres de mener l'interview complètement à leur guise en ce sens qu'ils ne pouvaient pas poser de questions autres que celles qui figuraient sur une liste qu'on leur donnait. La composition de cette liste est évidemment capitale pour le reste du déroulement de l'expérience : 1/3 des questions avait trait à l'extraversion (par exemple : "Que faites-vous lorsque vous voulez animer une soirée ?"), 1/3 avait trait à l'introversion (par exemple : "Que n'aimez-vous pas dans les sociétés bruyantes ?") et enfin, le tiers restant était complètement étranger et à l'extraversion et à l'introversion. Ce qui intéressait Snyder et Swann était évidemment de voir le genre de questions que posaient les sujets suivant qu'ils avaient reçu pour instruction de s'assurer de l'extraversion ou de l'introversion de leur interlocuteur. Les résultats sont absolument conformes aux attentes théoriques. Les sujets qui débutaient leur interview avec l'idée de détecter l'extraversion posaient préférentiellement des questions relatives à l'extraversion; à l'opposé, ceux qui étaient orientés vers l'introversion posaient surtout des questions de type introverti. En d'autres termes, les interviewers cherchaient essentiellement à confirmer leur idée de départ, leur théorie implicite 11).

Tous les interviews furent enregistrés et les réponses des interlocuteurs purent être jugées par des observateurs qui n'étaient absolument pas au courant des buts de l'expérience. Leur tâche était de jauger le caractère plus ou moins extraverti ou introverti des réponses. Les résultats sont édifiants : les personnes qui reçurent principalement des questions de type extraverti furent perçues comme davantage extraverties par des observateurs extérieurs, celles qui reçurent des questions de type introverti furent jugées davantage introverties. La prophétie se réalisait : le client-Pygmalion devenait ce qu'avait rêvé de lui au départ son thérapeute ou son psychologue-conseil ! Au vu de ces résultats, nous pouvons paraphraser Proust et le magistrat belge : les faits n'entrent pas dans le monde de nos croyances; ils ne les détruiront pas; <u>elles</u> les engendrent !

On comprendra maintenant l'introduction de ce chapitre : désireux d'un changement social mais prisonniers de TIP erronées, les psychologues sont souvent les apôtres inconscients du statu-quo. Ne considérant que la personnalité, ils occultent les problèmes de société; confondant science et naïveté, ils s'opposent à l'avancement de la science.

Et pourtant, il arrive que nos TIP changent ! Assez curieusement - à première vue du moins car n'est-ce pas normal d'après ce que nous venons de voir -, alors que dans le domaine des attitudes, c'est le changement qui a retenu l'attention des chercheurs, dans celui des TIP, c'est l'optique de la permanence qui a prévalu. Quant à nous, nous terminerons ce chapitre en choisissant un moyen terme : nous nous intéresserons moins aux conditions de changement des TIP qu'aux possibilités d'infléchir l'erreur fondamentale.

---

11) Selon Semin et Strack (1980), les résultats de Snyder et Swann ne sont pas aussi fiables qu'ils le paraissent. Toutefois, au vu de l'évidence empirique accumulée par Snyder (sous presse), il y a peu de doutes que nous ne soyons, en règle générale, enclins à chercher la confirmation plutôt que l'infirmation de nos croyances. Nous-mêmes, dans une expérience-pilote destinée à tester certains facteurs qui entraînent un changement de théorie, nous avons rencontré ce phénomène : les sujets qui croient en l'innocence d'un accusé posent des questions dont la formulation renforce la présomption de non-culpabilité.

a. Le problème de la formation théorique

La prédiction du comportement ne devrait pas se poser en termes dichotomiques, exclusifs : la personnalité ou la situation. C'est pourtant ce que les psychologues ont eu tendance à faire et, dans les pays francophones européens, moins influencés par le behaviorisme, la tendance a toujours été de favoriser la personnalité.

L'expérience de Langer et Abelson (1974) ayant montré que la sensibilité à l'erreur fondamentale dépendait de la formation théorique des psychologues, n'y aurait-il pas lieu de revoir celle-ci, de la rendre plus éclectique et moins dogmatique ? Je pense tout spécialement aux derniers développements que Bandura (1980) a donnés à sa théorie de l'apprentissage social : il insiste sur les déterminations réciproques qui existent entre la situation (stimuli et renforcements) et le sujet (voir notamment sa théorie de l'auto-efficacité, 1977).

b. Le problème des ressources thérapeutiques

Sans que l'on ne puisse distinguer la cause et l'effet, il y a souvent un parallélisme entre les conceptions théoriques en vigueur dans une société donnée et les moyens que celle-ci institutionnalise pour provoquer le changement. Là où la "folie" est considérée comme une tare psychologique, il y aura indubitablement plus d'hôpitaux psychiatriques qu'ailleurs où elle est une marque de l'intervention divine.

Intimement lié à celui des théories en usage et de la formation professionnelle, il y a donc le problème des ressources "thérapeutiques" dont les psychologues et psychiatres disposent ou croient disposer. Si un psychologue estime que les seules solutions thérapeutiques existantes sont orientées vers un changement de la personne, ne sera-t-il pas tout normalement conduit à exagérer l'importance des facteurs dispositionnels dans l'étiologie des troubles de comportement de son client ? C'est en tout cas ce que suggère une ingénieuse étude de Batson, Jones et Cochran (1979).

Leurs sujets étaient des étudiants de psychologie qui devaient fonctionner dans une simulation de consultation psychologique. Ils entendaient les interviews de différents patients qui insistaient sur l'origine situationnelle de leurs problèmes et devaient ensuite répondre à plusieurs questions, la plus importante et la seule à retenir notre attention ici étant de définir l'origine des troubles de chaque client. La seule variable

indépendante était la suivante : la moitié des sujets reçut une
liste de 6 traitements possibles, tous orientés à des degrés
divers vers un changement de la personne pour protéger la société
(par exemple, un hôpital psychiatrique). Le restant reçut une
liste de 6 autres possibilités de traitement, tous plus ou moins
destinés à favoriser une modification de la situation sociale
(par exemple, une action de la communauté). Comme on pouvait
s'y attendre, la simple manipulation des ressources prétendûment
disponibles a infléchi les attributions causales en ce qui concerne l'origine présumée des troubles de chaque patient. Les
sujets qui ont reçu la liste des "thérapies situationnelles"
sont plus nombreux que les autres à reconnaître une cause situationnelle aux problèmes des interviewés (48,2 % contre 34,7 %).
Comparant les résultats de cette étude à ceux d'une expérience similaire (Batson, 1975) pouvant servir de contrôle, les auteurs
remarquent que les deux listes ont influencé les réactions; suivant
celle qu'ils avaient reçue, les sujets étaient plus personnalistes
ou plus situationnistes qu'ils ne l'étaient normalement avec une
liste couvrant tout le spectre des solutions.

c. Le problème de l'empathie

Parmi les raisons susceptibles d'expliquer la propension
qu'ont les psychologues à tomber dans le piège de l'erreur fondamentale, nous avons fait état de la dichotomie entre acteurs
et observateurs. Pour montrer que la différence d'attributions
produites par ces deux rôles n'est pas nécessairement due à une
quantité inégale d'informations mais, parfois, à leur qualité
et leur traitement, des auteurs comme Regan et Totten (1975) ont
montré qu'il suffit de demander à l'observateur de faire preuve
d'empathie envers la personne qu'il juge : sous cette condition,
en effet, il arrivera aux mêmes conclusions que l'acteur, c'est-
à-dire, à des attributions moins dispositionnelles que celles
auxquelles il aurait abouti en tant qu'observateur neutre. La
conclusion du raisonnement est limpide. Si on veut restreindre
l'erreur fondamentale, il faut davantage faire preuve d'empathie
et oublier quelque peu les grandes catégories nosologiques. C'est
également la conclusion de Mischel (1973) qui veut que l'on garde
à chaque client sa spécificité plutôt que de l'enfermer dans les
cases d'une typologie aux prismes déformants.

A des fins de vérification de cette conclusion dans un
cadre clinique, Snyder, Shenkel et Schmidt (1976) ont demandé à
des étudiants d'écouter un extrait de thérapie au cours duquel
la patiente présentait son problème comme étant dû à des facteurs
situationnels. Selon la condition expérimentale, il s'agissait

d'une "malade chronique" ou, au contraire, d'une personne qui se présentait pour la première fois avec un problème psychologique. Les auteurs demandèrent à 1/3 de leurs sujets d'assumer le rôle d'un conseiller psychologique, et à un autre tiers celui de la patiente; le restant des sujets ne reçut aucune instruction spéciale. Comme l'indique le tableau n° 1, les résultats sont très clairs. Les sujets qui adoptent la position du conseiller psy-

Rôle Passé psychiatrique	Client	Conseiller	Contrôle
Chronique	5.07	6.47	6.47
Première	4.33	6.00	4.13

Tableau n° 1. Mesure selon laquelle les différents sujets attribuent la cause du problème à la situation (1) ou à la personnalité (9) (5 = le point neutre où ne dominent ni la situation ni la personnalité).

chologique incriminent plus la personnalité que ceux qui ont pris le rôle du client et les facteurs dispositionnels sont davantage mis en cause en cas de chronicité qu'en cas de première consultation. Les résultats les plus intéressants pour notre propos ont cependant trait à l'interaction entre rôle et passé psychiatrique. Lorsqu'il s'agit d'une patiente chronique, les sujets de contrôle, qui n'ont reçu aucune induction particulière de rôle, s'alignent sur les sujets-conseillers. Quand la patiente n'a pas d'antécédents psychiatriques, au contraire, ils adoptent la démarche des sujets-clients.

Encore une fois, donc, on s'aperçoit de l'importance du facteur empathique. Notons toutefois que rien de ce que nous avons dit ne nous assure de l'exactitude supérieure du diagnostic en cas d'empathie. Cela pourrait très bien être l'inverse et Nisbett et Wilson (1977) ont d'ailleurs démontré que les gens se trompent souvent lorsqu'ils essaient de spécifier les causes déterminantes de leur comportement. Tout ce que ce paragraphe voulait suggérer était que l'empathie, comme un avocat de la défense, amenait à prendre davantage en considération les facteurs situationnels susceptibles d'expliquer des réactions comportementales déterminées.

d. Le problème des taxonomies

A plusieurs reprises dans ce chapitre, nous avons évoqué les taxonomies utilisées par les psychologues et les psychiatres. Ce fut spécialement le cas lors de l'exposé de la recherche de Rosenhan (1973). Cet auteur reprochait d'ailleurs aux institutions psychiatriques d'avoir mal diagnostiqué ses pseudopatients et de leur avoir imposé un stigma pour le restant de leurs jours. Il y a donc ici une double question : 1) psychologues et psychiatres sont-ils en mesure d'employer valablement les taxonomies existantes ?; 2) celles-ci sont-elles suffisamment utiles pour compenser le stigma qu'elles créent ? Les discussions soulevées par ces deux questions ont donné lieu à une littérature tellement vaste qu'il serait vain de vouloir en esquisser ne serait-ce qu'un bref résumé. Nous nous contenterons donc de formuler quelques remarques qui ont un lien direct avec les TIP.

On a souvent reproché aux taxonomies psychologiques d'être vagues et de ne pas permettre un diagnostic valide. Il est vrai que dans la conception classique, les catégories de maladies mentales étaient définies par un ensemble de conditions nécessaires et suffisantes pour que tel individu y figure et pas tel autre. Or, de même que l'hirondelle est davantage un oiseau que n'importe quel gallinacée, il y a des schizophrènes qui sont davantage "schizophrènes" que d'autres. On en vient donc à une vue prototypique (Rosch, 1978) qui rend caduques certaines critiques. Il n'empêche que certains niveaux -ni trop généraux ni trop particularistes- de catégories sont davantage recommandables que d'autres (cfr. Cantor et Mischel, 1979; Cantor, Smith, Trench et Mezzich, 1980). Selon Millon (1975) et Spitzer (1975), ces catégories ont surtout une fonction de communication - entre spécialistes, je suppose - qui peut également avoir des répercussions sur le contrôle de la maladie mentale - c'est-à-dire son traitement-.

Personne ne nie que l'étiquetage en maladie mentale produise un stigma. On en a encore eu la preuve avec l'expérience de Snyder, Shenkel et Schmidt (1976) : les troubles de la malade chronique étaient considérés comme davantage sérieux et dispositionnels. C'est loin d'être une réaction aberrante : Lasky, Hover, Smith, Bostian, Duffendack et Nord (1959) n'ont-ils pas montré que, pour prédire une future réhospitalisation psychiatrique, il vaut mieux se fier au poids du dossier clinique qu'aux données du Rorschach ? De plus, dans quelle mesure dire de quelqu'un qu'il a des "hallucinations auditives" est-il moins stigmatisant que de déclarer cette personne "schizophrène" ?

La question attend une réponse empirique susceptible de varier historiquement et géographiquement.

Ma préférence en ce domaine repose sur l'examen du problème suivant.

e. Le problème des diagnostics nuancés

Nous nous formons très rapidement une impression d'autrui. Les psychologues n'échappent pas à cette règle. Rubin et Shontz (1960) ont montré que les cliniciens se forgent déjà un diagnostic sur la base de données aussi insignifiantes que : âge, sexe, race, religion, état marital, éducation, profession, nombre d'hospitalisation, etc. Et ce diagnostic ne change guère avec l'accumulation d'autres données (voir aussi Sines, 1959). Je crains donc que le recours à une taxonomie quelconque ne constitue un point d'ancrage - ne serait-ce que pour la communication entre spécialistes -, une réification, à partir desquels le psychologue ou le psychiatre ira à la recherche d'une confirmation. Je crains qu'en parlant de tel patient comme d'_un_ schizophrène, on ne le considère plus comme tel schizophrène _ayant_ des caractéristiques bien précises, mais comme _le_ schizophrène prototypique. J'avoue préférer une description en termes de comportements et de contingences de situation dont il faudra souligner _et_ les convergences _et_ les incohérences.

o

o o

J'ai écrit ce chapitre parce qu'à l'Université de Louvain (à Louvain-la-Neuve), j'enseigne la psychologie sociale expérimentale à des étudiants de psychologie qui ne deviendront jamais des psychologues sociaux expérimentaux. A ceux-là, quelle que soit leur pratique ultérieure, il me semble bon de montrer que la psychologie sociale a nécessairement quelque chose à dire et que ce quelque chose peut se révéler intéressant et important, même sous l'apparence d'une provocation.

BIBLIOGRAPHIE

Allport, G.W., Odbert, H.S. Trait names : a psycho-lexical study. Psychological Monographs, 1936, 47.

Bandura, A. Self-efficiency : toward a unifying theory of behavioral change. Psychological Review, 1977, 84, 191-215.

Bandura, A. L'apprentissage social. Bruxelles : Mardaga, 1980.

Batson, C.D. Attribution as a mediator of bias in helping. Journal of Personality and Social Psychology, 1975, 72, 455-466.

Batson, C.D., Jones, C.H., & Cochran, P.J. Attributional bias in counselors' diagnoses : the effect of resources. Journal of Applied Social Psychology, 1979, 9, 377-393.

Batson, C.D., & Marz, B. Dispositional bias in trained therapists' diagnoses : does it exist ? Journal of Applied Social Psychology, 1979, 9, 476-489.

Billiet, C., & Nizet, J. L'égalité des chances ou la grande illusion. Revue Nouvelle, septembre 1974, 145-154.

Bruner, J.S, & Tagiuri, R. Person perception. In G. Lindzey (Ed.) Handbook of social Psychology (Vol. 2) Reading, Mass. : Addison-Wesley, 1954.

Cantor, N., & Mischel, W., Prototypes in person perception. In L. Berkowitz (Ed.), Advances in experimental social Psychology (Vol. 12). New York : Academic Press, 1979.

Cantor, N., Smith, E.E., Trench, R.D., & Mezzich, J. Psychiatric diagnosis as prototype categorization. Journal of Abnormal psychology, 1980, 89, 181-193.

Chapman, L.J., & Chapman, J.P. Genesis of popular but erroneous psychodiagnostic observations. Journal of Abnormal Psychology, 1967, 72, 193-204.

Chapman, L.J., & Chapman, J.P. Illusory correlation as an obstacle to the use of valid psychodiagnostic signs. Journal of Abnormal Psychology, 1969, 74, 271-280.

Cohen, C.E., & Ebbesen, E.B. Observational goals and schema activation : a theoretical framework for behavior perception. Journal of Experimental Social Psychology, 1979, 15, 305-329.

Crown, S. "On being sane in insane places" : a comment from England. Journal of Abnormal Psychology, 1975, 84, 453-455.

Durlak, J.A. Comparative effectiveness of paraprofessional and professional helpers. Psychological Bulletin, 1979, 86, 80-92.

Farber, I.E., Sane and insane : constructions and misconstructions. Journal of Abnormal Psychology, 1975, 84, 589-620.

Farina, A., Fisher, J.D., Getter, H., & Fisher, E.H. Some consequences of changing people's views regarding the nature of mental illness. Journal of Abnormal Psychology, 1978, 87, 272-279.

Fisher, J.D., & Farina, A. Consequences of beliefs about the nature of mental disorders. Journal of Abnormal Psychology, 1979, 88, 320-327.
Golding, S.L., & Rorer, L.G. Illusory correlation and subjective judgment. Journal of Abnormal Psychology, 1972, 80, 249-260.
Harvey, J.H., Town, J.P., & Yarkin, K.L. How fundamental is "the fundamental attribution error" ? Journal of Personality and Social Psychology, 1981, 40, 346-349.
Hoffman, C., Mischel, W., & Mazze, K., The role of purpose in the organization of information about behavior : trait-based versus goal-bases categories in person cognition. Journal of Personality and Social Psychology, 1981, 40, 211-225.
Jones, E.E., The rocky road from acts to disposition. American Psychologist, 1979, 34, 107-117.
Jones, E.E., & Davis, K.E. From acts to dispositions : the attribution process in person perception. In L. Berkowitz (Ed.), Advances in experimental social Psychology, (Vol. 2). New York : Academic Press, 1965.
Jones, E.E., & Nisbett, R.E. The actor and observer : divergent perceptions of the causes of behavior. In E.E. Jones et al. (Eds.), Attribution : perceiving the causes of behavior. Morristown, J.J. : General Learning Press, 1972.
Kassin, S.M. Consensus information, prediction, and causal attribution : a review of the literature and issues. Journal of Personality and Social Psychology, 1979, 37, 1966-1981.
Langer, E.J., & Abelson, R.P. A patient by any other name...; clinician group differences in labeling bias. Journal of Consulting and Clinical Psychology, 1974, 42, 4-9.
Lasky, J.J., Hover, G.L., Smith, P.A., Bostian, D.W., Duffendack, S.C., & Nord, C.L. Post-hospital adjustment as predicted by psychiatric patients and by their staff. Journal of Consulting Psychology, 1959, 23, 213-218.
Machover, K. Personality projection in the drawing of the human figure. Springfield, III. : Charles C. Thomas, 1949.
Millon, T. Reflections on Rosenhan's "On being sane in insane places". Journal of Abnormal Psychology, 1975, 84, 456-461.
Mischel, W. Personality and assessment. New York : Wiley, 1968.
Mischel, W. On the empirical dilemmas of psychodynamic approaches: issues and alternatives. Journal of Abnormal Psychology, 1973, 82, 335-344.
Moscovici, S. La psychanalyse, son image et son public. Paris : P.U.F., 1961.
Moscovici, S. Psychologie des minorités actives. Paris : P.U.F., 1979.
Nisbett, R.E., & Ross, L.D. Human inference : strategies and shortcomings of social judgment. Englewood Cliffs, N.J.: Prentice-Hall, 1980.

Nisbett, R.E., & Wilson, T.D. Telling more than we can know : verbal reports on mental processes. Psychological Review, 1977, 84, 231-259.

Regan, D.T., & Totten, J. Empathy and attribution : turning observers into actors. Journal of Personality and Social Psychology, 1975, 32, 850-856.

Rosch, E. Principles of categorization. In E. Rosch et B.B. Lloyd (Eds.), Cognition and categorization. Potomac, Md : Erlbaum, 1978.

Rosenhan, D.L. On being sane in insane places. Science; 1973, 179, 250-258.

Rosenhan, D.L. The contextual nature of psychiatric diagnosis. Journal of Abnormal Psychology, 1975, 84, 462-474.

Ross, L. The intuitive psychologist and his shortcomings : distortions in the attribution process. In L. Berkowits (Ed.) Advances in experimental social Psychology (Vol. 10). New York : Academic Press, 1977.

Rubin, M., & Shontz, F.C. Diagnostic prototypes and diagnostic processes of clinical psychologists. Journal of Consulting Psychology, 1960, 24, 234-239.

Schneider, D.J. Implicit personality theory : a review. Psychological Bulletin, 1973, 73, 294-309.

Semin, G.R., Rosch, E., & Chassein, J.A. A comparison of the common-sense and "scientific" conceptions of extraversion-introversion. European Journal of Social Psychology, 1981, 11, 77-86.

Semin, G.R., Rosch, E., & Krolage, J. First and second order models of personality. Journal of Experimental Social Psychology, sous presse.

Semin, G.R., & Strack, F. The plausibility of the implausible : a critique of Snyder and Swann (1978). European Journal of Social Psychology, 1980, 10, 379-388.

Sines, L.K. The relative contribution of four kinds of data to accuracy in personality assessment. Journal of Consulting Psychology, 1959, 23, 483-492.

Snyder, C.R. "A patient by any other name" revisited : maladjustment or attributional locus of problems ? Journal of Consulting and Clinical Psychology, 1977, 45, 101-103.

Snyder, C.R., Shenkel, R.J., & Schmidt, A. Effects of role perspective and client psychiatric history on locus of problem. Journal of Consulting and Clinical Psychology, 1976, 44, 467-472.

Snyder, M. Seek, and Ye shall find : testing hypotheses about other people. In E.T. Higgings, C.P. Herman et M.P. Zanna (Eds.), Social Cognition : the Ontario symposium on personality and social psychology. Hillsdale, N.J. : Erlbaum, sous presse.

Snyder, M., & Swann, W.B. Jr. Hypothesis-testing processes in social interaction. *Journal of Personality and social Psychology*, 1978, 36, 1202-1212.

Spitzer, R.L. On pseudoscience in science, logic in remission, and psychiatric diagnosis : A critique of D.L. Rosenhan's "On being sane in insane places". *Journal of Abnormal Psychology*, 1975, 84, 442-452.

Srull, T.K., & Wyer, R.S. Jr. Category accessibility and social perception : some implications for the study of person memory and interpersonal judgments. *Journal of Personality and Social Psychology*, 1980, 38, 841-856.

Valins, S., & Nisbett, R.E. Attribution processes in the development and treatment of emotional disorder. In E.E. Jones et al. (Eds.), *Attribution : perceiving the causes of behavior*. Morristown : General Learning Press, 1972.

Weiner, B. "On being sane in insane places" : a process (attributional) analysis and critique. *Journal of Abnormal Psychology*, 1975, 84, 433-441.

ON BECOMING A PSYCHOLOGIST : A FIELD-STUDY IN ITALY

A. Palmonari

Istituto di Scienze dell'Educazione
Università di Bologna

This paper is a preliminary presentation and discussion of data gathered in the course of research concerning "the work of psychologists in Italy". This study was carried out as part of a broader project aimed at studying the conditions for the prevention of mental illness being sponsored by the Italian National Research Council (C.N.R.).

The objective of our research was to bring together first-hand information and documentary evidence concerning the ways psychologists (both researchers and pratitioners) actually work.

On the basis of this information the Council intends to open a broad-based discussion, as free as possible from any preconceived ideological scheme, about :

- the process of psychologists' professionalization;
- the training initiatives to be undertaken in order to fill the gaps in the present courses of psychological studies;
- the characteristics of the different professional activities of psychologists.

These problems are connected with other more general ones in present day Italian society. The exploratory research we carried out can already, at this stage, supply some useful information about :

- the organizational conditions and the programmes required in order to achieve efficiency and efficacy in new social and mental health services;

- the changes in habits and working procedures of a wide range of professional agents (not only psychologists) necessary in order to offer a satisfactory service in response to recently manifested and unprecedented social needs.

In other words, studying how psychologists' work can help us to gain insight into how doctors, social workers, nurses, managers of personnel, and public servants in state and local administration can best face the new circumstances which have arisen in their work as a consequence of recent social changes.

Our study considered only a limited sample of individuals which are not necessarily a statistical representation of the Italian situation in general, but which, we feel nonetheless, is highly indicative. This sample enables us to compare situations of varying professional standards and outlooks in relation to the formation and practices of three categories of agents working in the field of psychology. These situations are fairly representative of the overall one at a national level. In fact in all the towns which were considered, namely Arezzo, Bologna, Salerno and Trento, there are universities where one or more courses of psychology are taught (though there is not a faculty of psychology); psychologists work in public agencies; and in each case the local social policy towards mental health problems differs from one town to another.

These situations were also chosen because it was easy for our research group to get in touch with psychologists in these towns. Our study was made by conducting in-depth interviews with psychologists, some working in public agencies, others teaching at the University, and yet others who practice as private professional psychotherapists.

In Bologna, where more than two hundred psychologists work only a representative sample was studied. In the other centres all the local psychologists were interviewed.

The taped interviews were transcribed on special protocols and subjected to a content analysis.

In the different issues which emerged from the protocols similarities of outlook arose which did not correlate either with the category to which the psychologist belonged or with the town from which he came. Moreover although the interview itself was presented in such a way as to gather information about how a psychologist actually works, from the initial data we noticed that the responses of the interviewees tended to define ways of being a psychologist in a general sense. In the issues relating to ways of being a psychologist, ideological factors often played a major role in the definitions, which, in some cases, contradicted actual working experiences. This gave rise to various attempts at mediating between what was expressed in principle and what was carried out in practice. Likewise reference was often made to the importance of a specific theory (especially psycho-analysis) in the constitution of the psychologist, the relevance of which, however was rarely carried over into practice; or at least not in its entirety. Even when this was the case there ensued various attempts at trying to bring together what was felt to qualify as a psychologist and what the circumstances required him to do in practice.

As can be gathered from the above we found ourselves in the difficult position of trying to account for such diverse and contradictory material in as comprehensive a way as possible. On the one hand concepts such as "opinions" or "attitudes" are much too restrictive for this kind of data. In fact we not only had information about the opinions, the judgements, and the probable operative choices of each individual interviewed, but also many complex arguments where each point of view was supported and related to other points of view. In some cases these justifications and logical connections differed greatly from one case to another but in others they were very similar, even if the contexts in which the psychologists worked were highly different.

On the other hand, although these arguments were more cogent and logically well organized than simple attitudes or opinions they could hardly qualify as highly elaborated and strictly articulated closed systems of thought as, for example, ideologies and scientific theories.

We thought instead that the multifarious and complex data we had gathered could belong to that "sort of phenomena" which Moscovici(1961), refering to Durkheim, calls "social representations". Social representations are cognitive systems with a language and logic of their own. They are not just opinions or attitudes, but rather; naive theories or branches of knowledge used in the discovery and organization of reality. They are ideas and practices with a double function : firstly to establish an order that enables individuals to orient themselves in their material and social world, and secondly to make communication between members of a community possible, thus giving them a code for social exchange and a code for naming and classifying, in an unambiguous way, the various aspects of their world as well as of their individual and group history.

METHOD

It is useful to describe, step by step, the method we used for the content analysis of our protocols.

Step 1. Intuitive individuation of social representations

We tried to individuate how many social representations of a psychologist's work could be derived from the contents of the interviews. To this end all the protocols of the interviews were read several times by more than one researcher separately.

Thus, four social representations were intuitively individuated, corresponding more or less to four ways of being a psychologist which we labeled as:

    A) the political activist
    B) the interdisciplinary competent
    C) the clinical practitioner
    D) the psycho-therapist

Step 2. Building a grid for the content analysis

After having individuated these four social representations, we proceeded to analyze the thematic content of each interview by building a grid on the basis of the main topics, which emerged from the social representations themselves.

Each topic is divided into several points:

1) the scientific status of psychology
   - Science and social settings
   - Influence of psychology as a science on social life
   - The role of professionals and of the psychologist as a practitioner in social settings.

2) the working activity of psychologists
   - Objectives and strategy of intervention
   - Work programming
   - Working conditions

3) the psychologist's training
   - University education
   - Professional training
   - Supervision and permanent training

4) the professional identity of the psychologist
   - Main motives for being a psychologist
   - Self-definition in professional terms
   - Professional institutions (scientific associations, guild)
   - Fields of intervention (public and private)

Step 3. Classification of the interviews' contents according to the grid.

The contents of each interview were classified by means of the above grid. We obtained several tables, one for each item of the grid. Each table contained all the classified sentences (units of analysis) corresponding to that item. For each unit of analysis, we also took care to specify the interview from which it came. We then marked each sentence to indicate which social representation it could be ascribed to.

Step 4. Verification of the internal consistency of the protocols.

We examined the protocols of the interviews one by one in order to verify whether all the units of the same protocol could fit into the same social representation.

In other words, we wanted to verify if each person interviewed was more or less consistent in expressing his point of view about psychologists' work.

In fact, if the consistency of each interviewed psychologist was low, we would have to conclude that the social representations we thought we had individuated were nothing more than opinions lacking any profound relationship with the social agents expressing them and not representative of a shared category.

How then was this consistency tested ?

Each unit of analysis concerning one point of the grid was evaluated for its consistency in relation to the initially individuated representation. This was carried out by two judges chosen from among the researchers who worked independently one from the other.

When the two judges' evaluations of a unit where in accordance to ascribe it to one of the social representations, the sentence was considered compatible with that category; when they did not agree, the two judges discussed their evaluations in order to find a solution that satisfied both of them. A solution was not always found. In this case a third judge was called in, who after carefully considering the different points of view expressed by his colleagues, solved the problem in one of the two directions.

Not all the units of speech of each interview were entirely compatible with a single social representation, or, at least, it was not clear cut. It was necessary to find a discriminating criterion by which to make each protocol compatible with a single social representation.

The criterion for consistency chosen was that at least two thirds of the units of an interview had to correspond in a clear cut manner to a single representation in order for the protocol to be labeled under that "leading"/"category".

Out of the 113 protocols considered, 95 (that is to say 83,9 %) resulted consistent with one of the four ways of being a psychologist as is shown by the distribution in the following table :

Social representation	INTERVIEWS	
	A.S.	%
A	21	22.2
B	14	14.7
C	31	32.6
D	29	30.5
Total	95	100.0

Table N. 1. Distribution of psychologists in four social representations.

The remaining 18 interviews (16,1 %) show a consistency of about one half of all the units of analysis with one of the representations, and an equal consistency with another of them.

From this in-depth analysis of the protocols, there emerges a very high internal consistency, thus confirming the four social representations which we had individuated at a first reading.

From this high degree of internal consistency we can safely conclude that each representation corresponds to a sharply defined group of psychologists.

The following tables show the distribution of the psychologists in these groups, according to the professional fields they work in (table 2), the degrees with which they graduated (table 3), and their sex (table 4).

PROFESSIONAL FIELDS	A A.S.	A %	B A.S.	B %	C A.S.	C %	D A.S.	D %
SOCIAL SERVICES	17	81	7	50	15	48	2	7
UNIVERSITY	4	19	7	50	11	36	13	45
FREE PROFESSIONALS	/	/	/	/	5	16	14	48
Total	21	100	14	100	31	100	29	100

Table N. 2. Distribution of psychologists according to their professional field.

DEGREE	A A.S.	A %	B A.S.	B %	C A.S.	C %	D A.S.	D %
MEDICINE	/	/	3	21	10	32	16	55
PSYCHOLOGY	10	48	3	21	3	10	2	7
HUMANISTICS	11	52	8	58	18	58	11	38
Total	21	100	14	100	31	100	29	100

Table N.3. Distribution of psychologists according to their last University degree.

SEX	A		B		C		D	
	A.S.	%	A.S.	%	A.S.	%	A.S.	%
MALES	5	24	8	57	11	35	20	69
FEMALES	16	76	6	43	20	65	9	31
Total	21	100	14	100	31	100	29	100

Table N.4. Distribution of psychologists according to sex.

THE SCIENTIFIC STATUS OF PSYCHOLOGY

We will illustrate now some of the main topics which are part of the four representations.

A. Psychology is a science, science is an ideology

- Psychology is a science : science is an ideology because it serves the purposes of the dominant groups.
- Psychology is therefore the superstructure of an ideology it must serve.
- Science cannot affect social reality because every social change proceeds from the structural (and not from the superstructural) level.
- For this reason psychology, as a science, does not contribute to the solution of practical problems, but on the contrary it hides real problems.

Those who practice psychology create the conditions for "the oppressed" to submit to the present situation as it is. In these conditions what is the sense of carrying on working as a psychologist ? The psychologists who agree with this description do not answer the above question. Rather they state that they do not want to gain any technical competence(neither on the level of social work, nor on the level of teaching), because it creates an imbalance of power leading to the manipulation of people. The refusal to adopt such techniques represents a sort of warrant of their being on the side of the oppressed.

B. Psychology is a social science

- It is a social science because it uses scientific methods and techniques for the knowledge and analysis of social phenomena.
- The analysis of reality allows for the possibility of proposing changes. This is how psychology can affect social reality.
- The psychologist is competent in specific professional fields complementary to those of other social scientists.

But how can knowledge alone modify social reality ? The answer to this question, or at least a partial one, can be derived from a discussion about the psychologist's work.

C. Psychology is a science of the individual

This statement is based on the argument that psychology has a scientific method for obtaining knowledge about or from the individual.

- Thinking that it is possible to affect social reality is utopia. On this point the contrast between model B and C is very deep : according to C, you cannot say anything about the social world, but only about the individual.
- Scientific knowledge is a basis for the modification of what is particular, but not of the whole, the 'social'. (While in B 'social' means 'complex reality', in C it means 'abstract reality').

D. Psychology is a science of the single case

- Psychology uses a scientific method to obtain knowledge of the internal dynamics of an individual.
- Science cannot, in other words, describe a general reality, but only the single case.
- Psycho-analysis is a scientific method and therefore not a science. This logical short circuit is not followed by any further explanation.
- The concepts of competence and expertise which used to be employed, have been replaced by the concepts of power and potency of science.
The power of science thus becomes the power of the individual.
- This power is based on the therapist's personality and on his freedom of work.
- The psychotherapist, therefore, does not affect reality, but rather 'modifies the individual'. In this way, he can 'manipulate'.

It is worth dwelling upon the meaning attributed to the word 'manipulation' in all of the four models.

MANIPULATION

Model A - Technical intervention is manipulatory, because it hides social problems instead of highlighting them.

Model B - The psychologist's intervention can be manipulatory or emancipatory, the same as any other intervention carried out within the social sciences.

Model C - Political intervention in psychology's own field is manipulatory, because it does not allow for a deep knowledge of the single case which is the psychologist's only aim.

Model D - The psychotherapist's intervention may be manipulatory (provided that the 'contract' between him and his patient has been cleared up), the psychotherapist has the power of manipulating the patient for his own good.

WORKING ACTIVITY = GOALS AND INTERVENTION STRATEGY

A. <u>Psychologist's work only makes sense if connected with a political struggle</u> (that is to say if it opposes the present social system).

  - The general objective - to contribute to modifying the present social system - becomes concrete in everyday practice through the definition of some partial objectives that are strictly connected.
  - The psychologist's aim in intervening in personal problems is to prevent the individual from becoming an outcast (struggle against social exclusion).
  - To favour the awareness of citizens (and of students) that their psychological problems are in fact social-political ones, needing not technical, but political answers : the goal is, for example, to promote and organize a political debate about health problems.
  - To highlighten social contradictions and thus curtail or even diminish the influence of those agents who in applying the decision of policy makers would rather minimize these contradictions by advancing technical solutions to individual problems.

On the basis of past experience, there is a general recognition however, that this general objective is very difficult to

A	B	C	D
- Research, as an instrument of science, is a function of the political system.	- Research is a means of knowledge and analysis of reality	- Researcch increases the clinical knowledge of the individual	- Research concerns the single case
- Research can only bring about changes contemplated by the political system	- Research, in an interdisciplinary perspective, can bring about social changes	- Knowledge deriving from research is used by the psychologist in therapeutic practice	- The therapist establishes a research relationship with his patient
- Research takes place in Universities where dominant knowledge is transmitted	- Research must be carried out with different characteristics and objectives, both by University teachers and by practitioners	- Research is a task of people working at the University.	

Table N.6. Different meanings given to the concept of "research".

achieve, if not utopic.

It is worth noticing the repetition of the expression "struggle for" or "struggle against" which we find in 89 % of the psychologists belonging to this group.

We can also emphasize a strict connection between political and professional involvement : "there is no separation between struggle and work, it is a fundamental decision of life".

B. <u>Working activity must be emancipatory</u>.

- Psychologist's work can be emancipatory only within a general political project.
- It is emancipatory if it brings a <u>technical and scientific</u> contribution to the fulfillment of this project.
- The primary intervention is a preventive one. Prevention (as opposed to A) consists in a technical-scientific intervention. We must start from an analysis of <u>needs</u> in order to elaborate adequate professional solutions (within a political project).
- The fundamental technique used to prepare a serious way to work is through <u>research</u>.

It is interesting at this point to consider how psychologists belonging to different groups define the notion of "research".

C. <u>The psychologist's work consists of a technical intervention</u>.

- The aim is to help the person who has psychological problems.
- The work of the psychologist is based on professional competence : it is this competence which legitimates his professionalism and <u>qualifies his identity</u>.
- The intervention regarded as primary, is curative, that is psychotherapy. Other kinds of intervention (such as the organizational ones made by psychologists working in social services, and the didactic and research activities for psychologists working at the University) are considered noteworthy but not 'specific to the psychologist's work. The perspective these psychologists adopt for their work is that of "free profession".
- This kind of intervention enables us "to see" the result of this work (a modification of the patient) and is thus also a proof of the importance of the psychologist's status.

D. The psychologist's work is psychotherapy.

- The only actual function of a psychologist is psychotherapeutic activity. The objective is to alleviate the patient's suffering.
- This objective is achieved by establishing an affective interpersonal relationship. With regard to this, the human aspect of the work stands out as opposed to the mere technical side.
- The frequency with which this group makes use of the notion of "patient" requiring the psychologist's intervention is remarkable (see table 7)

	C	D
client	40 %	20 %
user	30 %	-
person	20 %	30 %
patient	10 %	50 %
Total	100 %	100 %

Table N. 7. How the psychologist sees "the other".

- The choice of the patient only depends on the therapist and is mainly based on the criterion of <u>personal</u> interest. This point is emphasized by everybody and is regarded as a fundamental expression of the <u>freedom</u> qualifying a free profession.
- There is a willingness to get personally involved because what is thought important is to establish a deep and satisfying relationship with patients.

Concerning this aspect there is also a difference in relation to the psychologists belonging to group C.

In fact, while according to C getting involved in the patient's problems is considered negative as a limitation to be overcome by means of technical competence, according to D getting involved is thought of as a positive aspect of one's professionalism.

PSYCHOLOGIST'S PROFESSIONAL TRAINING

A. <u>Psychologists have no specific professional training</u>.

 - It is senseless to try and provide psychologists with a specific professional training. It would only be a way of deceiving the powerless, of hiding the actual relationship of power from them.
 - A training problem does exist; however it concerns the general growth of the individual and his social and political maturation.
 - Training is therefore acquired as part of an active political involvement.
 - University studies provide only theoretical ideas (where 'theoretical' means 'abstract').
 - These are therefore useless in order to face the actual social and political situation.
 - You learn while working, while doing your training, offering yourself as a volunteer, undertaking the responsibility of an actual work practice.

B. <u>Training provides psychologists with specific capacities</u>.

 - The psychologist bases his work on specific capacities, which are strictly interdependent on other professional competences.
 - For this reason the psychologist needs a preparation that is not confined to clinical psycho-therapeutical competence.
 - Universities do not provide this type of professional preparation; they offer, however, the opportunity of acquiring relevant theoretical knowledge.
 - What is needed is a basic interdisciplinary preparation leading with time to a specific professional one. As a matter of fact, interdisciplinarity concerns every social science.
 - You cannot learn how to be a psychologist by studying only psychology.

C. <u>The real training is a technical-professional one</u>.

 - A psychologist's reliability depends on the competences he possesses : such competences legitimate his identity and his being different from other professionals.
 - What is taught at the University is not enough for a technical-professional preparation.
 - Gaps in training can only be filled by personally attending courses and seminars in professional centres. These courses

require an effort and are very expensive; they represent, however, a privileged position for those who attend them.
- It is a privilege, not only at a professional level, as the psychologist's task becomes clearer, but also on a personal level, as one feels self-confident and more satisfied with one's work.
- Being able to practice psychotherapy differentiates the psychologist from other social workers.

D. Training is a sort of personal apprenticeship.

- The psychologist's personality is the only important thing in the psychotherapeutic relationship (the only relevant relationship in psychology). There can only be a few psychotherapists.
- They cannot be trained in schools open to anybody interested. A psychotherapeutic preparation can only be acquired in noninstitutionalized circles, which are different from the University.
- Training is a personal matter, almost an initiation. Only those who have certain potential can be admitted.
- Similarly, what is of most importance in professional life is the psychotherapist's personality.
- The University is useful, but only for basic, not professional training. As part of the basic training valid philosophical culture is stressed as highly important.

THE PSYCHOLOGIST'S PROFESSIONAL IDENTITY

A. The psychologist is not a professional, but a social practitioner.

- The technical role is refused and substituted by a political one : professional distinctions do not exist anymore; anybody who is concerned with human and social problems is a social-practitioner.
- Any identification with a technical role is dangerous, for it legitimates the power that knowledge enables us to exert over others.
- During political controversies, roles become confused.

B. The search for a complex professional identity.

- A psychologist is one who gives a specific professional contribution to the knowledge of reality and elaborates proposals for intervention in society.

- Neither the psychotherapist alone nor the person who only stresses the political values of the profession is a psychologist.
- There is, therefore, a need for differentiating from other models and an endeavour to achieve a more complex formulation of a new professionality.

C. <u>The psychologist : a professional identity to be defended.</u>

- Identity is defined according to competences : for this reason there is a need to defend a specific nucleus of technical competences to be acquired and improved.
- It is necessary, therefore, to have a status and a role adequate to one's own preparation.
- The most convenient professional role to assume is that of a highly qualified specialist.
- The main difference from other practitioners consists in therapeutic ability.

D. <u>The few real psychologists are psychotherapists.</u>

- Those belonging to this group do not call themselves 'psychologists' (which implies a too vast and indefinite circle of intervention), but 'psychotherapists'.
- The mode of the psychotherapeutic relationship is not one implying specific competences, but is based on an interpersonal relationship : the therapist's whole personality plays a part in it.
- There is a deep relationship between personal and professional identity (which, therefore, is not meant, as in model C, as something "to be defended").

DISCUSSION

Let us briefly discuss the data we have presented. The analysis of the thematic contents gathered in our interviews enabled us to individuate four different images of the psychologist. We have defined these images as " social representations" in the sense Moscovici (1961) gives to this concept. What is the meaning of these social representations ? Can they improve our knowledge about the process of the psychologist's professionalization in our society ?

Moscovici states that social representations' main function is to make familiar what is unknown. An individual, who finds himself dealing with a highly relevant but unfamiliar social object will start a complex operation of redefinition in order to make this object more understandable and pertinent, compatible with the symbolic system of the group to which the individual belongs. This operation takes place both for totally unknown social objects, because completely different, and for unprecedented ones, which are only partially known.

The psychologist's work is actually a "social object" which is known and unknown at the same time. Public opinion knows it as something similar to the work done by physicians and psychiatrists, even though this relationship is only vaguely understood. It is new and in some ways strange as the psychologist's professional function is not based on a solid tradition and has not got a set of clear and widely held rules. Besides, public opinion does not identify psychology as a means of gaining knowledge about reality, but rather as a way of helping "by means of words" those who suffer (Smedslund, 1972).

What is more important, however, is that psychologists themselves have no clear idea about the meaning of their own work. This is proven by the fact that when talking about their work they sometimes emphasize its ideological side, and other times its political function. They sometimes criticize the scientific status of psychology to the point of denying the possibility of founding a new profession on this basis (Kanizsa, 1980). Other times they maintain that the psychologist's professionality must be defended legally as well as normatively.

From this concern, we can therefore understand why psychologists, when speaking about their work, as our interviews required them to do, use meanings and arguments which they most commonly have to deal within their every day interpersonal relationship. The discussion which ensued from the interviews organized practical considerations and elements relating to the work of psychologists in a logical sequence which ultimately depended upon the ways psychology was considered as a science. It should be added that the scientific status of psychology was taken for granted and was not considered as something to be proved.

The data introduced in this paper, in fact, seems to show that the social representations of psychologists are organized on the basis of the different meanings given to the concept of psychology as a science. Four clear-cut positions thus emerge concerning the psychologist's training, practice and identity which can all be reconducted to the interpretations of psychology as a science.

These logical sequences take the four following forms.

For A :

Psychology is a science; science is an ideology because it serves the purposes of the dominant group (etc.)

The psychologist's work only makes sense if connected with a political struggle (against the present social system) (etc).

A psychologist must not have any specific professional training (etc.)

A psychologist is not a professional but a social practitioner (etc.)

For B :

Psychology is a social science because it uses scientific methods for the analysis of social phenomena (etc.)

The scientific analysis of reality gives the possibility of proposing changes, that is how psychology can affect social reality (etc.)

Training provides psychologists with specific capacities which are interdependent on other professional competences (etc.)

The model for a psychologist is neither the psychotherapist nor the practitioner who only stresses the political value of the profession (etc.)

For C :

> Psychology is a science of the individual; it gives the opportunity to modify only that which is particular, not the whole, the social (etc.)

> The psychologist's training is a technical-professional one (etc.)

> The psychologist's professional identity has to be defended (etc.)

> The psychologist's work consists of a technical intervention (etc.)

For D :

> Psychology is a science of the single case; it knows the internal dynamics of the individual (etc.)

> Training is a sort of personal apprenticeship (etc.)

> The few real psychologists are psychotherapists (etc.)

> The psychologist's work is psychotherapy (etc.)

The contents of these representations are then construed by ordinary people as well as by psychologists themselves in relation to the kind of definition given of psychology as a science by assuming a set of meanings, rules, and values as consistent as possible on the basis of their partial knowledge of the social object in question. This knowledge can be more or less complete and more or less elaborate. In the former case we find, for example, the perception of the psychologist as a social service professional or as a new kind of doctor and so on. In the latter case, when the partial knowledge of the social object is more refined and sophisticated, the psychologist's training, profession and identity are seen as aiming at the formation of an "expert in intra-individual processes". This representation, incidentally, is also supported by Leyens' analysis of the implicit theories of personality, which the reader will be able to find in this volume.

But sophisticated as this representation may be, it cannot serve as a basis for elaborating a concrete model of the professional requirements and expertise necessary for the psychologist to be able to work and the kinds of interventions he can make. To do this we must leave aside any dogmatic statement or preconceived notion concerning the scientific status of psychology and aim principally at defining the psychologist's role as that of an expert in his own right who uses his specific knowledge for gaining insight into the workings both of social as well as individual processes. Only by making and firmly supporting choices of social policy which promote such a professional role can this goal be achieved.

REFERENCES

Kanizsa, G. Ristrutturare il corso di laurea ? Giornale Italiano di Psicologia, 1980, 2, 349-355.
Leyens, J.P. Implications des théories implicites de personnalité pour le diagnostic psychologique, Paper presented at the Summer School of E.A.E.S.P., Aix en Provence, 1981.
Moscovici, S. La psychanalyse, son image, son public. Paris : P.U.F., 1961.
Smedslund, J. Becoming a Psychologist. Oslo : Universitets-Forlaget, 1972.

EXPERIMENTAL STUDIES OF INTERGROUP BEHAVIOUR 1)

H. Tajfel

University of Bristol

I. EXPERIMENTAL SOCIAL PSYCHOLOGY AND THE REALITIES OF SOCIAL CONFLICTS

"The strenght of (social psychology) and the main feature distinguishing it from other social sciences were traditionally seen in its use of experimental methods of research. The aim was, some forty years ago, to create a reliably scientific approach to human social behaviour. This developed in due course into experimental social psychology which overwhelmingly dominated (and still does) the research and writing in the subject. But what started as an exciting new venture became over the years, as is often the case, a complacent and unquestioned old routine. It is therefore not surprising that the 'experimental' tradition found itself at the receiving end of most of the attacks directed in the last ten years or so at the kind of research done by social psychologists" (Tajfel, 1978a, p.IX).

It is, however, interesting that these attacks were mainly concerned with the inadequacies of the experimental studies of interpersonal behaviour. It has been said again and again that the contrived arrangements of laboratory experiments distorted out of all recognition the reality and richness of genuine human

---

1) This contribution has already been published in M. Jeeves (Ed.) : Survey of Psychology, N°3, London: Allen and Unwin, 1980. Copyright by Allen and Unwin and reproduced by permission.

encounters. They created, it was argued, an Alice-in-Wonderland world of their own which produced very little of interest or value, could not add to our common experience and even distorted it; methods of research needed to be closer to genuine articulations by the social "actors" of their experiences. It is not the aim of this chapter to enter this controversy. It is mentioned here solely because both the "old" and the "new" social psychologies seem to share their relative lack of interest in the dynamics and functioning of the relations between human <u>groups</u> as contrasted with their preoccupation with what happens between individuals. It is because of this common lack of interest that the experimental social psychology of intergroup behaviour has not become a direct target of the attacks against the experimental methods, although, by implication, it was undoubtedly included in them.

The purpose of the present brief and selective review of some recent experimental studies of intergroup behaviour is threefold : (i) to provide an account of the recent revival of interest in what has been a long-neglected area of social psychology; (ii) to show that, in this particular area, experimental studies are and will have to remain <u>one</u> of the indispensable tools of further research; and, (iii) to take stock, very briefly, of the present position and of the major requirements for further new developments.

It is possible to conceive of the psychological study of social interaction as containing a broad range of interests which can be simply defined, as it moves from one to the other of its extremes, in terms of the <u>numbers</u> of people who are the target of research. Thus, we have at one extreme the study of processes which are inherent in the individual, as in the case of cognitive dissonance, although they do intervene in many important ways in social interaction. From here we move to the study of interpersonal or dyadic relationships which has been at the core of many important developments in the subject in the last twenty years or so. Small groups - containing a few people who are in direct interpersonal contact - represent the next step in the range. From here, we move to the study of the relations between two or more such small groups. These relations are still affected by direct interpersonal involvements, both within each of the small groups and between members of the different groups. And finally, at the extreme of the range, there remains the social psychology of relations between large-scale human groups or categories, be they social, national, ethnic, racial, political or religious. As we move from the dyadic relationships to those between small groups, and finally to large social categories, an important question arises :

how much of the behaviour displayed in the encounters between members of small groups or, even more so, of large social categories is determined by interpersonal processes, and how much of it is due to the structure of the relations between the groups involved ?

This question must be discussed in terms of two transitions which concern two different segments of the range we have just described. The first transition is from interpersonal to inter-small group behaviour; and the second is the transition from small groups, which still remain inter-personal, to the large-scale social categories.

The first of these transitions has long been the major theme in the work of Sherif. As he wrote in one of his later books :

"The word "group" in the phrase "intergroup relations" is not a superfluous label. Our claim is the study of relations between groups and intergroup attitudes of their respective members. We therefore must consider both the properties of the groups themselves and the consequences of membership for individuals. Otherwise, whatever we are studying, we are not studying intergroup problems" (Sherif, 1966, pp.61-2).

Although Sherif appears to state here what should seem to be obvious, the tradition of studying intergroup relations as if they were an extension of individual and interpersonal processes has been, and still is, powerful in social psychology. Much of Sherif's work was based on the view that the structure and dynamics of relations between groups determine and direct, in all relevant situations, the course of personal encounters between people belonging to the different groups. The alternative perspective has been to consider the encounters between individuals which take place in the framework of issues posed by relations between groups as no more than a special category of other interpersonal encounters.

A good example of this perspective can be found in some approaches to the study of intergroup negotiations and bargaining in which are involved representatives of the groups in conflict. Stephenson and his colleagues have done over the years a great deal of work on these issues (e.g., Morley and Stephenson, 1977; Stephenson, 1978&; Stephenson et al., 1976). The "interpersonal" emphasis of much of the work in this field has recently led Stephenson to feel that he had to stress once more that "... in collective bargaining, interpersonal exchange between the participants is not the subject at issue, but is incidental to the dispute between the parties" (Stephenson, 1978b, p.6). This he contrasted with the assumption, still prevailing in some quarters, that "the intergroup or collective nature of the negotiation" is just one factor superimposed on "individual or interpersonal bargaining". "The fallacy in such reasoning is exposed when we realize that in collective bargaining the individuals would not be there but for the existence of a dispute which transcends their interpersonal relationship" (Stephenson, 1978b, p.6). A recent review by Druckman (1977) of studies on intergroup bargaining provides a good example that Stephenson is not tilting at windmills. Many of these studies assume "that role (i.e., group) obligations impinge - more or less detrimentally - on an otherwise interpersonal negotiation".

These interpersonal perspectives upon collective bargaining or intergroup negotiations are but one example of an approach to problems of intergroup relations which is still frequently found in social psychology. This neglects the need for a psychological analysis of the social context within which take place many encounters between individuals. Although such encounters may superficially appear to be "personal", they are structured and directed by a wider and extra-personal set of determinants. The example of negotiations will have to do for this brief survey of some present developments in the study of intergroup relations. More detailed discussions of a number of other similar issues which are still often conceived in "inter-individual" terms can be found in, e.g., Billig (1976) and Tajfel (1978b, 1979).

The transition from interpersonal behaviour to behaviour between members of small groups represents thus a shift in theoretical perspectives. This is needed in order to establish a correspondence between the nature of the intergroup problems and the requirements of the research concerning them. There exists a second transition which requires yet another shift of perspectives. The nature of personal interactions between individuals still affects in _some_ measure the relations between small and restricted groups, be they "natural" or created in social psychological experiments. When one approaches the issues of intergroup behaviour which derive from tensions or conflicts between large-scale social categories, such as ethnic or national groups, personal interactions become, in many situations, even less important in determining the individuals' reciprocal attitudes and their manner of behaving towards each other.

One of the major features of encounters between members of different social categories is the _interchangeability_ of the individuals who take part in them. In other words, behaviour towards members of an outgroup is often, in such cases, to a large extent determined by that membership rather than by any individual characteristics of the people involved. It is this interchangeability which casts the shadow of anonymity upon the "outsiders", and thus it is directly relevant to the study of what is often called "depersonalization". As I wrote elsewhere, "when in conditions of racial discrimination people find it difficult to obtain accommodation or employment, it is not because they are ugly or handsome, short or tall, smiling or unsmiling, but because they are 'black'" (Tajfel, 1978b, pp. 27-28).

The question then arises about the ways in which social psychologists can study phenomena of this kind. Field studies of conflicts, tensions and prejudices are one of the obvious solutions, and many such studies are in existence. They have evident advantages, such as their closeness to social reality and the possibility of getting to know "in depth" the attitudes and experiences of selected individuals (e.g., Weinreich, 1979). But their findings need to be seen _in combination_ with the results of research aiming at a more contrived and "artificial" isolation of one or another of the causal factors which may be involved. It is here that experimentation becomes a crucial adjunct to the field studies of intergroup processes, without in any sense being conceptually prior to field research or being able to compete with it in its closeness to raw social reality. It is not the role of such experiments to _simulate_ social reality; it is unlikely that they could ever achieve this. Their value lies in the possibility they offer of providing hints about the theoretical links between the innumerable strands which compose the maze of the world of real social conflicts; and thus, experimental studies can help to guide and direct the difficult selection of empirical questions on which must be based any adequate field study of intergroup behaviour. Experiments of this kind have two fundamental and inherent limitations : in time and in numbers. They cannot reproduce the complex history of any instance of conflict or tension between social groups; nor can they mobilize or reproduce the massive membership of multigroup clashes and encounters in complex social systems. But it is possible to contrive research on some selected aspects of these systems and to establish theoretical links from there to the half-hidden and closely interlocking complexities of natural social situations.

The next section of this chapter will be concerned with a selection of such experimental studies, centering around a few of the issues which may turn out to be important for our further understanding of intergroup behaviour at large.

II. THE INTERCHANGEABLE INDIVIDUALS

The characteristic of intergroup behaviour stressed in the previous section of this chapter was that, as one moved towards larger groups of individuals engaged in some form of conflict or competition, their reciprocal behaviour was increasingly determined by the structure of the relations between these groups. This does not, of course, apply to _all_ social behaviour of the people concerned; the intergroup determination is limited to those social encounters and interactions which are perceived by the participants as being in some ways relevant to the relations between the groups to which they respectively belong. Some of Sherif's studies provided a good example of this shift from the interpersonal to the intergroup context of behaviour. In some of these studies (e.g., Sherif and Sherif, 1953), the first stage of the activities in the holiday camp did not involve a division into competing groups. When such a division was introduced after about a week, "care was taken to separate close friends and to place them into opposing groups" (Billig, 1976, p.303). This did not prevent the development of intergroup antagonisms in the subsequent stages of camp activities. It was the intergroup conflict which structured the behaviour of the boys, and not their previous friendships across the groups' boundaries.

This kind of finding enables us to state a simple but fairly general proposition : the stronger is an individual's affiliation with a social group, the more it is likely that, in a variety of situations, his behaviour towards members of other groups will show uniformities which are largely independent of the individual differences between the members of the outgroup. Stated in this bare form, the proposition is, of course, much too general. The "variety of situations" must be specified and analyzed in terms of the nature of the outgroup, of its relations with the ingroup and of the classes of social situations which may be involved. Nevertheless, the general proposition provides a useful pointer towards research concerned with the conditions in which certain categories of other people become, in a sense, anonymous and irrelevant _as_ individuals. This kind of research is important not only for theoretical reasons; it is directly relevant to many social situations, too familiar to need illustrating or exemplifying, in which strongly drawn boundaries between groups seem to create forms of behaviour towards outsiders which are hardly conceivable, in usual circumstances, within an ingroup, large or small.

It seems, however, that an explicit conflict of interests (real or imaginary) between groups is not the only necessary condition for the appearance of many forms of discriminatory intergroup behaviour. It is not the purpose of this chapter to outline the substantial number of theoretical considerations which lead one to expect that this kind of behaviour can also occur in a variety of intergroup situations which do not appear, on the face of it, competitive or fraught with conflict. These outlines are available elsewhere (see p.243 for some of the references). We can do no more here than select a few empirical variables which seem particularly relevant to this treatment "en masse" or "interchangeably" of people from social categories other than one's own.

Social categorization and social competition

Can intergroup discrimination occur when groups are not in an explicit conflict of interests and their relationship is not based on previous hostility ? It was to answer these questions that some studies were conducted from which all factors were carefully eliminated, other than a simple and clear-cut division between two groups based on a trivial difference between them (Tajfel et al., 1971). The following criteria guided the experimental procedures : there was no face-to-face interaction either within the "groups" or between them; anonymity of group membership was preserved; the intergroup responses requested of the subjects were not in any way related to the original criterion for the intergroup division; these responses were not directly related to a personal gain or loss for the subjects making them; a strategy of not differentiating between the groups would have been more rational and advantageous to all the subjects, independently of their group membership; there was no previous hostility between the groups; the responses were not "trivial", in the sense that they consisted of decisions awarding amounts of money to two anonymous other subjects from the "ingroup" or from the "outgroup" (Tajfel et al., 1971, pp.153-154). The results showed a clear-cut differentiation in favour of the ingroup, even when this meant, in some cases, that in order to preserve a difference between the groups favouring one's own group, the subjects had to award less money to members of the ingroup than would have been otherwise possible. These results have since been replicated in various ways in a large number of other studies conducted in several countries with subjects ranging in age from seven-year old children (Vaughan, 1978a) to young adults (e.g., Doise et al., 1972). A review of some of these studies can be found in Brewer (1979).

There is little doubt that the anonymity of group membership (and thus, "depersonalization") had something to do with the appearance of intergroup discrimination in these "minimal" situations. In this way, these highly contrived experimental procedures paradoxically rejoin the reality of some social situations in which behaviour towards certain people is largely affected by their social "label" (or sometimes, as Goffman, 1971, put it, "stigma") and not by their other characteristics. Wilder (1978) recently reported a series of experiments in which a decrease in this "deindividuation", as he called it, of members of the outgroup led to a corresponding decrease in the bias shown against them.

Although anonymity of membership may contribute to intergroup discrimination, it cannot, by itself, explain its occurrence. Hostile attitudes and discrimination have traditionally been seen as consequences of an intergroup conflict of interests, real or imaginary. Most of the earlier studies on the subject, such as those of Sherif, explored in detail various aspects of these conflicts. There is now, however, an accumulating body of evidence showing that such conflicts are not the only necessary conditions for intergroup bias to occur. As Brewer (1979) puts it, "it appears... that ingroup bias does occur in the absence of explicit competitive interdependence between groups". But, as she adds, "the absence of implicit competitive orientation... is difficult to establish". Indeed, the evidence that such an implicit competition exists has been provided in a large number of recent studies.

It has already been mentioned that in the initial "minimal categorization" experiments of Tajfel et al. (1971), obtaining a relative gain for the ingroup was often more important for the subjects than increasing the absolute amounts of gain. This was also the case in a study by Billig and Tajfel (1973) in which the criteria for categorization into groups were even more flimsy than those used in the earlier experiments. Brewer and Silver (1978), using a simplified version of the distribution matrices employed in the previous studies, found the same maximization of "relative gain in favour of the ingroup over choice maximizing absolute ingroup gain or other alternatives "(Brewer, 1979). Co-action rather than explicit conflict seemed sufficient to cause here this discriminatory intergroup behaviour or attitudes (as also shown in the studies of, for example, Allen and Wilder, 1975; Dann and Doise, 1974; Janssen and Nuttin, 1976; Kahn and Ryen, 1972; Rabbie et al., 1974; Rabbie and Wilkens, 1971; Ryen and Kahn, 1975; etc.). As might be expected, the introduction in such conditions of explicit competition increases still further the amount of bias.

The question then arises about the nature and determinants of this "implicit" competitive orientation. Two different views about it have recently been formulated. Neither of them denies the overriding importance of "objective" conflicts of interests in intergroup behaviour and attitudes; but they also both agree that this competitive interdependence is by no means the whole story. As we wrote earlier, it will not be possible in this brief review to go into the detail of the theoretical considerations which are involved. Very briefly stated, the first of these views (as represented in, e.g., Doise, 1978) is an elaboration closely based on some earlier ideas about the functioning of social categorizations (cf., Tajfel, 1959, 1972; Eiser and Stroebe, 1972). It makes use of these views to argue that such categorizations, when applied by individuals to social groups, are a necessary and sufficient condition for intergroup bias and discrimination to occur.

As Doise wrote :

"Differentiation of aspects of the social reality occurs in association with other differentiations relevant to the same reality... Category differentiation gives rise to behavioural, evaluative and representational differentiations... When there is differentiation at one of these three levels... there is a tendency for corresponding differentiations to be made at the other levels" (1978, p.152).

This view is based on the general idea that "the categorization process not only enables the individual to organize his subjective experience of the social environment but also, and perhaps more importantly, constitutes a process by which social interaction is structured, differentiates among, and shapes individuals". (Doise, 1978, p. 151). In other words, the introduction by the experimenters of a categorization of subjects into "groups" in several of the experiments mentioned earlier was sufficient to create the ingroup biases that were observed, and no other variables need to be postulated in order to explain their existence.

Although these initial "minimal categorization" experiments were designed to ascertain whether social categorization *per se* can elicit intergroup bias and they produced findings that this indeed was the case, later theoretical and research developments led to the elaboration of the second of the two views mentioned above. It has been argued (e.g., Tajfel, 1974, 1978; Tajfel and Turner, 1979; Turner, 1975, 1978a; see also e.g., Brown, 1978a; Caddick, 1978; Eiser, 1979, for extensive reviews) that, although social categorization is a necessary condition for these intergroup phenomena to occur, it is not a sufficient condition. What was needed in addition was that the individuals' group membership be relevant in some ways to their positive or negative self-images. This leads to a search for a positive "social identity" through group membership, and -in turn - this search can only be conducted and its outcomes assessed through engaging in, or *creating*, social comparisons with other groups. These comparisons are selective, both in their choice of groups appropriate as objects of comparison and of dimensions on which these intergroup comparisons are made. A positive outcome of such a process would be the achievement, creation or preservation of a "positive distinctiveness" of the ingroup from the outgroup. From this general basis, a number of hypotheses were formulated concerning the conditions, modes and varieties of social actions attempting to achieve this "distinctiveness", these differentiations of the ingroup from the outgroups. The aim was to provide an explanation of the general ingroup bias *and* of the importance to the subjects of the ingroup's *relative* gain over the outgroup which was found in many studies. The theory provided at the same time the point of departure for a large number of new studies, in the laboratory and in the field, which cannot be summarized here (cf., Tajfel, 1978c, for some of the reports). In this survey we can do no more than outline very briefly some of the experimental attempts to support the "pure" categorization view and those which tried to show that the "social identity" requirements for engaging in certain kinds of intergroup social comparisons were a *sine qua non* condition for intergroup discrimination.

Turner (1975, 1978b) assumed that "where an intergroup situation allows a positive self-evaluation on *some* dimension, then the individual confronting this situation will define himself in social terms relevant to that dimension..." (1975,p.17). This was, according to him, the case in the initial minimal categorization experiments where distribution of amounts of money to members of ingroup and outgroup was the *only* such dimension available to the subjects. In his own experiments, Turner enabled each subject, in some of the conditions, to make distributions (of money or valueless "points") between himself and either a member of the ingroup or of the outgroup. When such a distribution came first in the order of tasks, there was no evidence that the members of the ingroup were being treated any better than members of the outgroup. When, however, this task was <u>preceded</u> by choices concerning two <u>other</u> people, one from the ingroup and one from the outgroup, the subsequent choices between self and others did show a clear difference, in the sense that less was awarded to self at the expense of a member of the ingroup than of the outgroup. In other words, group membership -when it was made more salient at the beginning of the study- led the subjects to make choices between themselves and a member of the ingroup which represented a direct sacrifice in the amounts they could have awarded to themselves. This was so despite the fact that, as Turner (1978b) wrote, the self is by no means a "minimal" category, while the "others" -both from the ingroup and the outgroup- remained anonymous throughout the study.

Turner's contention is further supported by his data that results of the same kind were even clearer when valueless "points" were being distributed by the subjects rather than amounts of money. What seems to matter here is the ingroup's <u>relative</u> position on a dimension on which a differential between the groups exists or can be created. In more general terms, "social competition", as the term is used by Turner, refers to attempts to achieve gains in relative distinctiveness on a dimension of comparison which is <u>commonly</u> valued by the separate groups. In this way, studies of this kind represent an experimental paradigm which is of direct theoretical relevance to the presently ubiquitous issues of "differentials". It will be clear, however, from the preceding discussion that "social competition" -i.e., the achievement of positive distinctiveness on criteria which are consensually valued in a multigroup social context -is one only of the possible modes of action open to groups to achieve, preserve or defend, through the outcomes of social comparisons of various kinds, a positively valued "social identity" (or personal integrity)of their members. As already mentioned, other possibilities of this kind are discussed elsewhere within a more general theoretical framework.

The evidence for the alternative position, favouring "pure" categorization as a determinant of intergroup bias, comes from a study by Deschamps and Doise (1978). They found that their results did "not confirm the view that there exists a preference for establishing distinctions between oneself and others as compared with the establishment of differentiations between one's own membership category and another one. On the contrary, it seems that, at least for the boys in our study, the two types of discrimination are inherently connected. When one of them appears ... so does the other; and they are both absent" in another experimental condition (pp. 154-5). As Deschamps and Doise imply, according to Turner's argument the two kinds of discrimination (self-other and ingroup-outgroup) should vary inversely, since the possibility of engaging in one makes the other less functionally relevant. The issue remains to some extent unresolved, although there exists now more recent evidence from a study by Oakes and Turner (1979) that the opportunity offered to subjects to establish a difference in favour of their own group through intergroup discrimination directly enhances their self-esteem. These findings would seem to support Turner's position since the enhancement of self-esteem occurs on measures which are unrelated to the nature of the favourable difference that the subjects have been able to establish in the experiments, and it does not appear when there is no possibility to engage in intergroup discrimination.

This issue of social categorization and social competition is one only of the many theoretical problems on which work is now continuing in the recent revival of interest in the social psychology of intergroup relations. The "differentials" remain a crucial element in many of the social and industrial conflicts of today. There is no doubt that the socio-economic and political objectives of groups in conflict must be given priority in any discussion of these conflicts. But it is also true that such discussions will remain incomplete until and unless the social psychological processes of intergroup categorization and comparison, not always directly related to "objective" gains, are accorded their due place in the total picture (cf., Brown, 1978b, for a particularly clear example from "real life"; cf., also Skevington, 1979).

Social comparison is the process which provides the links between various forms of categorization of human beings into social groups and the forms of individual and collective actions towards outgroups. It can be assumed that some general social labels, even when they are frequently used, remain fairly "neutral" and socially inactive- so long as the various differences between the groups involved are not endowed with strong value connotations. The origins and development of these value connotations cannot be discussed here, although they are amongst the crucial social psychological issues in intergroup relations (cf. e.g., Milner, 1975; Tajfel, 1978b). We shall attempt, however, a brief review of some recent studies of one of the underlying processes. This concerns the effects on social comparisons of an increase in people's awareness that they are members of a group which is immersed in an interacting system involving other groups as well as their own.

Social comparison and awareness of group membership

Social categorization cannot be considered as a "static" variable which somehow leads people to behave in a constant and uniform manner towards those who are classified as "outsiders". The conditions of interaction between groups, and the relevance of a group membership to an individual vary from situation to situation, from one period of time to another, and from one outgroup to another. The individual and social significance of the membership of a group (and, consequently, the importance of the presence of _other_ groups) vary continuously. Therefore, an individual's affiliation with a group and the functional relevance of social comparisons with other groups, or even with the same group from one situation to another, enter into a continuously changing dynamic relationship.

There are at least three separate lines of evidence that, in this diversity of conditions, an increase in the awareness of one's group membership determines the nature of intergroup comparisons, and thus has predictable effects on intergroup attitudes and behaviour. They are as follows : (i) the findings that individuals acting as members of a group, or representing a group, tend to be more competitive than they are in similar situations in which they act as individuals in relation to other individuals; (ii) studies showing the effects of an experimentally produced increase in the salience of a social categorization; and finally (iii) results of some of the studies concerned with attitudes towards their own group of children from various ethnic or racial minorities. It will be impossible to provide, within the limits of this brief survey, more than the barest outline of these studies, their results and their general significance; but the reader will find in the references an opportunity to pursue further any of these issues.

In an experiment by Billig and Tajfel (1973), it was shown that a categorization of people into "groups" on an explicitly random basis induced more discrimination against anonymous "outsiders" than did equally anonymous inter-individual dissimilarities. But this finding raises issues concerning the relative effects of inter-individual similarities and intergroup categorizations on prejudice (cf., Rokeach, 1960) which cannot be discussed here (cf., Brown, 1978a, for a detailed review and analysis).

There exists, however, a good deal of evidence concerning the effects on attitudes and behaviour of group membership, when intergroup disagreements are compared with inter-individual differences or disagreements. For example, Stephenson et al. (1976) found that differences in attitudes about the raising of the age of compulsory school attendance led to less bias against those of another opinion when they were considered as a collection of individuals than after they had been divided into two separate groups. Wilson and his collaborators showed in a number of studies (e.g., Wilson and Katayani, 1968) that subjects in pairs make more competitive choices in a game than when they compete individually. Rabbie and Visser (1977) also found that groups were more involved in pre-arranged competitions than was the case for individuals in the same situation. As they wrote, echoing Sherif:

"These experiments strongly suggest that groups may have different ways of handling conflicts than individuals. If we want to build theories of intergroup relations we should use groups instead of individuals in our experiments" (p.4).

There is also a good deal of evidence (cf.e.g., Morley and Stephenson, 1977; Stephenson, 1978a for reviews) that people acting as representatives of groups tend to show more competitive actions and attitudes than is the case in inter-individual negotiations.

All these studies share one characteristic : they show the effects of group categorizations superimposed on individual characteristics in situations which involve some kind of conflict or competition. These effects seem to consist of a bias against the "other" which is stronger in the case of intergroup than inter-individual relations. But situations of explicit conflict or competition are, once again, not the only necessary condition for showing the powerful effects of categorizing people into groups. It is apparently sufficient simply to make people more aware of the presence or potential presence of another group to elicit ingroup bias. A technique of this kind was first used by Doise and Sinclair (1973) who, in one condition, asked "group members to describe themselves without mentioning any other group" (p.149); in a second condition, the same request was made but an outgroup was "evoked", in the sense that the subjects knew that they would have to describe it afterwards. Using groups of apprentices and collégiens (i.e., approximately grammar-school pupils) in Geneva, Doise and Sinclair found that the induced awareness of another relevant group led the collégiens to evaluate their own group much more favourably than was the case in the "non-comparison" condition; the apprentices showed a trend in the same direction which did not reach statistical significance. A similar method was used in a study by Doise et al. (1978) on Swiss linguistic groups with results showing a clear tendency to accentuate ingroup similarities when relevant outgroups were brought symbolically into the situation. Van Knippenberg (1978) refined and improved the method in his recent study of engineering students from two Dutch educational institutions of unequal social and academic prestige. His complex results cannot be described here, but they also showed clear effects of increasing the salience of a social categorization. Similar results were obtained from studies of ethnolinguistic groups (cf., Bourhis et al., 1979; Bourhis and Giles, 1977) in Belgium and Wales.

Thus, the first of the three groups of studies mentioned above focuses on situations in which groups rather than individuals disagree. The second line of evidence, just discussed, is based on strengthening the salience of an existing intergroup categorization in experimental or controlled semi-natural situations. The third source of data comes from studies on the self-images of children from minority groups. There are many such studies, the first of which were conducted in the 'thirties in the United States (see Milner, 1975, for a detailed review). The consensus of data which emerged from them was that minority children (particularly those from racial minorities) tended, in specially devised tests, to show preference for stimuli (such as dolls, etc.) representing the dominant "white" outgroups over those representing their own group. Some of these results were criticised on methodological grounds (e.g., Greenwald and Oppenheim, 1968). There is little doubt, however, that most of the apparent discrepancies in the findings can be attributed to the functioning of a process which has repeatedly been referred to in this chapter. In relation to the studies on minority children, this can be stated as follows : the intensity of "ingroup devaluation" shown in these tests by children from racial minorities seems to be directly related to the degree of <u>explicitness</u> of comparisons with the outgroup which is built into the methods of testing. This fits in with data on desegregated schools in the United States obtained by Katz in the 'sixties who concluded (Katz, 1968) that anticipated comparisons with whites affected adversely the level of performance of black pupils. The outcomes of these comparisons are in the direction opposite to the findings from the first two groups of studies described above (although some of the data from the study by van Knippenberg, 1978, are consonant with the minority group data). In the case of these first two groups of studies, an increased salience of group membership or of social categorization led to an increase in ingroup bias or outgroup discrimination. In the case of the children studies, an increased salience of comparisons with the dominant outgroup led to what has come to be known as a more marked "ingroup devaluation".

In discussing these findings, we can thus return to the major theme of this chapter. The identity of minority children (as distinct from their conceptions of self based on individual interactions within their own group) is based on unfavourable comparisons with the majority. The nature of these comparisons is affected by the innumerable economic, social, political, ideological and linguistic influences in the society-at-large. It is therefore hardly surprising that when comparisons with the dominant outgroup are made more salient, be it in "natural" conditions or in controlled studies, young children are reduced to express aspects of their "social identity" through the only channels of comparison which are open to them. These negative self-images are by no means the only ones in existence; there exist many positive alternatives (cf., Tajfel, 1978d), and the negative ones change quickly in the wake of social change (cf., Vaughan, 1978b). Either way, they provide one further example of the importance of social intergroup comparisons in the general structure of social psychological processes underlying intergroup relations.

CONCLUSION

This brief survey was no more than a highly selective scratching of the surface. A few aspects of intergroup relations were discussed with some of the experimental studies related to them. After a fairly long period of relative inactivity, there has been in the last few years an upsurge of interest and revival of research into many social psychological issues of intergroup behaviour. Some of these issues which are quite fundamental were not even mentioned in this chapter. They include, for example, the problems of status relationships, of power and subordination, of stability and change in the relations between social groups, of competition and co-operation between groups which are similar or dissimilar, of the perceived legitimacy or illegitimacy of a social multigroup system, etc. A substantial amount of work on all these problems has recently been done and is continuing at present. Much of this work remains in the form of social psychological experimentation. The view defended in this chapter was that, however "artificial" or contrived much of this experimental work may appear to be, it has a substantial and continuing role to play in our further understanding of one of the most crucial social problems of our day. Social psychological experiments will not solve these problems, and they are not meant to do this. However, fruitful social psychological theories, seeking to combine their evidence from both the laboratory and the natural conditions of human social interaction, can undoubtedly contribute to a further unravelling of this tangled and difficult set of issues.

REFERENCES

Allen, V.L. and Wilder, D.A. Categorization, belief similarity and intergroup discrimination. Journal of Personality and Social Psychology, 1975, 32, 971-977.

Billig, M. Social Psychology and Intergroup Relations. London : Academic Press, 1976.

Billig, M. and Tajfel, H. Social categorization and similarity in intergroup behaviour. European Journal of Social Psychology, 1973, 13, 27-52.

Bourhis, R.Y. and Giles, H. The language of intergroup distinctiveness. In H. Giles (Ed.), Language, Ethnicity and Intergroup Relations. London,: Academic Press, 1977.

Bourhis, R.Y., Giles, H., Leyens, J.P. and Tajfel, H. Psycholinguistic distinctiveness : language divergence in Belgium. In H. Giles and R. St.Clair (Eds.), Language and Social Psychology. Oxford: Basil Blackwell, 1979.

Brewer, M.B. Ingroup bias in the minimal intergroup situation : A cognitive-motivational analysis. Psychological Bulletin, 1979, 86, 307-324.

Brewer, M.B. and Silver, M. Ingroup bias as a function of task characteristics. European Journal of Social Psychology, 1978, 8, 393-400.

Brown, R.J. Competition and Co-operation between Similar and Dissimilar Groups, Unpublished Ph.D. Dissertation, University of Bristol, 1978a.

Brown, R.J. Divided we fall : An analysis of relations between sections of a factory workforce. In H. Tajfel (Ed.), Differentiation between social groups. London : Academic Press, 1978b.

Caddick, B.F.J. Status, legitimacy and the social identity concept in Intergroup relations, Unpublished, Ph. D. Dissertation, University of Bristol, 1978.

Dann, H.D. and Doise, W. Ein neuer methodologischer Ansatz zur experimentellen Erforschung von Intergruppen-Seziehungen. Zeitschrift für Sozialpsychologie, 1974, 5, 2-15.

Deschamps, J.-C. and Doise, W. Crossed category membership in intergroup relations. In H. Tajfel (Ed.), Differentiation between social groups. London: Academic Press, 1978.

Doise, W. *Groups and Individuals : Explanations in Social Psychology*. Cambridge : Cambridge University Press, 1978.

Doise, W., Csepeli, G., Dann, H.D., Gouge, C., Larsen, K. and Ostell, A. An experimental investigation into the formation of intergroup representations. *European Journal of Social Psychology*, 1972, 2, 202-204.

Doise, W., Deschamps, J.-C. and Meyer, G. The accentuation of intra-category similarities. In H. Tajfel (Ed.), *Differentiation between social groups*. London : Academic Press, 1978.

Doise, W. and Sinclair, A. The categorization process in intergroup relations. *European Journal of Social Psychology*, 1973, 3, 145-157.

Druckman, D. (Ed.), *Negotiations : Social Psychological Perspectives*. London : Sage Publications, 1977.

Eiser, J.R. *Cognitive Social Psychology*. London : McGraw Hill, 1979.

Eiser, J.R. and Stroebe, W. *Categorization and Social Judgment*. London : Academic Press, 1972.

Goffman, E. *Relations in Public*. London : Allen Lane, 1971.

Greenwald, H.J. and Oppenheim, D.B. Reported magnitude of self-misidentification among Negro children : Artifact ? *Journal of Personality and Social Psychology*, 1968, 8, 49-52.

Janssens, L. and Nuttin, J. Frequency perception of individual and group successes as a function of competition, coaction and isolation. *Journal of Personality and Social Psychology*, 1976, 34, 830-836.

Kahn, A. and Ryen, A.H. Factors influencing bias towards one's own group. *International Journal of Group Tensions*, 1972, 2, 33-50.

Katz, I. Factors influencing Negro performance in the desegregated school. In M. Deutsch, I. Kahn and H.R. Jensen (Eds.), *Social Class, Race and Psychological Development*, New York: Holt, Rinehart and Winston, 1968.

van Knippenberg, A. *Perception and evaluation of intergroup differences*. University of Leiden, 1978.

Milner, D. *Children and Race*. Harmondsworth : Penguin Books, 1975.

Morley, I.E. and Stephenson, G.M. *The Social Psychology of Bargaining*. London : Allen and Unwin, 1977.

Oakes, P. and Turner, J.C. Social identity, social competition and self-esteem in the minimal group paradigm. Submitted for publication, 1979.

Rabbie, J.M., Benoist, F., Oosterbaa, H. and Visser, L. Differential power and effects of expected competitive and cooperative intergroup interaction on intragroup and outgroup attitudes. *Journal of Personality and Social Psychology*, 1974, 30, 46-56.

Rabbie, J.M. and Visser, L. Notes on the effects of intergroup competition and co-operation. Paper presented at the L.E.P.S. Colloquium on the social psychology of social conflict, Paris, 1977

Rabbie, J.M. and Wilkens, G. Intergroup competition and its effects on intragroup and intergroup relations. European Journal of Social Psychology, 1971, 1, 215-234.

Rokeach, M. The Open and Closed Mind. New York : Basic Books, 1960.

Ryen, A.H. and Kahn, A. Effects of intergroup orientation on group attitudes and proxemic behaviour. Journal of Personality and Social Psychology, 1975, 31, 302-310.

Sherif, M. Group Conflict and Co-operation : Their Social Psychology. London : Routledge and Regan Paul, 1966.

Sherif, M. and Sherif, C.W. Groups in Harmony and Tension. New York : Harper and Row, 1953.

Skevington, S. Intergroup relations and social change within a nursing context. British Journal of Social and Clinical Psychology, in press.

Stephenson, G.M. The characteristics of negotiation groups. In H. Brandstätter, J.H. Davis and H. Schuler (Eds.), Social Decision Processes. New York : Sage Publication, 1978a.

Stephenson, G.M. Intergroup bargaining and negotiation. Paper presented at the B.P.S. Social Psychology Section Conference on Intergroup Behaviour, Bristol, 1978b.

Stephenson, G.M., Skinner, M.R. and Brotherton, C.J. Group participation and intergroup relations : An experimental study of negotiation groups. European Journal of Social Psychology, 1976, 6, 51-70.

Tajfel, H. Quantitative judgement in social perception. British Journal of Psychology, 1959, 50, 16-29.

Tajfel, H. La catégorisation sociale. In S. Moscovici (Ed.), Introduction à la Psychologie Sociale, Vol. I, Paris : Larousse, 1972.

Tajfel, H. Social identity and intergroup behaviour. Social Sciences Information, 1974, 13, 65-93.

Tajfel, H. Foreword to the English edition. In W. Doise, Groups and individuals : Explanations in Social Psychology. Cambridge : Cambridge University Press, 1978a.

Tajfel, H. The psychological structure of intergroup relations. In H. Tajfel (Ed.), Differentiation between social groups. London : Academic Press, 1978b.

Tajfel, H. Differentiation between social groups : studies in the social psychology of intergroup relations. London: Academic Press, 1978c.

Tajfel, H. The Social Psychology of Minorities. London : Minority Rights Group, 1978d.

Tajfel, H. Individuals and groups in social psychology. British Journal of Social and Clinical Psychology, 1979, 18, 183-190.

Tajfel, H., Flament, C., Billig, M. and Bundy, R. Social categorization and intergroup behaviour. European Journal of Social Psychology, 1971, 1, 149-178.

Tajfel, H. and Turner, J.C. An integrative theory of intergroup conflict, in W.G. Austin and S. Worchel (Eds.), The Social Psychology of Intergroup Relations. Monterey, Calif.: Brooks/Cole, 1979.

Turner, J.C. Social comparison and social identity : Some prospects for intergroup behaviour. European Journal of Social Psychology, 1975, 5, 5-34.

Turner, J.C. The experimental social psychology of intergroup behaviour. Paper presented at the B.P.S. Social Psychology Section Conference on Intergroup Behaviour, Bristol, 1978a.

Turner, J.C. Social categorization and social discrimination in the minimal group paradigm. In H. Tajfel (Ed.), Differentiation between social groups. London : Academic Press, 1978b.

Vaughan, G.M. Social categorization and intergroup behaviour in children. In H. Tajfel (Ed.), Differentiation between social groups. London : Academic Press, 1978a.

Vaughan, G.M. Social change and intergroup preferences in New Zeeland. European Journal of Social Psychology, 1978b, 8, 297-314.

Weinreich, P. Cross-ethnic identification and self-rejection in a black adolescent. In G. Verma and C. Bagley (Eds.), Race Education and Identity. London : MacMillan, 1979.

Wilder, D.A. Reduction of intergroup discrimination through individuation of the outgroup. Journal of Personality and Social Psychology, 1978, 36, 1361-1374.

Wilson, W. and Katayani, M. Intergroup attitudes and strategies in games between opponents of the same or a different race. Journal of Personality and Social Psychology, 1968, 9, 24-30.

DIFFERENCIATIONS ENTRE SOI ET AUTRUI ET ENTRE GROUPES

Recherches sur la "covariation" entre les différenciations
inter-individuelles et inter-groupes 1)

J.C. Deschamps

Université de Lausanne

Avant d'aborder le point spécifique des différenciations
inter-individuelles et inter-groupes, nous mentionnerons, et sans
qu'il soit question de faire ici un historique de la notion d'identité, certains points de repère permettant de saisir dans quelles
perspectives la notion d'identité sociale s'est développée et a
évolué et la nécessité qui s'est manifestée, en psychologie sociale, d'articuler le champ de recherche sur l'identité et le
domaine des études sur les relations entre groupes.

Il semble qu'il faille mentionner avant tout le nom du philosophe social Georges Herbert Mead (1934) qui, dès le début du
siècle, s'est penché sur la définition du Soi. Chez Mead, on trouve l'idée que le Soi est constitué à la fois d'une composante
"sociologique", le Moi qui ne serait qu'une intériorisation des
rôles sociaux, et d'une composante plus personnelle, le Je.
Mead distingue donc deux aspects dans le Soi : le Je qui représenterait le Soi en tant que sujet et le Moi qui représenterait
le Soi en tant qu'objet. Plus exactement, le Je est la réaction
de l'organisme aux attitudes des autres, et le Moi est l'ensemble
organisé des attitudes des autres qu'on assume soi-même. Les attitudes d'autrui constituent le Moi organisé auquel on réagit comme
Je. Autrement dit, le Soi émerge d'une interaction entre le Je

---

1) Recherches effectuées dans le cadre du contrat No 1.707.0.78
avec le Fonds National Suisse de la Recherche Scientifique.

et le Moi qui ne sont que des éléments constitutifs du Soi. Le Je représente l'aspect créateur du Soi qui répond aux attitudes d'autrui alors que le Moi est justement cet ensemble organisé des jugements d'autrui que le Soi assume. C'est la "conversation du 'Je' et du 'Moi'" qui constitue le Soi et cette conversation est la transposition, au niveau de l'individu, du processus qui lie un organisme aux autres dans les interactions.

La notion d'identité a été utilisée dans une perspective psychanalytique "néo-freudienne" notamment par un auteur tel que Erikson (par exemple en 1963) et à la suite du courant qu'on a pu qualifier de "culturaliste" en psychanalyse. Cet auteur développe les notions de personnalité de base avancée par Kardiner (1939, 1945), mais aussi par Linton (1945), et de caractère social ou caractère national introduit par Fromm (1941, 1956) et décrivant la personnalité partagée par les membres d'une même société et résultant des expériences communes. L'identité se situe dans cette perspective, et comme chez Mead, à l'articulation entre l'individuel et le collectif, à l'articulation du personnel et de la culture commune.

Plus récemment, l'identité sociale a été l'objet d'une attention particulière de la part de la sociologie (mentionnons par exemple les travaux de Berger et Luckman, 1966) et on peut citer les recherches ethnologiques sur l'identité culturelle (avec le séminaire dirigé par Levi-Strauss publié en 1977).

En psychologie sociale, cette notion d'identité est liée aux recherches sur les rôles sociaux, sur les positions qu'un individu occupe dans une structure sociale. L'identité sociale est avant tout conceptualisée comme une variable dépendant des positions qu'un individu occupe dans la société. Cette conception est particulièrement claire chez Sarbin et Allen (1968) pour qui "l'identité sociale serait une partie du processus du Soi, représentant les cognitions découlant des placements dans l'écologie sociale" (p. 50). Plus récemment, chez Zavalloni (1973), on trouve l'idée que son "Inventaire d'Identité Sociale" doit permettre "d'analyser comment l'appartenance à des groupes donnés (nation, classe sociale, sexe, etc.) est-elle susceptible d'affecter la perception du Soi et les valeurs personnelles et réciproquement" (p.253); chez Tajfel (1972,p.292), "l"identité sociale' d'un individu est liée à la connaissance de son appartenance à certains groupes sociaux et à la signification émotionnelle et évaluative de cette appartenance". Bien d'autres auteurs, notamment Sherif pour ne mentionner que lui, insistent sur le fait que l'identité sociale d'un individu n'est pas indépendante de ses groupes d'appartenance. On considèrera donc ici, à la suite de ces travaux, que l'identité sociale a "quelque chose à voir" avec les groupes d'appartenance. Etant en rapport avec l'appartenance à certains groupes, l'identité va être aussi liée à la façon dont les membres de différents groupes sociaux se représentent leur propre groupe et d'autres groupes, et par là même, comme nous allons le voir, aux rapports entre groupes. En fait, on peut même dire que, par exemple, pour un auteur comme Tajfel, ce sont ses travaux sur les relations entre groupes et la catégorisation sociale qui l'ont conduit à élaborer une théorisation intégrant identité sociale et catégorisation sociale.

Des recherches sur les discriminations entre groupes et portant sur le contenu des stéréotypes ont été entreprises très tôt dans l'histoire de la psychologie sociale. La volonté de comprendre les racines, les bases de l'intolérance et des discriminations a donné lieu à de nombreuses recherches sur les préjugés et les stéréotypes entre groupes. Des centaines de recherches ont été effectuées, après le célèbre travail de Katz et Braly publié en 1933, afin de saisir quelles étaient les images que les membres de différents groupes sociaux avaient de leur propre groupe (auto-stéréotype) et d'autres groupes (hétéro-stéréotypes). Cependant, ces recherches ont été avant tout centrées sur le contenu des stéréotypes; elles ne permettent pas de déceler l'origine des stéréotypes d'un groupe à l'égard de divers autres groupes. En fait, les caractéristiques que les groupes s'attribuent réciproquement reflèteraient les modalités de leurs rapports. C'est ce qu'ont pu montrer Sherif et collaborateurs (par exemple Sherif et al., 1961). Pour ces auteurs, les attitudes à l'égard des autres groupes, les images de ces groupes sont les produits des relations entre groupes et non leur cause; l'hostilité, la rivalité sont à la source des stéréotypes entre deux groupes et non l'inverse (qui serait que ce sont les stéréotypes entre deux groupes qui sont à la source du conflit et donc de l'hostilité). De plus, les relations entre l'antagonisme, l'hostilité, le conflit donc d'une part, et les attitudes, les préjugés, les stéréotypes d'autre part, ne sont pas univoques : s'il est bien vrai que c'est dans l'interaction que naissent les préjugés, ceux-ci à leur tour conditionnent un certain type d'interaction. Les images ne sont pas seulement des reflets du déroulement de l'interaction des groupes : elles interviennent activement dans ce déroulement en justifiant la manière dont cette interaction se déroule (voir par exemple Avigdor, 1953).

Cependant, pour importante que soit cette perspective de recherche inaugurée par Sherif, elle porte avant tout sur les effets de l'interaction compétitive et coopérative entre groupes et est en cela insuffisante pour rendre compte de mécanismes plus généraux. Une analyse des processus psychologiques sous-jacents aux relations entre groupes nous est fournie par Tajfel (par exemple, 1972) à la suite des travaux de Bruner (1957, 1958) et de l'introduction de la notion de catégorie dans sa théorie de la perception; c'est le processus de la catégorisation qui porte sur la façon dont un individu organise son expérience subjective de l'environnement social. La simple induction, au niveau représentationnel, de l'appartenance à deux groupes distincts entraîne chez les sujets expérimentaux une discrimination en faveur des membres du groupe d'appartenance. En 1971, Tajfel, Billig, Bundy et Flament ont montré que lorsqu'on répartit, apparemment sur la base de leurs préférences esthétiques (mais en fait de façon arbitraire), les élèves d'une même classe en deux groupes, celui des élèves censés avoir préféré les oeuvres de Klee et celui de ceux censés avoir préféré les oeuvres de Kandinsky, et lorsqu'on demandait ensuite à ces élèves de décider de la rémunération que recevront leurs camarades pour la participation à l'expérience des normes de favoritisme à l'égard des membres du groupe d'appartenance gouvernent les comportements des sujets (bien qu'un souci de ne pas trop s'écarter d'une juste répartition des gains suggère l'existence conjointe d'une norme d'équité entre groupes). Depuis, de nombreuses recherches employant ce "paradigme minimal" utilisé dans la recherche citée de Tajfel et al. (1971) ont étudié comment les sujets répartissaient de l'argent (ou des points n'ayant qu'une valeur symbolique) entre des individus qui ont (ou n'ont pas) été placés dans l'une ou l'autre des catégories sociales "minimales" introduites expérimentalement. Il semblerait que la simple induction expérimentale du clivage d'une population en deux groupes "minimaux" et de peu d'importance entraîne les individus à se comporter différemment envers leur groupe et l'autre groupe. La compétition entre groupes ne serait donc pas une condition nécessaire pour créer des comportements différentiels entre et dans les groupes comme Sherif le supposait dans sa théorie du conflit objectif d'intérêt. Dès 1964, Fergusson et Kelley avaient d'ailleurs pu montrer qu'en l'absence de toute compétition explicite, les sujets avaient tendance à évaluer plus favorablement les productions des membres de leur groupe que celles des membres d'un autre groupe. 2)

---

2) Pour plus de détails, voir Doise (1976).

Ce courant de recherche sur la catégorisation sociale va apporter un renouveau dans les recherches sur l'identité sociale. Classiquement, en psychologie sociale, comme nous l'avons vu, l'identité était conceptualisée comme "découlant des placements dans l'écologie sociale". Autrement dit, l'idée de base était que la conduite d'un individu dépend de son identité et que son identité découle de la position qu'il occupe dans la société. Dans cette perspective, si on utilise la notion d'identité, c'est sans jamais étudier en tant que tels les processus qui lui sont sous-jacents. Par contre, à la suite des premiers travaux de Tajfel, Turner (1975), Tajfel et Turner (1979) ont élaboré une théorisation portant sur l'identité sociale. Un des postulats de base de cette théorisation est que les individus auraient le "désir" d'une auto-évaluation positive, un besoin de positivité individuelle. Les propositions théoriques qui sous-tendent ce courant de recherches expérimentales sur la notion d'identité sociale peuvent être résumées de la façon suivante : l'individu chercherait à préserver ou à accéder à une image positive de soi et un des moyens d'assouvir ce désir d'auto-évaluation positive serait la compétition sociale entre groupes 3) qui tend à introduire une différence positive en faveur du groupe d'appartenance par rapport à d'autres groupes. Les conclusions d'une des recherches de Turner (1975) faite dans le cadre de cette théorisation sont que les sujets n'agissent en terme d'une différenciation entre groupes que lorsque celle-ci représente pour eux le seul moyen d'avoir une auto-évaluation positive, d'accéder à une identité positive. S'ils peuvent agir en termes d'une différenciation entre soi et autrui, le "biais" entre groupes ne se manifeste pas. Ce serait alors lorsque des phénomènes d'identification au groupe permettent une identité positive que le biais entre groupes apparaît. Autrement dit, la catégorisation en soi, _per se_, ne serait pas suffisante pour qu'on observe une différenciation entre groupes et ce qui serait sous-jacent au processus de la catégorisation sociale serait la tendance à établir une distinction positive entre soi et autrui. En d'autres termes, cette théorisation nous conduit à un modèle homéostatique ou de l'équilibre dans lequel, si l'individu, par son identification à un groupe, accède à une identité positive, il n'a plus tendance à établir une différence d'avec autrui et si l'individu a la possibilité de se différencier

---

3) Compétition sociale entre groupes qui ne se résoud pas dans une compétition instrumentale comme chez Shérif mais qui est bea   plus à concevoir comme une comparaison sociale entre groupes.

d'autrui et par là même d'accéder à une évaluation positive de lui-même, il n'établit plus de discrimination entre les différents groupes de son entourage.

Dans un certain nombre de recherches (Deschamps, 1972-1973; 1977), nos résultats ne semblent pas aller dans le sens de ce modèle homéostatique et dans une autre recherche (Brown et Deschamps, 1980-1981) faite en Angleterre et en Suisse à la suite de l'expérience de Turner et reprenant le paradigme expérimental de cet auteur, nous n'avons pas pu répliquer ses résultats obtenus en 1975; les comparaisons avec les conditions équivalentes de l'expérience de Turner ne permettent pas de retrouver les résultats obtenus par ce dernier. Il semble bien plutôt que ces premiers résultats s'organisent en fonction d'une hypothèse plus structurelle en terme d'une "covariation" des différenciations entre groupes et entre soi et autrui.

Nous avons été conduit à suggérer (voir Deschamps, 1979) qu'un processus général de "centrisme" cognitif se manifeste lorsqu'on induit chez les sujets la représentation d'un univers dichotomisé, partagé en deux catégories mutuellement exclusives. En fonction de cette idée, à la fois le biais de favoritisme de l'intra-groupe (ce que l'on pourrait ranger provisoirement sous l'appellation de "sociocentrisme") et le biais d'auto-favoritisme (ce que l'on pourrait qualifier parallèlement d'"égocentrisme") seraient accrus lorsqu'une catégorisation devient plus saillante. En guise de proposition théorique de base, nous avons été amené à avancer, compte tenu de l'état des travaux dans ce domaine, qu'il semblait bien que les systèmes culturels pouvaient abriter de larges contradictions entre "universaux" (c'est-à-dire entre les valeurs qui sont censées inspirer les comportements de chacun). Au niveau inter-groupes, une de ces tensions (ou contradictions apparentes) serait celle entre solidarité et compétition ou concurrence. En effet, comme nous le rappelions précédemment, les résultats des recherches sur la catégorisation sociale montrent que des normes de favoritisme à l'égard de son groupe d'appartenance, mais aussi d'équité, régissent les comportements des sujets.

Notre hypothèse principale était alors que les tensions ou contradictions sociales qui peuvent se rencontrer à différents niveaux sont liées et qu'on retrouve, au niveau des relations entre soi et autrui, une tension parallèle à celle mise en évidence au niveau des relations entre groupes; cette tension ne serait plus en termes de solidarité/compétition, mais en termes de fusion/ individualisation. Au-delà de la simple mise en évidence de ces différentes normes antagonistes régissant le comportement des sujets, notre but était bien de montrer que ces différents systèmes contradictoires sont liés et varient ensemble (ou covarient) et qu'il suffit de renforcer expérimentalement le pôle compétition (ou concurrence, divergence, exclusion, en renforçant par exemple comme nous le verrons ci-dessous la saillance de la catégorisation induite dans une situation expérimentale pour que les sujets soient plus attirés par le pôle individualisation (ou différenciation de soi par rapport à autrui), et inversement.

L'objectif global des recherches que nous allons présenter peut donc être résumé de la façon suivante : il s'agissait de montrer que les différenciations inter-individuelles et inter-groupes sont liées et covarient ou varient de façon concomitante. Autrement dit, lorsque la différenciation entre groupes, pour une raison ou pour une autre est exacerbée, la différenciation que les individus établissent entre soi et autrui augmente et, parallèlement, lorsque la différenciation entre soi et autrui augmente, les différenciations que les individus établissent entre les groupes sont accrues.

RECHERCHES SUR LES DIFFERENCIATIONS INTER-INDIVIDUELLES ET INTER-GROUPES

Les expériences que nous rapporterons ne seront pas décrites ici dans leur intégralité; nous ne retiendrons que les éléments essentiels à notre propos (voir Deschamps, 1980; Deschamps et Lorenzi, 1981).

<u>Expérience 1</u>. Effet de la catégorisation inter-groupes sur les différenciations inter-individuelles

Les sujets de cette expérience étaient 88 élèves de l'Ecole Normale de filles de Délemont (Suisse), toutes âgées entre 16 et 20 ans.

La procédure de cette recherche, comme celle utilisée dans les recherches que nous mentionnerons ultérieurement, est proche de celle désormais classique élaborée par Tajfel et al. (1971).

La première partie de l'expérience, identique pour tous les sujets était présentée comme un travail sur les préférences esthétiques. On projetait sur un écran un certain nombre de couples de diapositives représentant des tableaux de Klee et de Kandinsky; chaque sujet indiquait alors sur une feuille de réponse individuelle laquelle des diapositives de chaque couple il avait préféré.

Figure 1. Exemple d'une page d'un carnet de matrice 8)

Carnet pour le groupe RILEY

Ces nombres sont des points pour :

	14	15	16	17	18	19	20	21	22	23	24	25	26
Vous-même, personne du groupe RILEY	–	–	–	–	–	–	–	–	–	–	–	–	–
Les personnes du groupe KABELAC	14	13	12	11	10	9	8	7	6	5	4	3	2

Ecrivez ci-dessous le détail des points de la case que vous avez choisie :

Points pour vous-même, personne du groupe RILEY : _____

Points pour les personnes du groupe KABELAC : _____

8) Exemple tiré de l'expérience 3, choix SA, condition Fusion.

La seconde phase de l'expérience était présentée comme une expérience sur les prises de décisions. Un carnet comprenant 32 matrices (une par page) était distribué à chaque sujet. On demandait aux sujets de lire attentivement la consigne se trouvant sur la première page du carnet et de répondre en fonction de ce qu'on leur demandait de faire dans ce texte. La consigne mentionnait : "Sur chaque page, vous choisirez une case et vous reporterez au bas de la page le détail des points de la case que vous aurez choisie. Les points figurant sur chaque page ne signifient rien de particulier, mais nous vous demandons de considérer ce travail comme un jeu où on joue pour des points et où le but est d'en obtenir le plus possible". 4)

Chaque matrice comprenait 13 cases contenant deux nombres. Dans les choix AA (choix autrui-autrui), les sujets distribuaient, dans chaque matrice, des points à deux autruis qui, en fonction des conditions expérimentales, étaient identifiés par leur appartenance catégorielle ou non; dans les choix SA (choix soi-autrui), chaque sujet distribuait des points dans chaque matrice à un autrui (identifié par son appartenance catégorielle ou non comme dans les choix AA) et à lui-même. L'ordre de passation des choix AA et SA était contrôlé pour chaque sujet.

A l'aide de ces matrices (voir figure 2, les matrices utilisées dans cette expérience sont celles de type 1(a) et 2(b), nous pouvons tester l'influence de certaines stratégies sur le comportement des sujets. Ces stratégies sont :

- RCM : Récompense Commune Maximale (colonne de la matrice correspondant au plus grand total de points qui peut être attribué)
- RIM : Récompense Intra-groupe Maximale ou favoritisme intra-groupe absolu (choix correspondant au plus grand nombre de points pouvant être attribué à un membre de l'intra-groupe)
- SM : Soi Maximum ou auto favoritisme absolu (choix correspondant au plus grand nombre de points pouvant être auto-attribué)
- DM : Différence Maximale en faveur de l'intra-groupe (ou de soi) ou favoritisme relatif de l'intra-groupe (ou de soi) (colonne de la matrice donnant la plus grande différence

---

4) Voir figure 1 l'exemple d'une page d'un carnet de matrice.

Figure 2. Matrices utilisées (tirées de Tajfel et al., 1971 et de Billig, 1972).

Matrices de type 1 : RCM versus RIM/SM + DM :

Matrice (a)   Choix AA   Choix SA 5)

19	18	17	16	15	14	13	12	11	10	9	8	7
1	3	5	7	9	11	13	15	17	19	21	23	25

                                                       I H   S I S H
                                                       H I   I S H S

Matrice (b)   Choix AA

23	22	21	20	19	18	17	16	15	14	13	12	11
5	7	9	11	13	15	17	19	21	23	25	27	29

                                                       I H
                                                       H I

Les matrices (a) et (b) de type 1 ont les mêmes propriétés : RCM est à droite; RIM/SM + DM sont aussi à droite lorsque les lignes du bas contiennent des points pour l'intra-groupe (I) ou soi (S), mais à gauche lorsque les lignes du haut contiennent des points pour l'intra-groupe ou soi.

Matrices de type 2 : DM versus RIM/SAM + RCM :

Matrice (c)   Choix AA   Choix SA

7	8	9	10	11	12	13	14	15	16	17	18	19
1	3	5	7	9	11	13	15	17	19	21	23	25

                                                       I H   S I S H
                                                       H I   I S H S

Matrice (d)   Choix AA

11	12	13	14	15	16	17	18	19	20	21	22	23
5	7	9	11	13	15	17	19	21	23	25	27	29

                                                       I H
                                                       H I

Les matrices (c) et (d) de type 2 ont les mêmes propriétés : RIM/SM + RCM sont à droite; DM est aussi à droite lorsque les points de la ligne du bas sont pour l'intra-groupe (I) ou soi (S), mais à gauche lorsque les points pour l'intra-groupe ou le soi sont dans les lignes du haut.

---

5) S = soi; I = intra-groupe; H = hors-groupe.

Matrices de type 3 : E versus RIM/SM + DM :

Matrice (e)

14	15	16	17	18	19	20	21	22	23	24	25	26
$\overline{14}$	$\overline{13}$	$\overline{12}$	$\overline{11}$	$\overline{10}$	$\overline{9}$	$\overline{8}$	$\overline{7}$	$\overline{6}$	$\overline{5}$	$\overline{4}$	$\overline{3}$	$\overline{2}$

Choix AA : I H / H I

Choix SA : S I S H / I S H S

Matrice (f)

17	18	19	20	21	22	23	24	25	26	27	28	29
$\overline{17}$	$\overline{16}$	$\overline{15}$	$\overline{14}$	$\overline{13}$	$\overline{12}$	$\overline{11}$	$\overline{10}$	$\overline{9}$	$\overline{8}$	$\overline{7}$	$\overline{6}$	$\overline{5}$

Choix AA : I H / H I

Les matrices (e) et (f) de type 3 ont les mêmes propriétés :
E est à gauche; RIM/SM + DM sont aussi à gauche lorsque les
points des lignes du bas sont pour l'intra-groupe (I) ou soi (S),
mais à droite lorsque les points des lignes du haut sont pour
l'intra-groupe ou soi.

possible de points en faveur de l'intra-groupe ou de soi)

Retenons ici que ce matériel nous permet d'accéder à des indices de différenciation soit entre groupes (dans les choix AA), soit entre soi et autrui (dans les choix SA) 6)

La moitié des sujets était alors placée dans une condition "Catégorisation". Les feuilles de réponse de la première phase de l'expérience avaient été corrigées (de façon fictive) par un assistant de l'expérimentateur afin de déterminer quel peintre avait été préféré par chaque sujet. En fait, on annonçait à chaque sujet sa préférence pour l'un ou l'autre peintre de façon aléatoire. En haut de la première page du carnet (consigne), était ajouté pour les sujets de cette condition Catégorisation : "Vous avez préféré les tableaux de (Klee ou Kandinsky). Vous êtes du groupe (Klee ou Kandinsky)", et en haut de chaque page du carnet était rappelé l'appartenance au groupe Klee ou Kandinsky. Dans chaque page pour les choix AA, les points de la ligne du haut étaient pour un membre de l'intra-groupe et ceux de la ligne du bas pour un membre du hors-groupe ou l'inverse; pour les choix SA, chaque sujet choisissait des points pour lui-même dans la ligne du haut, les points de la ligne du bas étant soit pour un membre de l'intra-groupe, soit pour un membre du hors-groupe ou l'inverse.

L'autre moitié des sujets était placée dans une condition "Non Catégorisation" dans laquelle on ne leur donnait pas les résultats supposés de la première phase de l'expérience; aucune induction de l'appartenance au groupe Klee ou Kandinsky n'était donc effectuée.

Conformément à notre hypothèse de la covariation des différenciations inter-groupes et inter-individuelles, les prédictions étaient que la différenciation de soi par rapport à autrui comme la différenciation intergroupes seraient plus importantes dans la condition Catégorisation que dans la condition Non Catégorisation.

---

6) Pour plus de détails sur ce type de matériel ainsi que sur la façon de traiter et d'analyser les résultats, voir Tajfel et al. (1971) et surtout Turner (1978) et en français Deschamps et Personnaz (1979).

Au niveau de la différenciation entre groupes, les résultats montrent une discrimination entre groupes dans la condition Catégorisation, discrimination en faveur de l'intra-groupe, et une absence d'effet de ce type dans la condition Non Catégorisation. 7) Cela montre bien, s'il fallait encore le prouver, que la simple induction chez les sujets de la représentation d'un environnement partagé en deux groupes, son groupe "minimal" d'appartenance et un autre groupe, entraîne une discrimination en faveur de son groupe d'appartenance.

Plus intéressants sont les résultats au niveau de la différenciation entre soi et autrui. Dans la condition Catégorisation, cette différenciation est significativement plus importante que dans la condition Non Catégorisation. Autrement dit, la simple introduction chez les sujets de la représentation d'un environnement composé de leur groupe et d'un groupe de non appartenance (dont un des effets est la différenciation entre groupes) a augmenté de façon significative le biais d'auto-favoritisme par rapport à la condition de Non Catégorisation (dans laquelle l'induction expérimentale d'une catégorisation sociale était absente).

Cette première expérience montre donc bien que la catégorisation, si elle est liée à la différenciation intergroupes, augmente aussi, comme c'était notre hypothèse, la différenciation inter-individuelle.

Expérience 2. Effet de la Solidarité / Compétition.

Cette recherche s'est déroulée collectivement dans un collège de Monthey en Valais (Suisse). Les sujets dont l'âge variait entre 12 et 13 ans étaient 44 garçons et filles.

L'expérience se déroulait de la façon suivante : on annonçait aux sujets que nous étions intéressés par les problèmes relatifs à la pratique du sport et plus particulièrement du ski et que nous allions leur demander de produire une réflexion sur la pratique du ski. "Pour des raisons pratiques", on avertissait les sujets qu'ils avaient été divisés en deux groupes et que chaque

---

7) Nous avons pu obtenir ces résultats en considérant, dans la condition Non Catégorisation, chaque alter comme étant tantôt du même groupe que le sujet, tantôt comme étant de l'autre groupe.

personne avait été mise au hasard dans le groupe "ROUGE" ou dans le groupe "BLEU". C'est alors que les conditions expérimentales étaient introduites.

Pour la moitié des sujets, ceux placés en situation de "Solidarité" on leur annonçait qu'on demanderait aux deux groupes, le groupe "BLEU" et le groupe "ROUGE", de travailler ensemble à l'élaboration de ce travail sur la pratique du ski et qu'ils auraient à produire un texte en commun. On amenait donc les sujets de cette condition à anticiper une relation coopérative entre groupes.

Pour l'autre moitié des sujets, ceux placés en situation de "Compétition", on leur annonçait que chaque groupe, le groupe "BLEU" et le groupe "ROUGE" devrait travailler séparément à l'élaboration de ce travail sur la pratique du ski et que chaque groupe aurait à remettre un texte, un seul texte devant être retenu par la suite par les expérimentateurs, celui qui aurait été jugé le meilleur. On amenait donc les sujets de cette condition à anticiper une relation compétitive entre groupes.

On prévenait ensuite les sujets, avant qu'ils réfléchissent et qu'ils effectuent une production sur la pratique du ski, que nous étions aussi intéressés par les "processus de prise de décision". Un carnet de 24 pages avec une matrice par page était alors distribué à chaque sujet. Cette recherche se déroulait alors comme la condition Catégorisation de la première expérience si ce n'est que les groupes Klee et Kandinsky étaient remplacés par les groupes "ROUGE" et "BLEU" et qu'un autre type de matrice (matrice de type 3 de la figure 2) avait été rajouté. 8) Une fois les carnets de matrices remplis, nous annoncions aux sujets que leur collaboration s'arrêtait là et nous leur dévoilions les buts de cette recherche.

L'effet direct de l'induction de la compétition et de la coopération (solidarité) nous permettait de prédire, au niveau des choix AA que la différenciation entre groupes en faveur de l'intra-groupe serait plus importante dans la condition Compétition que dans la condition Solidarité. De plus, conformément à notre hypothèse générale, au niveau des choix SA, un effet

---

8) Ce qui permet de tester en plus l'importance d'une stratégie d'Equité ($\underline{E}$: choix dans une matrice de la case correspondant à un nombre égal de points pour les deux bénéficiaires).

indirect de l'induction de la Solidarité et de la Compétition nous permettait de prédire que le biais d'auto-favoritisme ou la différenciation de soi par rapport à autrui serait plus important dans la condition Compétition que dans la condition Solidarité. Nos résultats montrent une tendance systématique dans le sens de ces prédictions, tant au niveau de la différenciation entre groupes qu'au niveau de la différenciation entre soi et autrui.

Ces deux premières recherches apportent un support empirique évident à la première partie de notre hypothèse de base, à savoir que les différenciations intergroupes et interindividuelles sont liées et qu'il suffit de renforcer expérimentalement la différenciation entre groupes pour que les sujets accroissent la différenciation qu'ils établissent entre soi et autrui.

Il nous reste maintenant à voir si l'inverse est vrai, en d'autres termes si lorsqu'on renforce la différenciation entre soi et autrui la différenciation entre groupes augmente.

<u>Expérience 3</u>. Différenciations entre groupes et entre individus identifiés par leur appartenance catégorielle.

Cette recherche s'est déroulée dans une école secondaire du canton de Vaud (Suisse). 56 garçons et filles dont l'âge variait entre 14 et 15 ans ont participé à cette expérience.

Le déroulement de cette expérience était identique à celui de l'expérience 1 si ce n'est que la première partie de la recherche portait sur des préférences esthétiques dans le domaine musical (préférences pour des extraits d'oeuvres de deux compositeurs contemporains : Kabelac et Riley) et non plus pictural.

Une façon de rendre plus saillante la dimension "Fusion" au niveau des relations inter-individuelles dans une recherche de ce genre consiste à demander aux sujets d'attribuer des points non plus à des individus caractérisés par leur seule appartenance catégorielle (points pour telle personne du groupe "X", ce qui correspondra dans cette expérience à la condition "Individualisation"), mais d'attribuer des points aux groupes dans leur ensemble (points pour les personnes du groupe "X"), ce qui correspond bien à une situation de "Fusion", au moins à l'intérieur de chaque groupe induit expérimentalement.

La manipulation expérimentale qui nous intéressera dans cette recherche était alors la suivante. A la moitié des sujets, ceux placés en condition de Fusion, on distribuait les carnets de matrices en leur indiquant leur appartenance au groupe Riley ou Kabelac en fonction d'une correction fictive de leurs réponses à la première phase de l'expérience. Pour les choix AA, dans chaque matrice, les points de la ligne du haut étaient pour "les personnes du groupe Riley", ceux du bas pour "les personnes du groupe Kabelac" ou l'inverse. Pour les choix SA, dans chaque matrice, les points de la ligne du haut étaient pour le sujet (par exemple, points pour "vous-même, personne du groupe Riley"), les points de la ligne du bas étant soit pour l'autre groupe ("les personnes du groupe Kabelac") soit pour le reste de son groupe ("les autres personnes du groupe Riley") ou l'inverse. L'autre moitié des sujets était placée dans la condition d'Individualisation dans laquelle, après leur avoir distribué les carnets de matrices et leur avoir indiqué leur appartenance au groupe Riley ou Kabelac comme dans la condition Fusion, ils devaient, pour les choix AA, attribuer des points non plus à des groupes mais à des individus caractérisés par leur appartenance à ces groupes dans chaque matrice, et pour les choix SA, attribuer des points à soi-même et à un individu de l'intra- ou du hors-groupe dans chaque matrice. Comme dans l'expérience précédente, les carnets comprenaient 24 matrices, matrices des trois types présentés figure 2.

Les prédictions que nous faisions étaient que, dans la condition Fusion, la différenciation entre soi et autrui serait plus faible que dans la condition Individualisation; de plus, au niveau de la différenciation entre groupes, la discrimination en faveur de son groupe devrait, conformément à notre hypothèse des variations concomitantes, être plus faible dans la condition Fusion que dans la condition Individualisation. Nos résultats montrent bien, effectivement, que la différenciation entre soi et autrui est significativement plus élevée dans la condition Individualisation que dans la condition Fusion. Pour ce qui est de la différenciation entre groupes, la discrimination en faveur de son groupe est aussi significativement plus élevée dans la condition Individualisation que dans la condition Fusion. Lorsque l'on augmente la différenciation entre soi et autrui, ici en centrant les sujets sur les individus caractérisés par leur appartenance groupale et non pas sur les groupes dans leur ensemble, la différenciation entre groupes augmente parallèlement, comme c'était notre hypothèse.

Expérience 4.   Effet de la Fusion / Individualisation.

Le cadre de cette recherche est le même que celui de l'expérience 2, les sujets étaient aussi au nombre de 44, des garçons et des filles âgés entre 12 et 13 ans.

Le but de cette recherche était de tester une autre opérationalisation de la dimension Individualisme / Fusion, dimension déjà abordée dans l'expérience précédente. On avertissait les sujets que nous étions intéressés par les "processus de prise de décision"; un carnet de 24 matrices était alors distribué à chaque sujet (matrices des 3 types représentés figure 2) et "pour des raisons pratiques", on annonçait aux sujets qu'ils avaient été placés, au hasard dans deux groupes et que chaque personne avait été mise aléatoirement dans le groupe "BLEU" ou dans le groupe "ROUGE". La tâche des sujets consistait alors à attribuer des points à un alter de leur groupe et de l'autre groupe dans chaque matrice pour les choix AA et à eux-même et à un autrui de leur groupe ou de l'autre groupe dans chaque matrice pour les choix SA.

La moitié des sujets était placée dans une condition Individualisation. Dans cette condition, on avertissait chaque sujet que les points qu'il aurait choisis pour une personne seraient donnés à cette personne. A l'autre moitié des sujets, ceux placés en condition de Fusion, on disait que les points qu'ils auraient choisis pour chaque personne d'un groupe entreraient dans une moyenne, moyenne des points que tous les sujets auraient attribués à ces personnes. Cette moyenne était censée être donnée à tous les membres d'un groupe, autrement dit, chaque personne d'un groupe devait recevoir le même nombre de points correspondant à la moyenne des points qui auraient été donnés aux personnes de ce groupe.

Les prédictions étaient alors que l'effet direct de l'induction de l'Individualisme et de la Fusion se traduirait, au niveau des choix SA par une plus grande différenciation entre soi et autrui dans la condition Individualisation que dans la condition Fusion. En accord avec l'hypothèse de la covariation des différenciations inter-individuelles et inter-groupes, pour ce qui est des choix AA, nous prédisions un effet indirect de l'induction de l'Individualisme et de la Fusion en fonction duquel la discrimination en faveur de l'intra-groupe devait être plus intense dans la condition Individualisation que dans la condition Fusion. Les résultats obtenus vont, et de façon systématique, dans le sens de ces prédictions, que ce soit en ce qui concerne la différenciation entre soi et autrui ou entre groupes.

Dans ces deux dernières expériences, nous avons pu apporter un début de validité empirique à la seconde partie de notre hypothèse selon laquelle lorsqu'on renforce expérimentalement la différenciation entre soi et autrui en augmentant le biais d'auto-favoritisme, la différenciation intergroupes en faveur de son groupe d'appartenance s'accroît.

Les résultats des recherches trop brièvement rapportées dans ce texte semblent être une base empirique sérieuse à notre proposition de départ, à savoir l'hypothèse de la covariation ou de la variation concomitante de la différenciation entre groupes et de la différenciation entre soi et autrui.

Nous avons pu montrer en effet, dans nos deux premières recherches, que lorsqu'au niveau intergroupes, on faisait en sorte que les sujets établissent une distance, une divergence entre groupes (que ce soit par l'induction de la représentation de l'appartenance à deux catégories "minimales" ou par l'anticipation d'une rencontre compétitive), la discrimination entre soi et autrui augmentait parallèlement. Dans les deux autres expériences que nous avons présentées ici, c'est lorsqu'on augmente la distance entre soi et autrui, la différenciation de soi par rapport à autrui (à l'aide de deux types d'opérationalisation de la dimension individualisme / fusion) que l'on peut observer une augmentation concomitante de la différenciation entre groupes.

BIBLIOGRAPHIE

Avigdor, R. Etude expérimentale de la genèse des stéréotypes. Cahiers Internationaux de Sociologie, 1953, 14, 154-168.

Berger, E. & Luckman, T. The social construction of reality. New York: Doubleday, 1966.

Billig, M.G. Social categorization and intergroup relations. University of Bristol : Ph.D. Thesis, 1972.

Bruner, J.S. On perceptual readiness. Psychological Review, 1957, 64, 123-152.

Bruner, J.S. Les processus de préparation à la perception. In J.S. Bruner, F. Bresson, A. Morf & J. Piaget (Eds.), Logique et perception. Paris, P.U.F., 1958, 1-48.

Deschamps, J.-C. Imputation de la responsabilité de l'échec (ou de la réussite) et catégorisation sociale. Bulletin de Psychologie, 1972-1973, 26, 794-806.

Deschamps, J.-C. L'attribution et la catégorisation sociale. Berne : Peter Lang, 1977.

Deschamps, J.-C. Différenciation catégorielle et différenciation de soi par rapport à autrui. <u>Recherches de Psychologie Sociale</u>, 1979, <u>1</u>, 29-38.

Deschamps, J.-C. Différenciations inter-individuelles et intergroupes. In P. Tap (Ed.), <u>Identité individuelle et personnalisation</u>. Toulouse : Privat, 1980, 187-190.

Deschamps, J.-C. & Lorenzi, F. "Egocentrisme" et "sociocentrisme" dans les relations entre groupes. Recherches expérimentales. <u>Revue Suisse de Psychologie Pure et Appliquée</u>, 1981.

Deschamps, J.-C. & Personnaz, B. Etudes entre groupes "dominants" et "dominés": Importance de la présence du hors-groupe dans les discriminations évaluatives et comportementales. <u>Social Science Information</u>, 1979, <u>18</u>, 269-305.

Doise, W. <u>L'articulation psychosociologique et les relations entre groupes</u>. Bruxelles : De Boeck, 1976.

Erikson, E.H. The problem of ego identity. In M. Stein, A. Vidich, D.N. White (Eds.), <u>Identity and anxiety</u>. Glencoe : Free Press, 1963.

Brown, R. & Deschamps, J.-C. Discriminations entres individus et entre groupes. <u>Bulletin de Psychologie</u>, 1980-1981, <u>34</u>, 185-195.

Fromm, E. <u>Escape from freedom</u>. New York: Farrar & Rinehart, 1941.

Fromm, E. <u>The sane society</u>. London: Routledge & Kegan, 1956.

Kardiner, A. <u>The individual and his society</u>. New York: Columbia University Press, 1939.

Kardiner, A., Linton, R., Dubois, C. & West, J. <u>The psychological frontiers of society</u>. New York: Columbia University Press, 1945.

Katz, D. & Braly, K. Racial stereotype of 100 colleges students. <u>Journal of Abnormal and Social Psychology</u>, 1933, <u>28</u>, 280-290.

Linton, R. <u>The cultural background of personality</u>. New York: Appleton Century, 1945.

Mead, G.H. <u>Mind, self and society</u>. Chicago: The University of Chicago Press, 1934.

Sarbin, T.R. & Allen, V.L. Role theory. In Lindzey, G.& E. Aronson (Eds.), <u>Handbook of social psychology</u>. Reading, Mass. Addison-Wesley, 1968.

Sherif, M., Harvey, O.J., White, B.J., Hood, W.R. & Sherif, C.W. <u>Inter-group conflict and cooperation, the Robber's cave experiment</u>. Oklahoma : Norma, 1961.

Tajfel, H. La catégorisation sociale. In S. Moscovici (Ed.) <u>Introduction à la psychologie sociale</u>. Paris; Larousse, 1972, vol. 1, 272-302.

Tajfel, H., Billig, M.G., Bundy, R.P. & Flament, C. Social categorization and intergroup behaviour. <u>European Journal of Social Psychology</u>, 1971, <u>1</u>, 149-178.

Tajfel, H. & Turner, J. An integrative theory of group conflict. In W.G. Austin & S. Worchel (Eds.), The social psychology of intergroup relations. Monterey, Calif.: Brooks/Cole, 1979.

Turner, J. Social comparison and social identity; some prospects for intergroup behaviour. European Journal of Social Psychology, 1975, 5, 5-34.

Turner, J. Social categorization and social discrimination in the minimal group paradigm. In H. Tajfel (Ed.), Differenciation between social groups. London : Academic Press, 1978,

Zavalloni, M. L'identité psychosociale, un concept à la recherche d'une science. In S. Moscovici (Ed.), Introduction à la psychologie sociale. Paris; Larousse, 1973, vol. 2, 245-265.

DIFFERENTIATING AND NON-DIFFERENTIATING BEHAVIOR : A COGNITIVE
APPROACH TO THE SENSE OF IDENTITY 1)

J.P. Codol

Laboratoire de Psychologie Sociale, Université de
Provence, Aix-en-Provence

There exist at least two possible approaches to the question of how the sense of identity is formed :
- The first and by far the most prevalent in the literature, might be called the "diachronic" approach : its focus is on the development of self-awareness and personal identity within the individual's life history and its development in the course of the socialization process.

Most of the theories advanced in genetic psychology, personality psychology, or clinical psychology (notably psychoanalytic theory), have attempted to determine the critical junctures for the sense of identity, its formative phases during childhood and adolescence, and its residue in the adult.

- The second approach (which, by contrast to the above-mentioned approach, might be called "synchronic") has, to the best of my knowledge, received only fragmentary attention. It is the object of this approach to investigate and define the sense of identity within the framework of a general study of cognitive mechanisms and structures.

---

1) A French version of this chapter was published, with a few minor modifications, in Social Science Information, 20, 111-136 (1980).

For anyone taking the individual's pursuit of social similarity and social differentiation as his main research focus, the individual's cognitive grasp of his environment, of himself and of other people necessarily provides the proper frame of reference. That is why, on the whole, I will operate within the framework of the second approach. "On the whole", as I must stress, since these two approaches are in fact by no means mutually exclusive. On the contrary, there is persuasive evidence (for which we are largely indebted to the Piagetian school) that developmentally, cognitive activities go hand-in-hand with socialization processes and are therefore nearly indissociable.

To avoid any possible misunderstanding, let us first spell out what we mean by the expression "cognitive activity". A common current usage in the field of psychology is to limit its meaning to purely intellectual operations. Obviously this perspective is too restrictive, and that is not the way in which I intend to use it here. What I have in mind by cognitive activity is any activity whereby a psychic apparatus organizes information into knowledge. When this information concerns the self, what we have to deal with is self-knowledge. And it is this self-knowledge - at any rate, this is the thesis I am submitting here - which is at the root of the sense of identity.

THE SENSE OF IDENTITY

The way in which an individual apprehends himself cognitively exemplifies several of the major mechanisms underlying cognitive apprehension generally : this will be the first point of our argument. We would of course need much more space to deal adequately with these mechanisms than can be done within the framework of this chapter. The following few points, which are certainly very well-established, may nevertheless serve as guidelines.

1. Cognitive apprehension - a few general points

Among the paramount processes for any kind of cognitive apprehension, those dealing with the <u>identification</u> and <u>recognition</u> of objects are certainly of the most fundamental importance. Identification and recognition of an object by an individual assumes specifically
a) that he is able to determine <u>resemblances</u> and <u>differences</u> between this object and other objects present in the environment;
b) and that, at the same time, this object has invariant characteristics, that is, a certain <u>consistency</u> and <u>constancy</u> over time.

It has become customary to view the determination of similarities and differences as a process that requires <u>categorizing</u> information provided by these objects. Within this categorization process, the information itself is <u>transformed</u>, inasmuch as information intake is subject to perceptive distortions governed by definite laws and processes, notably selection, simplification, rigidity, egocentricity, etc... 2). It is known, for instance, that individuals in most cases take in only what is <u>meaningful</u> for them, to wit, only those things that they can connect <u>directly</u> or remotely with objects that are already familiar and that have acquired a certain meaning for them, whether by prior exposure or by social transmission.

Since categories are made up of sets of characteristics that the subject attributes to the objects in his environment and these characteristics are <u>meaningful to him</u>, it would be wrong to view these categories as rigorously definitional and neutral with respect to the individual. Characteristics and properties of objects, which are always derived from personal experience or the impact of social norms, always have <u>values attached to them</u> in the eyes of the individual and are consequently linked with <u>behavioral patterns</u>.

Nevertheless, categorization and meaning are possible only because man lives in a <u>relatively stable</u> physical and social environment. The individual can identify these objects only because they have more or less invariant characteristics. The <u>constancy of objects</u> in turn relates to the <u>consistency of the individual's categorization system.</u> Thanks to this very stability of the environment and this psychological consistency, individuals are capable of making predictions about objects, persons, social events, etc.

---

2) Notwithstanding the modifications to which it may be subjected, the cognitive system could not function without a relative rigidity. Too great a flexibility would make any categorization inoperative. A counterpart of this rigidity is the fact that cognitive apprehension always implies a simplifying apprehension of reality. With respect to every kind of categorization, the <u>highlighting of differences or resemblances</u> is one of the ways in which simplification phenomena operate : by classifying different objects into one category, one stresses the perceived similarity of these objects; by classifying them into different categories, on the contrary, there is a cognitive stress on their differences.

In short, categorization seems to be an essential feature of information gathering. Each object is at the same time perceived as a whole and as possessing special characteristics distinguishing it from other objects and constituting its uniqueness. These characteristics, which the individual views as meaningful, are categorized either in isolation or within organized sets. The set of categories serves as a system for filtering and organizing new information. Only through this system can information acquire meaning for the individual.

Once a categorization system has been established, the individual can still perform some operations on his own system, and thereby build up new categories or objects that need have only a very remote relation to the reality of concrete objects.

The reader will certainly have noticed that these are blunt and lapidary assertions. At this point, all that the author would like the reader to retain from the foregoing are these three ideas:
a) any cognitive apprehension of an object presupposes the determination of differences - and similarities - whereby this object is specified from among other objects;
b) any cognitive apprehension presupposes a certain permanence and consistency as far as the object under consideration is concerned;
c) any cognitive apprehension is associated with a "valuation" or "valorization" (here the terminology remains in flux) with respect to this object.

2. Cognitive apprehension of the self - Dimensions of the sense of identity

The way in which an individual apprehends himself cognitively, as I stated earlier, derives from the same processes as those regulating any cognitive apprehension. One's self-image is thus simply a structured set of meaningful information items, which one has received or elaborated about oneself : it consists of an organization of traits, qualities, characteristics (taking these words in their most general meaning) that the individual attributes to himself.

In line with what we have just stated generally about cognitive apprehension, we shall now deal with three topics :
- When we speak of self-image, we assume that <u>it is possible to take oneself as an object, and that this object has characteristics distinguishing it from any other object</u>. Here we are dealing with the individual's sense of his own <u>difference</u>.

- As is true of any representation of an object, <u>the self-image offers a certain consistency and stability</u>; at stake here is the individual's sense of his own unity, of his <u>identity with himself</u>.
- As with any other representation, finally, the self-image reveals a <u>certain valorization about the object in question</u>. Here we will broach the topic of <u>self-valorization</u>, or the "value" one attributes to oneself.

2.1. The self as a unique object - the sense of difference

The only way that there can be a self-image is if the individual can <u>identify</u> a certain object as denoting himself. This identification presupposes that the individual can think of himself as a specific object and one that differs from any other object. The sense of self therefore perforce expresses an individual's awareness, on a cognitive level, of <u>his being different from any other object</u>, notably from those specific other objects constituted by other persons. The sense of difference is paramount in becoming aware of oneself. It is the root trait that allows the individual to view himself simultaneously as a subject and as an object, in short, as having both a material and a social existence.

Of course, this sense of difference can be experienced socially only <u>with reference to others</u>. For anyone to assert : "this is myself, this is not myself", others are absolutely indispensable. I have emphasized already that comparison alone allows categorization and therefore identification of the self among other selves. Comparison with others is thus <u>an intrinsic element of social existence as such</u>.

2.2. <u>Consistency and stability of the self-image - the sense of self-unity and self-identity</u>

There must always be a certain consistency, a certain stability, a certain constancy over time in the organization of traits into a structured whole. As far as one's self-image is concerned, this is where, strictly speaking, the <u>sense of self-identity</u> comes to the fore.

In the narrowest sense of the word, an individual's identity consists of whatever causes this individual to remain identical to himself over space and time. <u>Self-unity and its permanence are therefore the two major constituents of identity</u>. The sense of identity arises from the fact that the individual, by defining himself first of all as an particular object has a consistent image of himself and believes that the object to which this image refers (himself) has a certain constancy over time.

Strictly speaking, one should differentiate between the <u>sense of difference</u>, on the one hand, and the <u>sense of consistency and permanence</u> on the other. Practically speaking, the two phenomena are so inextricably tied together in one's self-image that common usage in the last analysis denotes them with a single concept : the concept of identity. I therefore subscribe wholeheartedly to Green's (1977, pp. 81-82) definition : "Several ideas come together under the term of identity. Identity is associated with the idea of permanence, of maintaining steady, constant reference points which are not subject to changes capable of affecting the subject or object over time. In the second place, identity refers to the setting of boundaries which assure the existence of a separate state of existence, allowing one to circumscribe unity, that totalizing consistency which is indispensable to the ability to make distinctions. Identity, finally, is one of the conceivable relations between two elements, whereby absolute similarity ruling between them is established and the two are recognized as identical. These three characteristics go hand-in-hand : constancy, unity, recognition of sameness".

2.3. <u>Self-valorization - the sense of autonomy and power</u>

Every global image, finally, is composed of a set of traits that are all valorized in a certain way and implies a certain valorization of the object in question.

If it is true that, in the last analysis, adaptation is the ultimate goal of every activity, it must be admitted (and evidence abounds for supporting this assumption !) that one's self-image, as a whole, can only be <u>positively valorized</u>. The fact that we attribute a certain <u>value</u> to ourselves is clearly revealed by the most fundamental physiobiological needs (assuring survival, etc...). Self-valorization is nothing but a more complex manifestation of this "value", which in man has a cognitive counterpart. Within the context of adaptation, self-valorization is not limited to attributing to oneself a set of qualities considered positive - either by the individual himself or by social transmission - (such as : I am good, likable, patient, tolerant, etc...); it also - and perhaps above all - implies attributing to oneself a certain <u>power</u> over one's material and social environment. Any positive image of the self is correlated with conceiving oneself as the source of specific effects and with the feeling of being able at least to a certain extent to influence things and people, of shaping or controlling events, etc.

3. Constructing the sense of identity

3.1. The individual's relations with his material and social environment

Several closely related dimensions taken together thus constitute each person's sense of identity : awareness of his uniqueness, of his permanence over time, of his internal consistency, of his positive value - and the sense of autonomy and power associated therewith 3).

Obviously, it is in the course of development that the foundation for the sense of identity is laid, in the individual's relations with his material and social environment.

One's self-image is of course not actually built up solely in a formal way, by distinguishing between oneself and others, by noting a relative consistency or a relative permanence. The various kinds of characteristics the individual attributes to himself have their share in providing a content for his self-image and giving sustenance to his sense of his own difference and his own identity.

The fact of the matter is that, essentially, these characteristics are an outgrowth of the cognitive integration on the individual's part of the information input he receives in the course of his interactions with his environment.

---

3) As is true of every other product of cognitive processes, apprehension of the self as a special object, the requisite sense of consistency and constancy, and valorization of the self all have an adaptive function within a given social framework. Proof thereof lies in the fact that - in our societies at least - the inverse phenomena are considered pathological symptoms. The feeling of non-differentiation between oneself and others, an inconsistent or shattered self-image, an exclusively negative valuation of the self : all these are symtoms by which mental illnesses are identified.

The specific sources of this information input are :
a) <u>behavior he adopts and the effects</u> (on objects, others, himself) <u>he perceives therefrom</u>. In this respect, the way in which an individual perceives his own behavior plays an important role in his elaboration of his self-image. One notable consequence of this fact is that the individual's adopting such and such a behavior may be determined by the self-image he wishes to receive from it.

b) <u>his integration into the social world, particularly, his belonging to certain social entities, groups, or categories</u>. Here the fundamental phenomenon is that of <u>introjective identification</u>. By means of introjective identification 4) the individual attributes to himself characteristics he attributes to other persons or groups 5).

---

4) I am taking up an expression here, whose use is hallowed in psychology. It must however be admitted that it is not altogether unambiguous. The word "identification" actually has two meanings. It may designate two things simultaneously : 1) the action whereby an object is identified and recognized - <u>and hence differentiated</u> from other objects and endowed with its own identity and 2) the action by means of which, in the pronominal sense, one pronounces oneself identical with another object - <u>and hence similar</u>. But perhaps this ambiguity reflects the difficulty we have in coming to terms with identity, since it represents the convergence point between identification as differentiation and identification as similarity.

5) The inverse phenomenon, which is its complement, may also be related to it. By <u>projective identification</u>, the individual attributes to others - whether persons or groups - characteristics he attributes to himself.

Projection and introjection are two processes whereby an individual establishes a <u>similarity</u> between himself and others. The establishment of this similarity does not have the same meaning in each of these cases : in the case of introjection, the similarity is established with reference to the subject himself. As I have shown elsewhere (Codol, 1979), generally similarity is more acceptable to the subjects in the second case than in the first, because the subject's own existence is more strongly asserted.

c) __and finally, what image of himself his environment sends back to him__. In this respect, the individual's social images 6) and his perception thereof play a fundamental role in his self-image. As matters stand, a person's social images derive in part from the way the people around him perceive his behavior, and from his being associated with certain groups or categories. As a result, both the adoption of a certain behavior on an individual's part, and his sense of belonging to certain groups, are partially determined by the self-image the individual wishes to convey to others.

3.2. Social images and introjective identification - stereotyping and discrimination

To a certain extent at least, social images are shaped in a way that can be compared to introjective identification. People around one most commonly assume that one has those traits and characteristics that are typical of the categories to which one belongs.

This is what Tajfel (1969, 1972; see also Doise, 1976) calls the "deductive" aspect of social categorization. By this he refers to the process whereby each member of a category is assigned those traits that presumably characterize the category as such. Conversely, he speaks of an "inductive" aspect, whereby a whole category is attributed a feature perceived as characterizing a single one of its members, who is assumed to be typical or exemplary.

As I mentioned earlier, all cognitive apprehension, by its reliance on categorization, leads to simplification and tends specifically to accentuate the similarity of objects within categories and to accentuate differences between categories 7).

---

6) By "social image" I am referring here to the image people around him generally have of that particular individual.

7) There are many experimental verifications in the literature about this point (for instance : Tajfel and Wilkes, 1963; Marchand, 1970, etc.) With reference to perception, the gestalt theory has amply demonstrated analogous phenomena in perceptive organization: the tendency to separate objects from each other on the one hand, and to homogenize them internally on the other.

This is true irrespective of the fact that the objects in question are persons and the categories are social categories 8) : in these processes, each social category starts out, in fact, as a cognitive category. On the social level, stereotypes reflect the attribution of similar characteristics to different members of one and the same group.

The effect of stereotyping is to homogenize and de-individualize the members of a group. "These individuals become perceptually interchangeable because they are perceived in terms of their shared category characteristics and not their personal idiosyncratic natures " (Turner, 1981) 9).

In a complementary way, social discrimination, conversely, reflects the expression of an exaggeration of differences between individuals belonging to different categories 10).

---

8) As is shown, for instance, in studies by Tajfel, Sheikh, and Gardner (1964).

9) Turner (1981) adds that stereotyping occurs not only in relation to external groups but also with respect to one's own group. To this he ascribes the biases generally affecting intra-group perceptions and behaviors : perception of similarity between members, uniformity of attitudes, mutual attraction and esteem, intra-group favoritism, etc... For that reason, he considers the definition of groups in terms of "social cohesion" as inappropriate, preferring a definition in terms of categorial affiliation and identification. For Turner, individuals who perceive themselves as members of the same social category - and who thereby share a common identification - can be said to constitute a group. Social cohesion, where it exists, is in his opinion only a result of categorial identification.

10) Several experiments have shown that the mere act of categorizing individuals, even on a purely arbitrary basis, into two groups ("the others" and "ourselves") gives rise to discriminatory behavior between the groups (downgrading of "the others" and valorization of "ourselves"). See for instance Tajfel et al., 1971 ; Billig, 1971; Billig and Tajfel, 1973.

The fact of belonging simultaneously to groups with different cultural guidelines and values raises significant questions in this context. This is true not only because under these circumstances it is obviously difficult for an individual to create a consistent self-image of himself, but also because, as a result of stereotyping on the basis of social categories, he is to a certain extent viewed as an outsider by each of these groups. The upshot is that those who belong in this way to two worlds are generally not fully accepted by either one of them.

Any individual may in principle be faced with such situations as a consequence of his belonging simultaneously to different groups. It is clear, however, that, depending on the nature and the "weight" of the groups in question, these situations do not affect all individuals involved with equal force. They must weigh particularly heavily on the children of North African immigrants in France, for example, caught as they are between two noticeably different cultural models and torn between what they experience in their families and what they experience at school or in the street. For them this type of experience must obviously be far more dramatic than it is for others.

3.3. Forms of social identification - "personal" identification and "social" identity

One may therefore be justified in thinking that there are altogether two major forms of <u>social identification</u> :
- one form corresponds to a cognitive activity <u>carried out by the individual himself</u>, whereby he attributes to himself characteristics associated with the groups or categories to which he belongs (introjective identification);
- the other form relates to an activity occurring <u>outside the individual</u> and involving the perception of characteristics assigned to him by the people around him because of these affiliations (as perceived by the people around him) with certain groups or categories.

The two forms of social identification delimit what one can call an individual's "<u>social identity</u>".

Two observations seem pertinent to me in this connection :
a) <u>the first involves the relations between these two forms of social identification</u>; their content, obviously, need not be identical. The social categories the individual applies to define himself do not, in truth, always coincide with the ones applied to him by the people around him 11). And even if there happened to be a perfect coincidence between these two sets of social categories, they would not necessarily mean the same thing to the individual and to those around him. To be a "researcher", for instance, does not have either the same meaning or the same connotations for the person who is a researcher as it does for the person who is not one himself.
b) <u>the second involves the relations between social identity and what I have introduced under the term "personal " identity</u> : while social identity is in fact one of the essential dimensions of identity, it does not, in my eyes, represent a comprehensive whole.

Published research - in particular publications in social psychology - may be responsible for this mistaken view, since most studies deal with identity only in terms of social affiliations.

Sometimes the authors themselves avoid this ambiguity by stating explicitly that they are limiting themselves to the study of social identity. Tajfel (1972) for instance is particularly cautious in that he writes in his chapter on social categorization : "(...) we shall define "identity" exclusively in relation to the topic of this chapter, without making any claims to generalizations (...). Suffice it to say that an individual's social identity is associated with the knowledge of his affiliation with certain social groups and with the emotional and valuational meaning derived from this affiliation" (p.292). And a few pages further : ("The individual's social identity can be defined) only in terms of the effects of social categorization, by means of which the social environment is compartmentalized so as to delimit clearly his own group from the other groups" (p.296).

Marisa Zavalloni (1973) is not equally explicit on this point in her studies, although she has developed interesting theoretical and methodological concepts in her research on identity.

---

11) There is no question, for instance, that ethnologists have great trouble defining ethnic identities in such a way that the definitions are objectively valid and at the same time recognized as applicable by the populations involved.

She suggests an analytical method for studying "psychosocial identity" and states its objectives in these terms : "The objective is to discover the functional relations between subjective awareness of identity (personal identity) and its objective social attributes (social identity) " (p.253).

How can one fail to applaud such a project ? All the more since Zavalloni claims to use a theoretical framework that coincides in every respect with my own concerns in this chapter : " (it is possible) to conceive psychosocial identity as a cognitive structure linked with representational thinking. It would therefore be essential to approach the question of identity both theoretically and methodologically within the general framework of the study of cognitive processes" (p.251).

And yet, what is the content of the method she proposes ? "In concrete terms, we shall attempt to analyze in what way affiliation with particular groups 12) (...) is likely to be affected by one's self-perception and personal values and the converse" (p.253).

Zavalloni's subjects are thus asked <u>in the first place</u> to define themselves by their affiliation with different groups or categories. Zavalloni's approach -which is quite complex - does not stop there; her subjects are induced, through several stages, to situate themselves, and to situate others within these groups. But "psychosocial identity" takes <u>social affiliations as a starting point</u> before it is further refined.

I have no doubt that one can obtain most instructive and interesting results by applying this type of method, and such is indeed the case. But in my eyes, this approach exclusively deals with social identity; it is not an all-inclusive approach to identity, at least as I have defined it.

In any case, social identifications, whether based on the individual's own judgment or on the judgment of the people around him, are inevitably structured within a comprehensive self-image and therefore subject to transformations. Consequently <u>identity cannot be derived from the sum or the resultant of various social identifications</u>.

---

12) These are the "groups" ; nation, sex, religion , origin, profession, social class, political affiliation, age group, civil status.

Other types of information input (such as the adoption of particular behaviors) surely have their own role to play in the shaping of one's self-image and hence in the definition of a comprehensive sense of identity.

To differentiate "personal identity" from "social identity" Turner (1981) takes up a distinction first made by Gergen (1971). According to it, each individual would have a two-fold characterization :
- on the one hand, he would have social traits, denoting his belonging to certain groups or categories (such as sex, nationality, relation, etc...)
- on the other hand, he would have certain personal traits, that would be specifically attributable to the individual (physical or psychological characteristics, etc...).

The former would then define a person's "social identity", and the latter his "personal identity".

The truth of the matter is that a distinction based on these criteria runs into many practical problems. The criteria for differentiating between the social and the personal realm are by no means clear-cut. Would one say, for instance, that wearing a beard is a personal attribute, while being a "student" would involve a social category ? In the real world, being bearded puts one in as well-defined a category as being a student. Under some circumstances, it may even be a more clearly defined one : what about the "beards" of South American revolutionary movements ? One can see that the question is by no means as simple as one might think at first.

Moreover, how could an attribute be completely personal, how could it be a specific trait of a particular person ? In so far as this attribute can be perceived and verbalized, it inevitably is a social object, relevant at least in a number of cases. To the extent that one can speak of a person's specificity, this can in fact only be the result of the particular combination of certain characteristics which, if taken in isolation, are surely shared by other people as well.

3.4. Variability in the ways of shaping a sense of identity

The part attributable to environmental "input of information" in the shaping of the sense of identity is likely to vary for different individuals, at different times, or for different groups.

J. Williams (1978), for instance, has pointed out a certain number of differences between the sexes on the basis of empirical research. From her studies it would seem that women (statistically, and in our societies) are more susceptible than men to the reactions of their surroundings and the social images reflected back to them in the way that they define themselves; that identifications with others play a greater role in shaping their identity; that their self-definition is more stereotyped, and that these stereotypes are expressed more in relational terms (for instance : mother, wife, etc.); that interpersonal comparisons play a greater role with them, and that they are more sensitive than men to prevailing social stereotypes, such as the prevailing conception of the "ideal woman".

In a related approach, J.C. Deschamps (1978) takes up an idea of Guillaumin's (1972) and suggests that persons belonging to a socially "dominant" group (a group that can exert a certain amount of social control) have a different way of shaping and expressing their sense of identity than persons belonging to a group that is socially "dominated".

He bases these conclusions on a certain number of empirical observations and experimental results. According to these, persons who belong to a minority and/or dominated social category are more likely to define themselves in terms of those characteristics that are related to their minority or dominated status. In a study done in the United States, Gordon (1968) for instance discovered that women answered the question "Who am I ?" more frequently by referring to their sex than was true of men, that blacks referred to their skin color more frequently than whites, Jews to their religious affiliation more than Christians, etc.

For their self-definition, therefore, the dominated were more likely to refer to collective characteristics, while those in a dominant category gave more personal and idiosyncratic responses (cf. Doise et al., 1976).

These tendencies are likely to be reinforced by the social images reflected to each one by his surrounding images which are at least partially internalized. Studies have shown, for example, that the behavior of persons with a high social status is perceived not only by themselves (cf. Doise et al., 1976) but also by other people, as being directly attributable to themselves. These persons are therefore perceived as the subjects of their actions. The same behavior, when attributed to lower-status persons, is more likely to be perceived as due to external causes (other people, chance, etc.) (cf.for instance Thibaut and Riecken, 1955, or Deaux and Emswiller, 1974).

These different types of identifying references have a linguistic counterpart as well, according to Deschamps. As Bernstein (1975) shows, the pronoun "I" is more frequently used by subjects belonging to the upper class of society, whereas, Bernstein asserts, "working-class subjects tend to use a relatively non-individualized speech". Bisseret (1974) similarly observes a wider use of the indefinite pronoun "one" than of the definite pronoun "we" in the speech of "dominated" groups. According to Deschamps, these are manifestations of a sense of belonging to a collective object (rather than a collective subject) and to an impersonal mass of people 13).

Irrespective of the validity of Deschamps' hypotheses (which must be subjected to specific empirical tests), 14) they are surely correct in stressing that the shaping and the expression of the sense of identity cannot be accounted for by simple mechanisms unrelated to situational and social contexts.

However, nobody can be satisfied with having a personal sense of identity. This sense of identity requires <u>social recognition</u>. The second part of this chapter proposes to provide some insight into the reasons why each of us desires this social recognition and what is the impact of this desire on the behavioral level -in particular the pursuit of similarity and differentiation.

---

13) Deschamps offers another interesting hypothesis on this point. Since the dominated groups are not entirely able to free themselves from the dominant norms - for the very reason that they are dominated - they work out a double system of identifying references, which results in their suffering a greater uncertainty as to what they are themselves.

14) And, with all due reservations attributable to their vagueness; thus the relationship between groups defined here as minority and those labelled dominated must be spelled out. As a matter of fact, everybody can think of himself as dominant in terms of his affiliation with a certain number of groups, and dominated in terms of his affiliation with other groups.

IN SEARCH OF A SOCIAL RECOGNITION OF IDENTITY

1. Self-image and social images of the self

Differentiation, constancy and consistency, valorization, these are the paramount dimensions of personal identity.

While it is true that personal identity is built up gradually in the course of the individual's development - some, like Erikson (1968) specifically view adolescence as the time of a normative identity crisis - it is actually never permanently established; nobody can be said to be settled for good within a completed identity.

J. Williams (1978), for instance, has shown the modifications in the sense of identity in certain women as they grew older, inasmuch as these women largely defined themselves in terms of their status as wives and mothers. To them the marriage of their children, or the loss of their spouse, implies not only the loss of roles whereby they can define themselves, but even the obliteration of the reference points for their personal identification. In addition, with advancing years, many women find that interpersonal comparison - an essential component of self-definition - becomes more painful with respect to some socially valorized dimensions of identity : in terms of physical comparison, by adding wrinkles to their body, the passage of time makes it less and less attractive and desirable.

The reason that one can never think of identity as having reached its final form is due to the fact that the characteristics one attributes to oneself are not stationary either. They change with the course of events, with the behavior one has adopted, with the categories to which one belongs, the groups that serve as guide-posts. Not surprisingly, identity conflicts arise quite frequently and alter our sense of consistency and constancy over time. The positive value we attach to ourselves is constantly challenged by facts; there is always a discrepancy between what one is aware of being and doing and what one desires to be doing. The conquest and establishment of an identity are therefore never more than the provisional result of a constantly renewed effort.

Personal identity is not only in a perpetual state of motion; it is also constantly <u>threatened</u> by the social environment or <u>jeopardized</u> by material conditions. In truth, <u>there is an unavoidable discrepancy between an individual's sense of his own identity and the way he thinks that this identity is perceived by others</u>. It is inconceivable that this discrepancy can be a matter of indifference to the individual. If the social images associated with a person play a fundamental role in that person's self-image, the hiatus 15) between these two images presents a direct challenge to his sense of identity. The reduction of this hiatus is therefore a matter of urgency.

The reduction can take place <u>in the cognitive realm</u> : in that case the person will persuade himself that the discrepancy is really quite insignificant and dissonance will be eliminated. It can also be implemented <u>in the behavioral realm</u>. In that case, the person will try to act in such a way that the people around him will perceive him as he perceives himself - or, to be more accurate, as he would like to be perceived - and will adopt behavior conducive to this result.

In any case, the desire on the part of every individual to have his identity socially acknowledged involves all the dimensions of his identity, particularly the most fundamental ones : each person wishes others to acknowledge his individual difference, his unity and constancy, his positive value, his autonomy, and his power.

In actuality, however, it is very difficult to make a clear distinction between each of these dimensions. How can one tell, for instance, whether a given behavior reflects primarily a search for differentiation rather than a search for a positive valuation, in a situation where the two are associated ? We shall however illustrate this point with a few typical observations.

---

15) What is conventionally called the identity "crisis" of adolescence stems from this discrepancy between the way the adolescent visualizes himself and the way others visualize him. He himself no longer conceives of himself as a child but his surroundings still refuse to recognize him as an adult. In short, the adolescent is no longer quite sure who he is. This gives rise to his sometimes confused pursuit of social identifications, which allow him to regain his sense of identity. The extreme conformism which is an occasional by-product of these identifications is thus a reaction to this fundamental anguish arising from a shattered image of the self.

1.1. Gaining recognition for one's individual difference

Everybody normally has the capacity to distinguish between separate objects. Specifically, everybody normally has the capacity to establish a cognitive discrimination between himself and others (between "myself" and "not myself"); everybody can also discriminate between various other people.

It is extremely likely, however, that everybody discriminates more accurately the object "myself" than he does between the various "not myself" objects. For one thing, he has much greater experience in dealing with himself - and a different sort of experience - than he does with others. Besides, as we have seen, every categorization results in a simplification, which reinforces differences between categories and at the same time stresses similarities within categories.

As a result, each individual has a much clearer sense of his own individual difference than do the people around him; and there is an unavoidable discrepancy between each person's idea of his own specific nature and how it is perceived by others.

The quest for identity therefore involves asserting one's individual difference and having this difference acknowledged by others.

I have elsewhere (Codol, 1979) described at great length a few of the behavioral manifestations of this quest : social visibility (cf. Ziller, 1964; Maslach, 1974; Fromkin, 1970), emphasis of one's incomparability with others (cf. Lemaine, 1974) etc.

1.2. Showing oneself to be consistent and constant

Personal consistency and constancy are often affected or thrown into disarray by the turn of events and the facts of life. Nonetheless, they are so indispensable for the assertion of personal identities that they have assumed a normative value on the social level; it is a good thing to appear consistent and true to oneself.

Numerous behaviors thus reflect the desire on the part of individuals to present a consistent and constant image of themselves.

Consistency and constancy, for that matter, are themselves important factors in social recognition, for they convey to others an image of personal unity, of someone who matters, of someone who has some "weight". It is known, for instance, that in group situations, consistency and constancy on the part of a minority are tokens of its influence on a majority (cf. for example Moscovici, 1976).

1.3. Conveying a favorable image of oneself to others

The desire on the part of individuals to relate to others so as to appear in a socially favorable light is one of the most powerful human motives. It cannot be left out of account by any theory of social psychology. As I stated earlier, this valorization is an intrinsic element in any cognitive apprehension of the self and a positive evaluation is essential for the establishment of a normally adapted identity.

Here too, as is true for the other dimensions of identity, the message that the social environment sends back to the individual is a component of his own self-image. <u>Self-valorization therefore correlates with the perception of being positively evaluated by others</u>. The individual will therefore adopt behaviors that place him in a favorable light not only in his own eyes but also in the eyes of the people around him. Many strategies to accomplish this come into play, and we can hardly enumerate them all.

Depending on whether individuals want to assert their difference or, on the contrary, display their similarity to others, these strategies can nevertheless be grouped into two major categories.

a) In the first category we include those behaviors with which the individual aims to enhance his personal value by his uniqueness. A few illustrations for the many facts that come to mind will have to do. It is known, for instance, that when individuals are faced with a personal <u>failure</u>, they tend to blame it publicly on uncontrollable <u>external factors</u> (chance, the situation, other people...), whereas they always take credit <u>themselves</u> for <u>success</u>. 16) As Durandin (1972) points out in a

---

16) Facts of this sort have been fully investigated, particularly within the framework of the so-called "locus of control" theory (see for instance Rotter, 1966).

study about lying, "we tend to blame others for reprehensible lies and to assume the responsibility for generous lies" (p.16) : others are said to lie out of self-interest or malice, while our own lies have only the noblest motives : to avoid hurting people, protect a friend, etc.

All the strategies in this category, no matter what form they assume, have the result (if not the conscious aim) of embellishing factual reality in some fashion. Each person generally presents himself in a way that stresses his autonomy or his power 17); or, conversely, tries to hide his faults or dependence.

b) At the same time, the attempt to enhance one's positive evaluation by others need not by any means involve assertion of one's own uniqueness. Far from it : <u>social support and public approval are generally bestowed on an individual only at the price of his submission to the common rule</u>. Consequently, as demonstrated by the studies on the "PIP effect" (Codol, 1975), each person is likely, under many circumstances, to emphasize his similarity with others and his conformity with social norms.

An individual's group affiliation or categorical attribution has some bearing on his desire for a positive self-valorization. Tajfel (1974) has proposed several hypotheses on this matter. For individuals belonging to devalued categories, there are several possibilities.

If, for one reason or another, this negative valuation of their category strikes them as legitimate, two ways are open to them. They may try to gain a positive valorization within their category, by means of interpersonal comparisons, or else they may try to dissociate themselves from this category and "slip into" more highly valued categories.

If, on the contrary, they consider the negative valuation of their group or category illegitimate, particularly in comparison with other groups or categories, they will opt for strategies aiming to enhance the social value of their own groups.

---

17) As soon as individuals feel that their autonomy or their freedom of choice is threatened, they adopt behaviors that aim to restore their sense of autonomy and freedom of choice. Brehm (1966) has theorized about behaviors of this type, which he analyzed within the framework of his studies on "reactance".

For instance, they may suggest a new and positive definition of their group characteristics, which had previously been assigned a negative value (a typical case would be the regionalist movements, whose aim it is to present regional ways and speech patterns in a positive light, or the movement of American blacks with their "Black is beautiful" slogan, etc.). They may also establish new dimensions permitting their own group to acquire a positive distinguishing feature compared to other groups, etc.

No matter what shape they assume, interpersonal relations, in the final analysis, always involve relations in which individuals seek to be positively evaluated by others. On the whole, each person wants to feel socially meaningful and deserving. <u>To be somebody for somebody else, that is, after all, the way in which the desire for identity makes itself manifest</u>.

2. The desire for social recognition of the self : limits and conflicts

Even though the desire to be noticed, recognized, and accepted by others may assume a great number of behavioral guises, an individual may nevertheless, despite his efforts, fail to secure the desired social recognition and feel deprived thereby.

It is quite conceivable, indeed, that an individual's self-assertion may assume forms that those around him experience as threatening and damaging to their own sense of identity. Examples occur both in the individual and the collective realm. J. Williams (1978) for instance cites a number of male behavior patterns in response to the "rise" in feminine assertiveness. An alternate strategy is simply not to acknowledge the new threat to male distinctiveness. This is what happens when identical behavior in males and females is perceived in a different light by males or when women who have acceded to positions traditionally limited to men are viewed as exceptional cases. Or, when the threat is recognized, many other strategies can be devised to eliminate its cause. An illustration is the fact that the adoption of traditionally masculine behavior patterns by women is met with derision and ridicule and is penalized and discouraged in a number of ways.

On the other hand, an individual's search for recognition by others of his own uniqueness, constancy, or positive value will sooner or later <u>meet with some barriers</u>. We know, for instance, that differentiation is not carried beyond a certain threshold, where it might be perceived as <u>deviance</u> (Freedman and Doob, 1968;

Fromkin, 1972; Codol, 1979); it stops short of implying a socially negative self-image or social exclusion 18). Similarly, a consistency that is too pronounced may be socially interpreted as rigidity, obstinacy or even stubbornness; an excessive constancy as dullness and monotony. Even the effort to enhance one's valorization may strike others as insufferable, whether it is perceived as pride, lack of modesty and conceit on the one hand, or obsequiousness, servility, and baseness on the other.

Different desires thus are frequently at odds with each other. I have mentioned, for instance, that the attempt to acquire a positive public image may lead individuals to adopt conformist behaviors, thereby frustrating the desire for visibility and uniqueness 19). Conforming to the expectations of others thus often enters into conflict with the self-image one wishes to promote.

---

18) It is a common enough observation that individuals who are too conspicuous because of some special characteristic - and who for this reason may feel excluded from the mainstream - make a particular effort to have their similarity with others acknowledged rather than their difference. A major demand of the handicapped, for instance, is to be treated like everybody else : "Treat us as you would anybody else". This type of demand, as a close observation of social facts reveals, is often only an intermediary stage in the development of individual or collective identities. The history of feminism shows, for instance, that after having sought equal rights and duties for men and women, militant feminists now demand that their differences as women be recognized. Similar observations apply to the black and Indian movements in the United States, as well as to the regionalist movements within national communities.

19) There are cases of course, where social affiliation offers a means of gaining social visibility. Belonging to a marginal group, for instance, may give an individual the feeling of a unique personal identity. But this uniqueness actually exists only with respect to persons not belonging to this group. Within the group, the individual must experience the fact that he is as marginal as the others - hence similar to them from this point of view.

In a very general way, it is safe to assume that in every instance where there is a conflict between diverging desires for social recognition, behavior will be guided by the mode of recognition that the individual deems as <u>the most important</u> at the moment under consideration.

To give an example, it is commonly observed that within a hierarchic order individuals often prefer to be <u>last</u> rather than <u>second-to-last</u> - at the risk of being even further down-graded in the eyes of others 20). This should in truth come as no surprise : in such a situation, undoubtedly, there is a greater urge on the part of individuals to occupy a unique position than to value a position that, in any case, falls within the bottom of the hierarchy.

Should one conclude from certain cases that individuals are in pursuit of a negative self-image and decide that the pursuit of a positive value for the self, is not a general phenomenon ? That would be a mistake : the uniqueness of a position bestows a value on it that is far from negligible, by giving visibility to the individual occupying it. The studies on the PIP effect (Codol, 1975, 1979) have clearly shown that attributing oneself a special place, even if that place is not desirable, has something important to contribute to personal valorization.

The pursuit of a social recognition for personal identity thus forces individuals constantly to present others with a two-fold vision of themselves. Asserting that they are similar, while considering themselves to be different, they try to prove both things simultaneously, through an unending series of social gymnastics, in which movements of approach and distanciation are in constant alternation, as the search for the proper stance continues.

No matter from what angle one views the matter, in the final analysis the problem of the interaction between one's self-image and social recognition of the self- and hence the question of both personal and social identity - is fought out in this difficult and precarious balancing act between differentiating and non-differentiating behaviors.

---

20) It is also sometimes less important to do well than to be noticed: everybody knows, for instance that in the Tour de France bicycle race, the one who comes in last receives a special award, while nobody pays any attention at all to the racers who come in after the winners.

REFERENCES

Bernstein, B. *Langage et classes sociales*. Paris : Editions de Minuit, 1975.

Billig, M.G. Categorization and Similarity in Intergroup Behavior. Unpublished manuscript, University of Bristol, 1971.

Billig, M.G. & Tajfel, H. Social categorization and similarity in intergroup behavior. *European Journal of Social Psychology*, 1973, 3, 21-52.

Bisseret, N. Langage et identité des classes : les classes sociales se parlent. *L'Année sociologique*, 1974, 25, 237-264.

Brehm, J.W. *A theory of Psychological Reactance*. New York : Academic Press, 1966.

Codol, J.P. On the so-called 'Superior conformity of the self' behavior : Twenty experimental investigations. *European Journal of Social Psychology*, 1975, 5, 457-501.

Codol, J.P. *Semblables et différents. Recherches sur la quête de la similitude et de la différenciation sociale*. Thèse d'Etat. Université de Provence, 1979.

Deaux, K. & Emswiller, T. Explanations of successful performance on sex-linked task : What is skill for the male is luck for the female. *Journal of Personality and Social Psychology*, 1974, 29, 80-85.

Deschamps, J.C. L'identité sociale et les relations entre les groupes. Paper presented at the Colloquium on Social Identity, Rennes (France), 1978.

Doise, W. *L'articulation psycho-sociologique et les relations entre les groupes*. Bruxelles : de Boeck, 1976.

Doise, W., Meyer, G. & Perret-Clermont, A.N. Etude psychosociologique des représentations d'élèves en fin de scolarité obligatoire. *Pratique et théorie* (Cahiers de la Section des Sciences de l'Education de l'Université de Genève), 1976, 2, 15-27.

Durandin, G. *Les fondements du mensonge*. Paris : Flammarion, 1972.

Erikson, E.H. *Identity : Youth and Crisis*. London : Faber and Faber, 1968.

Freedman, J.L. & Doob, A.N. *Deviancy : The Psychology of Being Different*. New York : Academic Press, 1968.

Fromkin, H.L. Effect of experimentally aroused feelings of undistinctiveness upon valuation of scarce and novel experiences. *Journal of Personality and Social Psychology*, 1970, 16, 521-529.

Fromkin, H.L. Feelings of interpersonal undistinctiveness : An unpleasant affective state. *Journal of Experimental Research in Personality*, 1972, 6, 176-185.

Gergen, K.J. *The concept of Self*. New York : Holt, Rinehart and Winston, 1971.
Gordon, C. Self-conceptions : Configurations of content. In C. Gordon & K. Gergen (Eds.), *The Self in Social Interaction*. New York : Wiley, 1968.
Green, A. Atome de parenté et relations oedipiennes. In C. Lévi-Strauss (Ed.), *L'identité*. Paris : Grasset, 1977.
Guillaumin, C. *L'idéologie raciste. Genèse et langage actuel*. Paris : Mouton, 1972.
Lemaine, G. Social differentiation and social originality. *European Journal of Social Psychology*, 1974, 4, 17-52.
Marchand, B. Auswirkung einer emotionalwertvollen und einer emotional neutralen Klassifikation auf die Schätzung einer Stimulus-Serie. *Zeitschrift für Sozialpsychologie*, 1970, 1, 264-274.
Maslach, C. Social and personal bases of individuation. *Journal of Personality and Social Psychology*, 1974, 29, 411-425.
Moscovici, S. *Social influence and social change*. London : Academic Press, 1976.
Rotter, J.B. General expectancies for internal versus external control of reinforcement. *Psychological Monographs*, 1966, 60 (1).
Tajfel, H. Cognitive aspects of prejudice. *Journal of Social Issues*, 1969, 25, 79-97.
Tajfel, H. La catégorisation sociale. In S. Moscovici (Ed.), *Introduction à la psychologie sociale*, Tome I. Paris : Larousse, 1972.
Tajfel, H. Social identity and intergroup behaviour. *Social Science Information*, 1974, 13, 65-93.
Tajfel, H., Billig, M., Bundy, R.P. & Flament, C. Social categorization and intergroup behaviour. *European Journal of Social Psychology*, 1971, 1, 149-178.
Tajfel, H., Scheik, A.A. & Gardner, R.C. Content of stereotypes and the inference of similarity between members of stereotyped groups. *Acta Psychologica*, 1964, 22, 191-201.
Tajfel, H. & Wilkes, A.L. Classification and quantitative judgment. *British Journal of Psychology*, 1963, 54, 101-114.
Thibaut, J.W. & Riecken, H.W. Some determinants and consequences of the perception of social causality. *Journal of Personality*, 1955, 24, 113-133.
Turner, J. Social comparison and social identity : Some prospects for intergroup behaviour. *European Journal of Social Psychology*, 1975, 5, 5-34.
Turner, J. Towards a cognitive redefinition of the social group, *Cahiers de psychologie cognitive*, 1981, 1, in press.
Williams, J. Identity conflicts in women : some personal and social consequences. Paper presented at the Colloquium on Social Identity, Rennes (France), 1978.

Zavalloni, M. L'identité psychosociale, un concept à la recherche d'une science. In S. Moscovici (Ed.), <u>Introduction à la psychologie sociale</u>, Tome II, Paris : Larousse, 1973.

Ziller, R.C. Individuation and socialization. <u>Human Relations</u>, 1964, <u>17</u>, 341-360.

AUTHOR INDEX

A

Abelson, 8, 16, 48, 54, 55, 75, 77, 78, 82, 83, 86, 92, 94, 103, 110, 112, 121, 122, 130, 148, 149, 189, 190, 197, 203
Abric, 115, 147
Adams, 93, 99, 113
Ajzen, 21, 23, 45, 51, 52, 55, 56, 57, 65, 66, 67, 69, 83, 84
Allen, 2, 44, 235, 243, 248, 265
Aloisio, 165, 168
Allport, 181, 202
Alwin, 21, 23, 44
Anderson, D., 103, 110
Anderson, R., 2, 8, 9, 12, 13, 14, 44, 55, 57, 65, 83, 89, 91, 95, 102, 110
Argyle, 1, 16, 17, 44
Aronson, 54, 83
Asch, 1, 2, 3, 7, 10, 20, 44, 118, 147
Atkinson, 63, 85
Audierne, 167, 168
Avigdor, 249, 264

B

Bales, 19, 44
Balley, 48
Bandura, 72, 73, 83, 197, 202
Barjonet, 133, 147
Bartlett, 9, 44, 75, 83, 88, 110
Battig, 89, 91, 113
Batson, 126, 147, 186, 189, 191, 197, 202
Bechterew, 128
Bellin, 30, 44
Bem, 60, 62, 83
Benoist, 244
Bentler, 55, 56, 57, 61, 62, 83
Berger, 248, 264
Berman, 62, 84
Bernstein, 282, 291

Berscheid, 150
Billig, 230, 232, 234, 239, 243, 250, 256, 264, 265, 276, 291, 292
Billiet, 172, 202
Billinger, 153, 158
Bisseret, 282, 291
Black, 77, 79, 83
Bobrow, 75, 83, 116, 147
Boring, 1, 45
Bostian, 200, 203
Boulanger, 168
Bourhis, 241, 243
Bower, 77, 79, 83
Bowers, 88, 111
Bowm-Gardner, 102, 111
Braly, 249, 265
Brehm, 287, 291
Brewer, 234, 243
Brotheron, 245
Brown, 20, 45
Brown, R., 236, 238, 239, 243, 252, 265
Bruner, 172, 202, 250, 264
Bundy, 250, 265, 292
Burnstein, 88, 89, 102, 109, 110, 113

C

Cacioppo, 88, 110
Caddick, 236, 243
Campbell, 66, 83, 87, 112
Cantor, N., 123, 150, 200, 202
Carlsmith, 54, 84
Carlston, 92, 108, 110
Carrol, 142
Chapman, J., 124, 131, 147, 174, 175, 180, 202
Chapman, L., 124, 131, 147, 174, 175, 180, 202
Chassein, 180, 204
Chombart-De-Lauwe, 115, 147
Clark, 63, 85
Clarke, 16, 45

Cochran, 197, 202
Codol, 147, 247, 285, 287, 289, 290, 291
Cohen, C.E., 182, 202
Cohen, 55, 86
Collett, 16, 45
Collins, 116, 147
Constanzo, 7, 49
Cook, 17, 44
Coombs, 6, 35, 45, 46
Cowdry, 30, 45
Craik, 88, 103, 108, 111
Crocker, 75, 77, 82
Crockett, 5, 7, 45
Cross, 66, 85
Crowder, 103, 111
Crown, 184, 202
Csepeli, 244
Cupchik, 71, 72, 83, 85
Curtis, 71, 85

D

Dann, 235, 243, 244
Darley, 20, 48
Datan, 60, 61, 84
Daveney, 54, 84
Davis, J., 156, 168
Davis, K., 177, 203
Deaux, 282, 291
Delbeke, 35, 45
De Leeuw, 13, 48, 49
Deschamps, 237, 238, 243, 244, 252, 253, 258, 264, 265, 281, 282, 291
Deutsch, 61, 84
Deutscher, 62, 84
Dewes, 35, 45
Dohrenwend, B.S., 60, 61, 84
Dohrenwend, B.P., 60, 61, 84
Doise, 115, 147, 234, 235, 237, 238, 240, 241, 243, 244, 250, 265, 275, 281, 291
Doob, A., 288, 291
Doob, L., 66, 84
Druckman, 230, 244
Dubois, 265

Dudycha, 9, 45
Duffenback, 200, 203
Durandin, 286, 291
Durkheim, 163, 168
Durlak, 192, 202
Dwyer, 97, 111
Dyer, 92, 111

E

Ebbesen, 88, 91, 111, 182, 202
Eckman, 8, 45
Edelman, 125, 134
Edwards, 53, 84
Eiser, 235, 236, 244
Ellis, 132, 147
Emswiller, 282, 291
Erikson, 248, 265, 283, 291

F

Farber, 184, 185, 202
Farina, 130, 147, 193, 202, 203
Farr, 115, 147
Faucheux, 2, 48, 85, 115, 147
Fergusson, 250
Feshbach, 80, 84
Festinger, 1, 3, 45, 54, 60, 62, 84, 118, 147
Fincham, 15, 45
Fischer, E., 147, 193, 202
Fischer, J., 130, 147, 193, 202, 203
Fischhoff, 65, 84
Fishbein, 21, 23, 45, 51, 52, 55, 56, 57, 62, 63, 65, 66, 67, 69, 83, 84
Fiske, 102
Flament, 7, 45, 115, 144, 147, 151, 156, 157, 158, 160, 161, 168, 169, 250, 265, 292
Flaubert, 138, 148
Freedman, 288, 291
Fremontier, 133, 148
Friedman, 92, 111
Friesen, 45
Fromkin, 285, 289, 291

Fromm, 248, 265
Fryda, 8, 45

G

Gabel, 133, 148
Galanter, 61, 85
Gardner, 276, 292
Gergen, 2, 46, 127, 148, 280, 292
Getter, 147, 193, 202
Geva, 93, 102, 111, 112
Giles, 241, 243
Gilligan, 144, 148
Ginsberg, 60, 61, 83
Goffman, 234, 244
Goldberg, 35, 46
Golding, 194, 203
Gordon, 281, 292
Gouge, 244
Graumann, 120, 121, 148
Green, 272, 292
Greenwald, 87, 88, 111, 241, 244
Gugter, 150
Guillaumin, 281, 292
Guttman, 53, 84

H

Hagendoorn, 9, 16, 46
Harary, 153, 169
Harré, 1, 2, 16, 18, 46, 146, 148
Harvey, 3, 46, 176, 203
Harvey, O.J., 265
Hayes-Roth, 99, 111
Hays, 97, 111
Heider, 1, 2, 3, 5, 24, 46, 54, 84, 129, 136, 148, 151, 164, 169
Herrnstein, 20, 45
Herzlich, 115, 148
Hewstone, 141, 148
Hoffman, 9, 46, 109, 111, 123
Hofstadter, 116, 148
Holmes, 148
Holt, 89, 113

Holzkamp, 2, 4, 6
Hood, 265
Houel, 157, 169
Hover, 200, 203
Hovland, 18, 149

I

Ickes, 3, 46
Indermuhle, 150
Insko, 87, 111
Israel, 13, 46

J

Janis, 80, 84
Janssen, 235, 244
Jaspars, 6, 7, 12, 13, 14, 15, 17, 21, 33, 34, 35, 45, 46, 141, 148
Jodelet, 115, 148
Johnson, J.E., 80, 84
Johnson-Laird, 144
Johnson, 21, 23, 46, 48
Jones, C., 197, 202
Jones, E., 176, 177, 179, 203
Jordan, 5
Judd, 101, 102, 111

K

Kahle, 62, 84
Kahn, 235, 244, 245
Kalber-Matten, 150
Kanizsa, 223, 226
Kardiner, 248, 265
Kassin, 135, 143, 148, 195, 203
Katayani, 240, 246
Katz, 241, 244, 249, 265
Keele, 92, 112
Kelley, 121, 148, 250
Kelly, 1, 9, 18, 47
Kendall, 47
Kendon, 1, 16, 17
Kenniston, 30, 45
Koffka, 5
Köhlberg, 47
Köhler, 5

Krantz, 55, 85
Krauss, 52, 86
Kriesberg, 31, 44
Krolage, 179, 204
Kruglanski, 127, 143, 148
Kulik, 101, 102, 111

L

Lalljee, 17, 44
Langer, 130, 148, 189, 190, 197, 203
La Pierre, 8, 20, 56, 85
Larsen, 244,
Lasky, 200, 203
Latane, 20, 48
Layer, 69, 86
Le Bon, 128, 148
Le Goff, 116, 148
Leippe, 102, 111
Lemaine, G, 285, 292
Leonard, 152, 169
Lepper, 149
Lerner, 144, 148
Leventhal, 71, 72, 80, 81, 82, 83, 84, 85
Levi-Strauss, 248
Lewin, 5, 9, 48, 63, 64, 85, 118, 149
Leyens, 126, 149, 226, 243
Lichtenstein, 2, 9, 10, 13, 14, 49, 65, 84
Lickert, 53, 85
Lingle, 93, 102, 111, 112
Linton, 248, 265
Lodge, 66, 85
Lord, 123, 149
Lorenzi, 253, 265
Lowell, 63, 85
Lowery, 150
Luce, 9, 12, 48
Luckman, 248, 264

M

Mack, 66, 71, 86
Machover, 174, 203
Mandler, 102, 111
Marais, 29, 48
Marchand, 275, 292
Markley, 71, 85
Marz, 189, 191, 202
Maslach, 285, 292
Mazze, 182, 203
Mauss, 134, 149
McClelland, 63, 85, 97, 112
McDougall, 128
McGuire, 54, 83, 87, 113
McGurk, 136
Mead, 247, 265
Meinon, 5
Merleau-Ponty, 143, 149
Merton, 1, 48
Meyer, G., 244, 291
Meyer, 80, 81, 82, 93, 112, 113
Mezzich, 200, 202
Milgram, 2, 20, 48
Miller, D.T., 144, 148
Miller, G., 61, 185
Miller, N., 87, 112
Millon, 184, 186, 191, 200, 203
Milner, 238, 241, 244
Minsky, 92, 112
Mischel, 55, 85, 172, 182, 198, 200, 202, 203
Monnier, 160, 161, 169
Morley, 229, 240, 244
Moscovici, 2, 48, 61, 85, 115, 131, 138, 144, 147, 149, 172, 180, 203, 209, 222, 226, 286, 292

N

Nayen, 9, 45
Nerenz, 80, 81, 82
Newcomb, 5, 7, 48, 54, 83, 85
Newtson, 91, 112
Neisser, 145, 149
Nisbett, 126, 128, 149, 179, 192, 195, 199, 203, 204, 205
Nizet, 172, 202
Nord, 200, 203
Norman, 8, 48, 75, 83
Nuttin, 20, 48

Nuttin, Sr., 235, 244

O

Oakes, 238, 244
Odbert, 181, 202
Oosterbaa, 244
Oppenheim, 241, 244
Ortony, 75, 85, 88, 92, 112
Osgood, 1, 3, 48, 53, 67, 85, 118, 149
Ostell, 244
Ostrom, 53, 70, 85, 93, 102, 111, 112

P

Parducci, 70, 85, 94, 112
Payne, 142
Peak, 103, 112
Perret-Clermont, 291
Personnaz, 258, 265
Petty, 88, 110
Piaget, 6, 48
Pichevin, 154, 157, 165, 166, 167, 169
Plon, 2, 48
Poitou, 154, 162, 164, 165, 166, 167, 169
Posner, 92, 94, 97, 112
Pribram, 61, 85
Proust, 149
Pryor, 93, 112

R

Rabbie, 235, 240, 244, 245
Regan, 198, 204
Riecken, 281, 292
Rokeach, 65, 85, 239, 245
Roqueplot, 115, 149
Rorer, 194, 203
Rosch, E.K., 179, 180, 204
Rosch, E., 200, 204
Rosenberg, 8, 54, 83, 103, 112, 120, 149
Rosenhan, 184, 185, 200, 204
Ross, D., 72, 73, 83

Ross, L., 126, 128, 149, 176, 177, 195, 203, 204
Ross, S., 72, 73, 83
Rossignol, 156, 157, 169
Rotter, 286, 292
Rubin, 201, 204
Rule, 71, 85
Rumelhart, 75, 86, 88, 92, 112
Ryen, 235, 244, 245

S

Sabin, 30, 45
Sarbin, 48, 248, 265
Schachter, 43, 48
Schenkel, 150, 198, 200, 204
Schmidt, A., 198, 200, 204
Schneider, 121, 149, 172, 204
Schorr, 93, 99, 113
Schul, 109, 110, 113
Schumann, 21, 23, 48
Schümer, 13, 48, 55, 86
Schvaneveldt, 93, 112, 113
Secord, 2, 146, 148
Sedlak, 120, 149
Semin, 179, 180, 196, 204
Shank, 8, 16, 48, 75, 77, 78, 86, 92, 112, 121, 122, 149
Shaw, 7, 49
Sheik, 276, 292
Sherif, C., 232, 245, 265
Sherif, M., 118, 149, 229, 232, 245, 248, 249, 250, 251, 265
Shontz, 201, 204
Silver, 234, 243
Simmel, 3, 46
Sinclair, 240, 244
Sines, 201, 204
Skevington, 238, 245
Skinner, 245
Slovic, 2, 9, 10, 13, 14, 49, 65, 84
Smedslund, 223, 226
Smith, E., 93, 99, 113, 200, 202
Smith, G., 49
Smith, P., 200, 203
Snyder, C., 94, 112, 126, 150, 190, 198, 200, 204

Snyder, M. 74, 86, 123, 125, 129, 150, 195, 204, 205
Sommer, 120, 121, 148
Speckart, 55, 56, 61, 62, 83
Spitzer, 184, 185, 200, 205
Srull, 181, 205
Steedman, 144
Stephenson, 229, 230, 240, 244, 245
Stevens, G., 66, 71, 86
Stevens, S., 66, 71, 86
Strack, 196, 204
Stroebe, 235, 244
Stuart, 47
Suci, 48, 53, 85
Swann, 74, 86, 123, 125, 129, 150, 195, 205
Swets, 69, 86

T

Tajfel, 46, 227, 230, 231, 233, 234, 235, 236, 238, 239, 242, 243, 245, 248, 249, 250, 251, 253, 256, 258, 265, 266, 275, 276, 278, 287, 291, 292
Tagiuri, 172, 202
Takane, 48, 49
Tanenhaus, 66, 85
Tanke, 150
Tannenbaum, 48, 53, 54, 83, 85, 118, 149
Taylor, 75, 77, 82
Tesser, 89, 113
Thibaut, 281, 292
Thurstone, 53, 57, 65, 86
Toglia, 89, 91, 113
Torgerson, 13, 33, 49
Totten, 198, 204
Town, 176, 203
Trench, 200, 202
Trope, 88, 113
Tukey, 9, 12, 48
Tulving, 88, 103, 108, 111
Turner, C.F., 52, 86
Turner, J., 236, 237, 238, 244, 246, 251, 258, 266, 276, 280, 292

Turner, T.G., 77, 79, 83
Tursky, 66, 85
Tversky, 35, 45, 55, 85
Tyler, 102, 103

U

Upmeyer, 68, 69, 70, 82, 86
Upshaw, 66, 70, 85, 86, 94

V

Valins, 192, 205
Van den Dever, 47
Van de Geer, 6, 7, 46
Van der Kloot, 13, 37, 47
Van Gils, 47
Van Knippenberg, 241, 244
Van Kreveld, 47
Vaughan, 234, 242, 246
Verhoeven, 13, 15, 49
Vinokur, 88, 89, 102, 109, 110, 113
Visser, 240, 244, 245
Von Cranach, 145, 150

W

Weinreich, 231, 246
Warr, 13, 14, 15, 49
Watts, 87, 89, 113
Wegener, 66, 86
Weiner, 184, 205
Wertheimer, 5
West, 265
White, 265
Wicker, 21, 49, 52, 55, 86
Wilder, 235, 243, 246
Wilensky, 77, 79, 82
Wilkes, 275, 292
Wilkens, 235, 245
Williams, 281, 283, 288, 292
Wilson, T., 199, 204
Wilson, W., 240, 246
Wishner, 103, 113
Wyer, 2, 5, 14, 49, 94, 113, 181, 205

Y

Yarkin, 176, 203
Yntema, 13
Young, 13, 48, 49

Z

Zajonc, 2, 5, 6, 49, 103, 113, 117, 150, 151, 169
Zavalloni, 248, 266, 278, 279, 293
Ziller, 285, 293
Zimbardo, 20, 49

SUBJECT INDEX

A

actor-observer differences, 178, 179
additivity, 13, 15
affiliation, 232
announcements, 67
artificial intelligence, 78
attitudes, 2, 20-21, 51-82, 118, 209
attitude polarization, 87
attribution, 3, 7, 9, 15, 60, 143
availability, 181, 182

B

balance theory, 5-6
bargaining, 229-230
Bayesian model, 14-15
behavior, 62
behavioral intention, 55-56
beliefs, 57

C

categorization, 233-239, 250-251, 269-270
cognitive consistency, 3, 16, 54, 94
cognitive representation, 1-2, 6-8, 19-20
correspondences, 69, 72-73
cross-modality matching, 66

D

decision, 94, 107-110
differentiation, 164-167, 267-290
disposition vs. situation, 184-191
dissonance theory, 54, 118

E

egocentrism, 252
empathy, 198-199
encoding (elaborative), 92-93, 107-110
encoding (initial), 91-92, 107-110
equilibrium bias, 151-168
ethogenics, 1, 16, 18-19
expectations, 69, 73

F

fundamental error, 126, 176-177

G

goals, 63-64, 79
goal-attitude, 64-65, 81

I

identification, 268, 274
identity, 221-222, 267-290
ideology, 163-165, 214
illusory correlation, 174-175, 194
implications, 88, 107
implicit theory of personality, 7, 120, 172-176, 194, 226
impression formation, 7, 10, 55, 95
information integration, 2-3, 7, 12
instrumental attitude, 65-66, 82
integration, 93, 107-110
intergroup behaviour, 227-243
intergroup differentiation, 233-243, 247-264
interindividual differentiation, 247-264

L

lay-epistemology, 122-141

M

magnitude estimation, 70-71
manipulation, 216
measurement approach, 53
memory, 79
minority, 240-242

N

negociation, 229-230

O

opinion formation, 91-94, 101

P

personalism, 126
personal identification, 277-283
personality, 25, 179-180
persuasion, 87-110
positivity effect, 7
prejudice, 141, 249
prototype, 200
pseudo-cognitions, 7, 11, 15

R

representation, 7, 9, 15, 23, 32, 74, 102

S

sanctions, 68, 72-73
schema, 9, 74-77, 80-81, 88, 108-110, 121, 152
scripts, 74-77
self-identity, 271-283
self-image, 283-290
semantic matching, 93, 95
social change, 171-172
social cognition, 7-9, 19, 123-141
social comparison, 238-242
social competition, 233-239, 250
social conflicts, 227-232, 250
social identity, 237, 247-249, 273-283
social judgements, 2, 9, 13, 19-20, 30-31, 33, 119
social representation, 115, 128-146, 152, 162-168, 209-210. 222-226
social skill, 1, 16-19
sociocentrism, 252
stereotype, 141, 249, 275-277

T

taxonomy, 200